# SpringerBriefs in Economics



## Development Bank of Japan Research Series

This series is characterized by the close academic cohesion of financial economics, environmental economics, and accounting, which are the three major fields of research of the Research Institute of Capital Formation (RICF) at the Development Bank of Japan (DBJ). Readers can acquaint themselves with how a financial intermediary efficiently restructuring firms in financial distress can contribute to economic development.

The aforementioned three research fields are closely connected with one another in the following ways. DBJ has already developed several corporation-rating methods, including the environmental rating by which DBJ decides whether or not to make concessions to the candidate firm. To evaluate the relevance of this rating, research, which deploys not only financial economics but also environmental economics, is necessary.

The accounting section intensively studies the structure of IFRS and Integrated Reporting to predict their effects on Japanese corporate governance. Although the discipline of accounting is usually isolated from financial economics, structural and reliable prediction is never achieved without sufficient and integrated knowledge in both fields.

Finally, the environmental economics section is linked to the accounting section in the following manner. To establish green accounting (environmental accounting), it is indispensable to explore what the crucial factors for the preservation of environment (e.g., emission control) are. RICF is well equipped to address the acute necessity for discourse among researchers who belong to these three different fields.

Titles in the series are authored not only by researchers at RICF but also by collaborating and contributing researchers from universities and institutions throughout Japan. Each proposal is carefully evaluated by the series editor and editorial board members, who submit written reports that appraise each proposal in terms of academic value and rigor and also provide constructive comments for further improvement. At times, the editorial board appoints external referees to provide additional comments. All prospective authors also present their research findings to the editorial board in face-to-face editorial board meetings, where the series editor and editorial board members provide further detailed comments on the findings, methodology, overall presentation, and advice in preparing the book manuscript in English.

Any opinions, findings or conclusions contained in this series are those of the author and do not reflect the views of the Development Bank of Japan Inc.

More information about this subseries at http://www.springer.com/series/13542

Kohei Kamaga

# Social Welfare Evaluation and Intergenerational Equity

Springer

Kohei Kamaga
Sophia University
Tokyo, Japan

ISSN 2191-5504 ISSN 2191-5512 (electronic)
SpringerBriefs in Economics
ISSN 2367-0967 ISSN 2367-0975 (electronic)
Development Bank of Japan Research Series
ISBN 978-981-15-4253-4 ISBN 978-981-15-4254-1 (eBook)
https://doi.org/10.1007/978-981-15-4254-1



This Springer imprint is published by the registered company Springer Nature Singapore Pte Ltd.
The registered company address is: 152 Beach Road, #21-01/04 Gateway East, Singapore 189721, Singapore

The original version of the book was revised: With correct copyright holder name as "© Development Bank of Japan". The correction to the book is available at https://doi.org/10.1007/978-981-15-4254-1_7

# Acknowledgements

I am very grateful to Tsuyoshi Adachi, Walter Bossert, Susumu Cato, and Takashi Kojima, with whom I jointly worked on the research used in this book, for my discussions with them. I would also like to thank Geir B. Asheim and Stéphane Zuber for their discussions and help with ongoing research projects related to the contents of this book. Also, I would like to thank Conchita D'Ambrosio for her discussions about an ongoing research project related to the contents of this book. For providing useful comments to the research used in this book, my thanks go to Marc Fleurbaey, Yoshio Kamijo, François Maniquet, Kaname Miyagishima, Paolo G. Piacquadio, Marcus Pivato, Tomoichi Shinotsuka, Koichi Suga, and Kotaro Suzumura. I appreciate the editorial team of the Research Institute of Capital Formation, Development Bank of Japan for their support. In particular, my thanks go to Yuko Hosoda and Katsuhisa Uchiyama. Needless to say, all remaining errors are my own. Finally, this book is dedicated to Masayuki Otaki, who passed away too early in July 2018, and whom I would like to thank for encouraging me to complete this work.

# Contents

# About the Author

**Kohei Kamaga** is Associate Professor of Economics at Sophia University, Japan; a Visiting Associate Professor at Graduate School of Economics and Management, Tohoku University; and a Visiting Scholar of the Research Institute of Capital Formation, Development Bank of Japan. Born in 1980, Prof. Kamaga received a Bachelor of Arts in Economics at Waseda University in 2004 and a Doctor of Economics at Waseda University in 2011. His research interests include social choice theory, welfare economics, intergenerational equity, and population ethics.

# Chapter 1
# Introduction

**Abstract** This chapter presents a brief overview of the axiomatic analysis of social evaluation criteria for intra- and intergenerational utility distributions. Analyzing finite-horizon and infinite-horizon utility distributions instead of social alternatives is called the "welfarist approach," which has a firm theoretical background in social choice theory. Our main concern in analyzing the evaluation criteria for infinite-horizon utility distributions will be the logical compatibility between the two basic axioms requiring the efficiency and impartiality of the evaluation: the strong Pareto principle and an anonymity axiom.

**Keywords** Social choice theory · Intergenerational equity · Axiomatic analysis · Welfarism

## 1.1 The Aim of This Book

Evaluating the relative goodness of social alternatives such as among economic policies is an indispensable in selecting what is socially best. As a matter of course, the selection crucially depends on the evaluation criteria used. Consequently, we ultimately face a fundamental question: What evaluation criteria should we use in evaluating social alternatives? The search for normatively appealing evaluation criteria has been studied in social choice theory. This book presents a social choice theoretic analysis of evaluation criteria for both intragenerational and intergenerational social welfare evaluation. Specifically, we will analyze (i) intragenerational social welfare evaluation, (ii) intergenerational social welfare evaluation, and (iii) intergenerational social welfare evaluation with variable generation population sizes.

Social choice theory has applied the axiomatic approach to social welfare evaluation criteria. The axiomatic analysis of evaluation criteria considers several axioms, each of which is a mathematical representation of a normatively appealing property to be satisfied by an evaluation criterion; then, the evaluation criterion (or class of evaluation criteria) that satisfies a set of axioms is identified. Identifying an evaluation criterion that satisfies a set of axioms is called an "axiomatization" or an "axiomatic characterization" of the evaluation



K. Kamaga, *Social Welfare Evaluation and Intergenerational Equity*,
Development Bank of Japan Research Series,
https://doi.org/10.1007/978-981-15-4254-1_1

criterion. An axiomatization of an evaluation criterion shows the normative foundation of the evaluation criterion in terms of the axioms used. Specifically, it shows that the evaluation criterion (or class of evaluation criteria) axiomatized is the only criterion that satisfies the axioms considered. Therefore, once we think of those axioms as acceptable, the chosen evaluation criterion is the only permissible one. In this sense, axiomatization results provide an answer to the fundamental question of which evaluation criterion should be used.

Selecting the socially best alternative from several social alternatives is a collective decision-making problem. The collective decision making within a generation—within the current generation, for instance—does not necessarily require a social welfare evaluation criterion in order to select the socially best alternative because there are several methods of doing this, such as voting. However, when the social alternatives affect the well-being of not only near but far future generations and when the choice must be made right now—like taking an action to deal with climate change—a normatively appealing evaluation criterion is indispensable for selecting the socially best alternative because current and future generations cannot interact, and the current generation's choice needs to take the interests of future generations into account in a normatively justifiable way. Two basic axioms will be employed to explore normatively appealing intergenerational social welfare evaluation criteria: the strong Pareto principle and the finite or extended anonymity axioms. The strong Pareto principle is an efficiency requirement whereby the evaluation must be positively sensitive to each generation's well-being. An anonymity axiom formalizes the equal treatment of generations using permutations of generations. Specifically, it postulates that two situations that coincide by a permutation of generations (in terms of utility distribution) are deemed equally good. Some distributional equity axioms will also be considered to deal with the inequality of well-being between generations.

By analyzing both intragenerational and intergenerational social welfare evaluation criteria, this book intendes to shed light on the close linkage between them. Specifically, we will analyze intragenerational and intergenerational social welfare evaluation criteria in a unified manner to examine to what extent the value judgment within a generation is extendable to intergenerational value judgment and to what extent it restricts a permissible intergenerational value judgment. As we will see in the following chapters, the study's general extension results enrich a large body of literature by offering important insights into the exploration of normatively appealing intergenerational social welfare evaluation criteria.

## 1.2 Historical and Philosophical Background

Modern social choice theory was initiated by Arrow (1951). In his celebrated impossibility theorem, Arrow showed that there is no reasonable preference aggregation rule $f$ that transforms the preferences $(R_1, \ldots, R_n)$ of the finite and fixed $n$ individuals to a social preference (ordering) $R = f(R_1, \ldots, R_n)$ over social alternatives $\{x, y, z, \ldots\}$. What is meant by "reasonable" is that the aggregation rule satisfies three properties: the weak Pareto principle (respect for unanimous preferences of individuals), the binary independence of irrelevant alternatives (the use of the information on individuals' preference only over a pair of social alternatives when socially ranking those two alternatives), and non-dictatorship (the non-existence of an individual whose preference determines the social preference in any case). Restating the Arrow impossibility theorem in term of the utilities of individuals, this means that there is no reasonable social evaluation criterion for the distributions of utilities of individuals as long as we assume that the utilities of individuals are ordinally measurable and interpersonally non-comparable. Meanwhile, once we accept the assumption that the utilities of individuals are ordinally or cardinally measurable and interpersonally comparable, there are social welfare evaluation criteria for the distributions of the utilities of individuals that satisfy some axioms, including the strong Pareto principle and the anonymity axiom, both of which are formulated for the distributions of the utilities of individuals, as well as the binary independence of irrelevant alternatives. These include classical utilitarianism, which formalizes Bentham's (1776, 1789) principle of the greatest happiness of the greatest number, and the leximin principle, which is the welfarist reformulation of Rawls's (1971) lexical difference principle. In this connection, it should be noted that Rawls (1971) focuses on the difference principle instead of the lexical difference principle because it is simpler. The welfarist reformulation of the difference principle is well-known as the maximin principle. In Rawls (1971), the lexical difference principle is discussed with reference to the work of Sen (1970) where the leximin principle appears in the context of examining Rawls's concept of fairness and he citets Rawls's works, e.g., Rawls (1958, 1963, 1967).

A social evaluation criterion for the distributions of the utilities of individuals is analyzed in the form of a social welfare ordering, or a social welfare quasi-ordering. (see Chap. 2 for their detailed definitions.) It ranks utility distributions instead of social alternatives. However, ranking utility distributions is related to ranking social alternatives. An aggregation rule $F$ that transforms a profile $(u_1(\cdot), \ldots, u_n(\cdot))$ of the utility functions, not the preferences, of individuals to a social preference $R = F(u_1(\cdot), \ldots, u_n(\cdot))$ over social alternatives $\{x, y, z, \ldots\}$ was first analyzed by Sen (1970) under the name of "social welfare functional." The welfarism theorem, established by d'Aspremont and Gevers (1977) and Hammond (1979), shows that a social welfare functional defined on the unlimited domain of profiles of utility functions satisfies the binary independence of irrelevant alternatives (reformulated for a social welfare functional) and Pareto indifference (asserting that any two alternatives are socially equally good if each individual receives the same utility level in them) if and only if the social preference associated by the social welfare functional is represented by an ordering $\succsim$ defined for utility distributions $(u_1, \ldots, u_n)$ irrespectively of what profile $(u_1(\cdot), \ldots, u_n(\cdot))$ of utility functions and which social alternatives, say $x$, generate those utility distributions $(u_1, \ldots, u_n) = (u_1(x), \ldots, u_n(x))$. Therefore, the analysis of aggregation rules for profiles of utility functions is equivalently done by analyzing an ordering (or a quasi-ordering) for utility distributions. The analysis focusing on an evaluation criterion for utility distributions instead of an aggregation rule is called the "welfarist approach," which is what we will employ in the following chapters.

The axiomatic analysis of intergenerational social welfare evaluation can be traced back to Diamond (1965) and Koopmans (1960). Each of these seminal contributions shows, in a slightly different setting, that there is no social welfare ordering $\succsim$ for infinite streams of utilities of generations $\boldsymbol{u} = (u_1, u_2, \ldots, u_i, \ldots)$ in a way that respects the strong Pareto principle and the finite anonymity axiom if we insist that the ordering satisfy a suitable continuity property, such as the sup norm continuity, that guarantees its numerical representation. On the other hand, Svensson (1980) has shown that, once we allow the evaluation to be incomplete or require only a weaker continuity property, the strong Pareto principle and finite anonymity are compatible with each other.

Since these seminal contributions were made, three main types of approaches have been taken in the literature. The first approach examines which continuity properties are compatible with the strong Pareto principle and finite anonymity. (see, e.g., Banerjee and Mitra (2008) for the development of this approach.) The second approach is to drop the completeness of the evaluation while retaining transitivity and reflexivity, as done by Svensson (1980), and to explore evaluation criteria that satisfy additional axioms as well as the strong Pareto principle and finite anonymity. Finally, the third approach is to retain the completeness of the evaluation while weakening transitivity to quasi-transitivity (e.g., Fleurbaey and Michel 2003). Among these approaches, this book focuses on the second. As we will see in Chaps. 3 and 4, those who have taken this approach have proposed and axiomatically characterized many intergenerational social welfare evaluation criteria. (See also Asheim (2010) and Lauwers (2016) for reviews of the development of this approach.)

In the infinite-horizon framework, several versions of an anonymity axiom can be defined by employing different sets of permissible permutations (see Chap. 4). Finite anonymity is the weakest anonymity axiom, and is defined by the set of finite permutations that exchange the positions of the finite number of generations. The strongest anonymity axiom is obtained by employing the set of all possible permutations of generations. Although finite anonymity is a weak requirement of the equal treatment of generations, it implies that the utilities of future generations should be taken into account without discounting them, so that, once we accept the weakest form of the anonymity axiom, it is no longer acceptable to use discounted utilitarianism, which compares the sums of the geometrically discounted utilities of generations by assigning greater weights to earlier generations. (See the next section for the formal definition of discounted utilitarianism.) Arguments against discounting the utilities of future generations have appeared in (among others) Pigou (1920), Ramsey (1928), and Sidgwick (1907), who insisted that there is no moral rationale for treating generations unequally. It is not a coincidence that they all are British scholars because, first, utilitarianism was employed as an evaluation criterion by British academics of the time, such as in the welfare economics of Pigou (1920); and, second, the prohibition against discounting utilities severely restricts the range of application of utilitarian evaluation due to the divergence of the utility sum.

The problem of the infinite-horizon application of utilitarianism could be seen as a specific form of the general incompatibility between the strong Pareto principle and finite anonymity that was first suggested by Fleurbaey and Michel (2003). They conjectured that an evaluation ordering for infinite utility streams that satisfies the weak Pareto principle and finite anonymity is a non-constructible object in the sense that it necessarily relies on the use of the Axiom of Choice or Zorn's lemma.[1] This conjecture was proven true by Zame (2007) and Lauwers (2010) using the strong Pareto principle and by Dubey (2011) using the weak Pareto principle. These impossibility results mean that any evaluation ordering that satisfies the strong Pareto principle and finite anonymity cannot be explicitly described, and thus does not help us in any practical way. In light of this impossibility, exploring incomplete evaluation criteria that can be explicitly described, the approach this book takes, is meaningful.[2]

## 1.3 Relevance to Climate Change

The axiomatic analysis of social welfare evaluation is a purely theoretical approach to evaluation criteria; some may therefore think of it as hardly relevant to practical issues. However, it has relevance to several social and economic issues. In particular, the axiomatic analysis of the social welfare evaluation of intergenerational welfare distributions has important implications for the economic analysis of climate change. Chapter 2A of the Stern Review (Stern 2007) explains the relevance of welfare economics for resolving conflicts between current and future generations. The review is a report submitted to then Prime Minister Tony Blair and the Chancellor of Exchequer of the United Kingdom in 2016. It provides a comprehensive economic analysis of the impacts of climate change, including suggestions regarding policy and institution making.

Despite their great impact on the debate regarding climate policies, Chap. 2A of the review and related research deal only with the suitable choice of discount factor $\beta \in (0, 1)$ used in the social welfare evaluation criterion called *discounted utilitarianism*. (see Nordhaus (2007) for reviews and critical assessments of the Stern Review.) Discounted utilitarianism is represented by the following real-valued function:

$$W(\boldsymbol{x}) = \sum_{i=1}^{\infty} \beta^{i-1} u(x_i),$$

where $\boldsymbol{x} = (x_1, x_2, \ldots, x_i, \ldots)$ is an infinite stream of the consumptions of infinitely many generations, and $u$ is the utility function that measures the welfare level of each generation. Reformulated in the welfarist framework, discounted utilitarianism

[1] Szpilrajn's (1930) lemma, or its variant presented by Arrow (1963), is usually used to prove the existence of an ordering extension.

[2] It should be noted that this also applies to the third approach we mentioned earlier—exploring complete and quasi-transitive evaluation criteria. (See, for instance, Sakai (2010)).

is represented by the real-valued function $W^*$ as follows:

$$W^*(\boldsymbol{u}) = \sum_{i=1}^{\infty} \beta^{i-1} u_i,$$

where $\boldsymbol{u} = (u_1, u_2, \ldots, u_i, \ldots)$ is an infinite utility stream (generated by the consumption path and utility function considered). Since, even if $\beta$ is close to one, discounted utilitarianism assigns a greater weight to earlier generation, it does not satisfy finite anonymity, and thus, cannot realize the equal treatment of generations in this sense.[3] In this book, we will examine some forms of utilitarianism, the leximin principle, and their intermediate variants, which we can use to evaluate infinite utility streams treating generations equally.

It should be noted, however, that insisting on evaluation criteria that satisfy anonymity axioms has an analytical drawback. As discussed in Stern (2007), an ethical basis for the use of utility discounting can be established by referring to the uncertainty of the existence of distant future generations. Exploring evaluation criteria that satisfy anonymity axioms, such as finite anonymity, means that we will put aside the consideration of this uncertainty.

## 1.4 The Structure of This Book

As noted before, the purpose of this book is to clarify how intragenerational social welfare evaluation is extended to an intergenerational one following the axiomatic approach. Thus, we start with the axiomatic analysis of intragenerational social welfare evaluation and then extend it to an intergenerational one with additional analytical structures.[4]

In Chap. 2, we begin by reviewing early and recent researches on social welfare evaluation in the finite and fixed population case, focusing on axiomatizations of utilitarianism, the leximin principle, and several forms of their compromises. This chapter outlines the preliminaries that readers may require to better understand how the intragenerational evaluation criteria can be extended to and reformulated as intergenerational welfare evaluation criteria.

In Chaps. 3 and 4, we will examine social welfare evaluation criteria for intergenerational utility distributions that are represented by an infinite utility stream. Our purpose is to establish general extension results that clarify how a finite-horizon evaluation criterion can be extended to the infinite-horizon setting in a way that realizes the equal treatment of generations. Chapter 3 focuses on a finitely anonymous eval-

[3]The limit case where $\beta$ goes to one is studied by Jonsson and Voorneveld (2018) under the name of "limit-discounted utilitarianism," which realizes the equal treatment of generations.

[4]For a discussion of the finite-horizon social welfare evaluation with variable population and its relationship with the finite-horizon fixed-population social welfare evaluation, we refer readers to the excellent monograph by Blackorby et al. (2005).

uation criterion, which guarantees the equal treatment of finitely many generations. Applying the general extension results, we will present axiomatizations of infinite-horizon extensions of utilitarianism, the leximin principle, and their compromises.

Chapter 4 examines infinite-horizon evaluation criteria that satisfy extended anonymity axioms. Extended anonymity axioms are logically stronger than the finite anonymity axiom and are intended to realize the equal treatment of infinitely many generations. We will begin by looking into the incompatibility between the strong Pareto principle and the strong anonymity axiom that is formulated with the set of all permutations of generations and that asserts that any two infinite utility streams are equally good if they are related by a permutation of generations. Then, we establish general extension results that show how a finite-horizon evaluation criterion can be reformulated as an infinite-horizon evaluation criterion that satisfies Pareto-compatible extended anonymity axioms. Again, the general results are applied to the establishment of axiomatizations of infinite-horizon extensions of utilitarianism, the leximin principle, and their compromises.

In Chap. 5, demographic change across generations is explicitly taken into account in an analysis of intergenerational social welfare evaluation. We begin with the welfarism theorems in this extended framework. Then, social welfare evaluation criteria for infinite streams of generational utility vectors are analyzed. We present axiomatizations of infinite-horizon extensions of the critical-level (generalized) utilitarian criterion. Moreover, the relationship between the choice of the critical-level parameter and population ethics axioms are discussed.

In Chap. 6, we will briefly discuss some other possible approaches to intergenerational social welfare evaluation. Specifically, the issues of numerically representable evaluation criterion, a strongly anonymous infinite-horizon evaluation criterion, and the choice function approach are discussed.

## References


Arrow, K. J. (1951). *Social choice and individual values* (2nd ed., 1963). New York: Wiley.

Asheim, G. B. (2010). Intergenerational equity. *Annual Review of Economics*, *2*, 197–222.

Banerjee, K., & Mitra, T. (2008). On the continuity of ethical social welfare orders on infinite utility streams. *Social Choice and Welfare*, *30*, 1–12.

Bentham, J. (1776). *A fragment on government*. London: Payne.

Bentham, J. (1789). *An introduction to the principle of morals and legislation*. London: Payne.

Blackorby, C., Bossert, W., & Donaldson, D. (2005). *Population issues in social choice theory, welfare economics, and ethics*. Cambridge: Cambridge University Press.

d'Aspremont, C., & Gevers, L. (1977). Equity and the informational basis of collective choice. *Review of Economic Studies*, *44*, 199–209.

Diamond, P. (1965). The evaluation of infinite utility streams. *Econometrica*, *33*, 170–177.

Dubey, R. S. (2011). Fleurbaey-Michiel conjecture on equitable weak Paretian social welfare order. *Journal of Mathematical Economics*, *47*, 434–439.

Fleurbaey, M., & Michel, P. (2003). Intertemporal equity and the extension of the Ramsey criterion. *Journal of Mathematical Economics*, *39*, 777–802.

Hammond, P. J. (1979). Equity in two person situations: Some consequences. *Econometrica, 47*, 1127–1135.

Jonsson, A., & Voorneveld, M. (2018). The limit of discounted utilitarianism. *Theoretical Economics, 13*, 19–37.

Koopmans, T. C. (1960). Stationary ordinal utility and impatience. *Econometrica, 28*, 287–309.

Lauwers, L. (2010). Ordering infinite utility streams comes at the cost of a non-Ramsey set. *Journal of Mathematical Economics, 46*, 32–37.

Lauwers, L. (2016). The axiomatic approach to the ranking of infinite streams. In G. Chichilnisky, & A. Rezai (Eds.), *The economics of the global environment catastrophic risks in theory and policy*. Cham: Springer.

Nordhaus, W. (2007). Critical assumptions in the Stern review on climate change. *Science, 317*, 201–202.

Pigou, A. C. (1920). *The economics of welfare*. London: Macmillan.

Ramsey, F. (1928). A mathematical theory of saving. *Economic Journal, 38*, 543–559.

Rawls, J. (1958). Justice as fairness. *Philosophical Review, 64*, 167–194.

Rawls, J. (1963). Constitutional liberty and the concept of justice. In C. J. Friedrich & J. Chapman (Eds.), *Nomos VI: Justice*. New York: Atherton Press.

Rawls, J. (1967). Distributive justice. In P. Laslett & W. G. Runciman (Eds.), *Philosophy, politics, and society* (3rd Series). Oxford: Basil Blackwell.

Rawls, J. (1971). *A theory of justice*. Cambridge, MA: Harvard University Press.

Sakai, T. (2010). Intertemporal equity and an explicit construction of welfare criteria. *Social Choice and Welfare, 35*, 393–414.

Sen, A. K. (1970). *Collective choice and social welfare*. Amsterdam: Holden-Day.

Sidgwick, H. (1907). *The methods of ethics*. London: Macmillan.

Stern, N. (2007). *The economics of climate change-the stern review*. Cambridge: Cambridge University Press.

Svensson, L.-G. (1980). Equity among generations. *Econometrica, 48*, 1251–1256.

Szpilrajn, E. (1930). Sur l'extension de l'order partiel. *Fundamenta Mathematicae, 16*, 386–389.

Zame, W. (2007). Can intergenerational equity be operationalized? *Theoretical Economics, 2*, 187–202.

# Chapter 2
# Intragenerational Social Welfare Evaluation

**Abstract** This chapter examines the axiomatic foundations of social welfare orderings and quasi-orderings for intragenerational utility distributions assuming that the population size is fixed and finite. Utilitarianism, the leximin and maximin principles, and their compromises formulated in the forms of lexicographic composition and convex combination are, respectively, axiomatized using several versions of equity axioms as well as Pareto and anonymity axioms. Diagrammatic proofs are given for some of the results. Important in its own right, this chapter is also intended to serve as preliminary to the analysis of intergenerational welfare evaluation in the subsequent chapters.

**Keywords** Social welfare ordering · Utilitarianism · Leximin · Maximin

## 2.1 Introduction

The welfaristic analysis of social welfare evaluation is formally represented by the framework of ranking fixed- and finite-dimensional utility vectors. Each utility vector is interpreted as an attainable utility distribution under some social alternative, such as alternative economic policy options. A social welfare evaluation criterion for utility distributions compares relative goodness between utility distributions, and thus serves as an evaluation criterion for the underlying social alternatives. A social evaluation criterion is formalized as a reflexive, complete, and transitive binary relations on a set of utility vectors, which is called a "social welfare ordering." An evaluation criterion that is not necessarily complete is called a "social welfare quasi-ordering."

Two social welfare orderings are firmly rooted in moral philosophy. One is the utilitarian social welfare ordering, and the other is the maximin social welfare ordering, or leximin social welfare ordering, its lexicographic modification. The former reflects Bentham's (1776, 1789) principle of the greatest happiness of the greatest number, while the latter, or its lexicographic modification, is a welfarist analogue of Rawls's (1971) difference principle. A generalized utilitarian social welfare ordering takes a generalized form of utilitarianism, which compares the sums of transformed utilities. A generalized utilitarian social welfare ordering can exhibit inequality



K. Kamaga, *Social Welfare Evaluation and Intergenerational Equity*,
Development Bank of Japan Research Series,
https://doi.org/10.1007/978-981-15-4254-1_2

aversion using a concave transformation of utilities. In this sense, it is in-between the utilitarian and leximin or maximin social welfare orderings regarding the attitude to distributional equity. Other forms of a compromise between the utilitarian and leximin or maximin social welfare orderings are proposed by Roberts (1980) and Kamaga (2018). Roberts (1980) considers a convex combination of utilitarianism and the maximin principle, which is also analyzed by Bossert and Kamaga (2020) under the name of "mixed utilitarian-maximin social welfare ordering." Bossert and Kamaga (2020) also present two classes of social welfare orderings, each of which includes mixed utilitarian-maximin social welfare orderings. Kamaga (2018) proposes lexicographic compositions of the utilitarian social welfare ordering and the leximin social welfare ordering.

This chapter presents the axiomatizations of those social welfare orderings obtained in the literature on social choice theory. While some informational invariance axioms are considered, we will mainly focus on distributional equity axioms as well as the two basic axioms—the strong Pareto principle and anonymity. The next section presents the analytical framework for the welfarist analysis of social welfare evaluation. Section 2.3 provides the formal definitions of the social welfare orderings and quasi-orderings we consider. Axiomatizations of those evaluation criteria are given in Sect. 2.4. Diagrammatic expositions of the axiomatization proofs will be presented for readers unfamiliar with the axiomatic analysis of social evaluation criteria. Section 2.5 provides concluding remarks.

## 2.2 Preliminaries

Let $\mathbb{R}$ be the set of all real numbers and $\mathbb{R}_{++}$ be the set of all positive real numbers. The sets of all integers and all positive integers are denoted by $\mathbb{Z}$ and $\mathbb{N}$, respectively. Our notation for vector inequalities is given by the symbols $\geq$, $>$, and $\gg$. The symbols $\subseteq$ and $\subset$ are used for weak and strict set inclusion.

Let $N = \{1, \ldots, n\}$ be the set of individuals, where we assume $n \geq 2$. The set of all possible utility vectors $u = (u_1, \ldots, u_n)$ for $N$ is the $n$-dimensional Euclidean space $\mathbb{R}^n$, where $u_i$ is the utility level of individual $i \in N$. For each $u \in \mathbb{R}^n$, $u_{()} = (u_{(1)}, \ldots, u_{(n)})$ is a non-decreasing rearrangement of $u$, ties being broken arbitrarily. The $n$-dimensional vector that consists of $n$ ones is denoted by $1^n$.

A binary relation $\succsim^n$ on $\mathbb{R}^n$ is a subset of $\mathbb{R}^n \times \mathbb{R}^n$. For simplicity, we write $u \succsim^n v$ for $(u, v) \in \succsim$. The asymmetric and symmetric parts of $\succsim$ are denoted by $\succ^n$ and $\sim^n$, respectively. Thus, for all $u, v \in \mathbb{R}^n$, $u \succ^n v$ if and only if $u \succsim^n v$ and not $v \succsim^n u$, and $u \sim^n v$ if and only if $u \succsim^n v$ and $v \succsim^n u$. A social welfare quasi-ordering on $\mathbb{R}^n$ is a reflexive and transitive binary relation. A social welfare ordering on $\mathbb{R}^n$ is a complete social welfare quasi-ordering.

Given social welfare quasi-orderings $\succsim_A^n$ and $\succsim_B^n$ on $\mathbb{R}^n$, we say that $\succsim_A^n$ is a subrelation of $\succsim_B^n$ if, for all $u, v \in \mathbb{R}^n$, $u \succ_A^n v$ implies $u \succ_B^n v$, and $u \sim_A^n v$ implies $u \sim_B^n v$. Further, $\succsim_B^n$ is said to be an ordering extension of $\succsim_A^n$ if $\succsim_A^n$ is a subrelation of $\succsim_B^n$ and $\succsim_B^n$ is a social welfare ordering.

## 2.3 Utilitarianism, Leximin, and Compromised Criteria

We present the definitions of the utilitarian social welfare ordering, generalized utilitarian social welfare orderings, and the leximin social welfare ordering. We also present social welfare quasi-orderings that are compromises between the utilitarian and leximin social welfare orderings.

The *utilitarian* social welfare ordering is defined as the following binary relation $\succsim^n_U$ on $\mathbb{R}^n$. For all $u, v \in \mathbb{R}^n$,

$$u \succsim^n_U v \Leftrightarrow \sum_{i \in N} u_i \geq \sum_{i \in N} v_i. \tag{2.1}$$

We say that a social welfare ordering $\succsim^n$ on $\mathbb{R}^n$ is *weakly utilitarian* if $\succ^n_U \subseteq \succ^n$.

*Generalized utilitarian* social welfare orderings constitute a class of social welfare orderings that includes the utilitarian social welfare ordering as a special case. Let $G$ be the set of all continuous and increasing functions $g : \mathbb{R} \to \mathbb{R}$ with $g(0) = 0$. Given $g \in G$, the generalized utilitarian social welfare ordering associated with $g$ is defined as the following binary relation $\succsim^n_{U,g}$ on $\mathbb{R}^n$. For all $u, v \in \mathbb{R}^n$,

$$u \succsim^n_{U,g} v \Leftrightarrow \sum_{i \in N} g(u_i) \geq \sum_{i \in N} g(v_i). \tag{2.2}$$

If $g$ is linear, the associated $\succsim^n_{U,g}$ is the utilitarian social welfare ordering. If $g$ is strictly concave, the associated $\succsim^n_{U,g}$ exhibits strict inequality aversion.

The *leximin* social welfare ordering is the welfarist analogue of Rawls's (1971) lexical difference principle, which is extremely inequality averse. The leximin social welfare ordering is defined as the following binary relation $\succsim^n_L$ on $\mathbb{R}^n$. For all $u, v \in \mathbb{R}^n$,

$$u \succ^n_L v \Leftrightarrow \text{there exists } m \in N \text{ such that } u_{(m)} > v_{(m)} \text{ and } u_{(i)} = v_{(i)} \text{ for all } i < m, \tag{2.3a}$$

$$u \sim^n_L v \Leftrightarrow u_{(i)} = v_{(i)} \text{ for all } i \in N. \tag{2.3b}$$

The utilitarian social welfare ordering and the leximin social welfare ordering contrast with each other in their distributional equity properties. We present possible compromises between them. First, following Sen's (1973) intersection approach, the agreement of their evaluations can be formalized by taking their intersection. The *intersection* of the utilitarian and leximin social welfare ordering on $\mathbb{R}^n$, which we denote by $\succsim^n_\cap$, is defined by

$$\succsim^n_\cap = \succsim^n_U \cap \succsim^n_L, \tag{2.4}$$

that is, for all $u, v \in \mathbb{R}^n$, $u \succsim^n_\cap v$ if and only if $u \succsim^n_U v$ and $u \succsim^n_L v$. The intersection $\succsim^n_\cap$ first appeared in Blackorby and Donaldson (1977). Note that $\succsim^n_\cap$ is an incomplete quasi-ordering. Its asymmetric and symmetric parts are characterized as follows; see Kamaga (2018) for details. For all $u, v \in \mathbb{R}^n$,

$$u \succ^n_{\cap} v \Leftrightarrow u \succsim^n_U v \text{ and } u \succ^n_L v, \tag{2.5a}$$

$$u \sim^n_{\cap} v \Leftrightarrow u \sim^n_L v. \tag{2.5b}$$

The leximin social welfare ordering is an ordering extension of $\succsim^n_{\cap}$. Another ordering extension is given by the lexicographic composition of the utilitarian and leximin social welfare orderings. The *utilitarianism-first and leximin-second* social welfare ordering is defined as the following binary relation $\succsim^n_{UL}$ on $\mathbb{R}^n$. For all $u, v \in \mathbb{R}^n$,

$$u \succsim^n_{UL} v \Leftrightarrow \text{(i) } u \succ^n_U v \text{ or (ii) } u \sim^n_U v \text{ and } u \succsim^n_L v. \tag{2.6}$$

It is easy to verify that the asymmetric and symmetric parts of $\succsim^n_{UL}$ are given as follows. For all $u, v \in \mathbb{R}^n$, $u \succ^n_{UL} v$ if and only if (i) $u \succ^n_U v$ or (ii) $u \sim^n_U v$ and $u \succ^n_L v$, and $u \sim^n_{UL} v$ if and only if $u \sim^n_L v$. Therefore, $\succsim^n_{UL}$ is weakly utilitarian. Further, $\succsim^n_L$ and $\succsim^n_{UL}$ are the two possible lexicographic compositions of the utilitarian and leximin social welfare orderings since the lexicographic composition that applies the leximin first is the leximin social welfare ordering.

A compromise between the utilitarian social welfare ordering and the maximin principle was presented by Roberts (1980). It is a convex combination of them. In Bossert and Kamaga (2020), Roberts's (1980) criterion is called *mixed utilitarian-maximin* social welfare ordering. Let $\mu(u) = (1/n) \sum_{i \in N} u_i$ for all $u \in \mathbb{R}^n$. Given $\theta \in [0, 1]$, the mixed utilitarian-maximin social welfare ordering associated with $\theta$ is defined as the following binary relation $\succsim^n_{UM,\theta}$ on $\mathbb{R}^n$. For all $u, v \in \mathbb{R}^n$,

$$u \succsim^n_{UM,\theta} v \Leftrightarrow \theta\mu(u) + (1-\theta)u_{(1)} \geq \theta\mu(v) + (1-\theta)v_{(1)}. \tag{2.7}$$

If $\theta = 1$, the mixed utilitarian–maximin social welfare ordering represents the utilitarian social welfare ordering. Further, if $\theta = 0$, it represents the *maximin* social welfare ordering. See Bossert and Kamaga (2020) for generalizations of mixed utilitarian–maximin social welfare orderings.

## 2.4 Axiomatizations

We provide axiomatizations of the social welfare quasi-orderings presented in the previous section. We begin with axiomatizations of the utilitarian social welfare ordering and the generalized utilitarian social welfare orderings. To this end, we consider seven axioms. The first three axioms are concerned with efficiency, impartiality, and distributional equity, respectively.

Strong Pareto requires that the evaluation be positively sensitive to individuals' utilities.

**Strong Pareto**: For all $u, v \in \mathbb{R}^n$, if $u > v$ then $u \succ^n v$.

Anonymity postulates impartiality of the evaluation asserting that names of individuals do not matter in social welfare evaluation.

**Anonymity**: For all $u, v \in \mathbb{R}^n$, if there exists a bijection $\pi : N \to N$ such that $u_i = v_{\pi(i)}$ for all $i \in N$, then $u \sim^n v$.

Incremental equity asserts that any utility transfer between two individuals does not change social welfare. This axiom was introduced by Blackorby et al. (2002).

**Incremental Equity**: For all $u, v \in \mathbb{R}^n$, if there exist $i, j \in N$ such that $u_i - v_i = v_j - u_j$ and $u_k = v_k$ for all $k \in N \setminus \{i, j\}$, then $u \sim^n v$.

Note that incremental equity implies anonymity.

The following theorem shows that the utilitarian social welfare ordering is axiomatized by strong Pareto and incremental equity. This axiomatization was established by Blackorby et al. (2002), who consider a complete social welfare quasi-ordering (i.e., a social welfare ordering). However, their proof does not rely on the completeness of a social welfare quasi-ordering.

**Theorem 2.1** (Blackorby et al. 2002) *A social welfare quasi-ordering* $\succsim^n$ *on* $\mathbb{R}^n$ *satisfies strong Pareto and incremental equity if and only if* $\succsim^n = \succsim^n_U$.

***Proof*** The proof we present basically replicates the proof of Blackorby et al. (2002, 2005). Let $u \in \mathbb{R}^n$ and $s = \sum_{i \in N} u_i$. We begin by showing that $u \sim^n (0, \ldots, 0, s)$; see Fig. 2.1, which illustrates the proof for the case where $n = 3$ assuming that $u_i > 0$ for each $i \in \{1, 2, 3\}$. From incremental equity, we obtain

$$u \sim^n (0, u_1 + u_2, u_3, \ldots, u_n) \sim^n \left(0, 0, \sum_{i=1}^{3} u_i, u_4, \ldots, u_n\right) \sim^n \cdots \sim^n (0, \ldots, 0, s).$$

Since $\succsim^n$ is transitive, it follows that for all $u \in \mathbb{R}^n$,

$$u \sim^n (0, \ldots, 0, s). \tag{2.8}$$

Since $\succsim^n$ satisfies strong Pareto, it follows that for any $u_n, v_n \in \mathbb{R}$,

$$(0, \ldots, 0, u_n) \succsim^n (0, \ldots, 0, v_n) \Leftrightarrow u_n \geq v_n.$$

Thus, from (2.8) and the transitivity of $\succsim^n$, we obtain that for all $u, v \in \mathbb{R}^n$,

$$u \succsim^n v \Leftrightarrow \left(0, \ldots, 0, \sum_{i \in N} u_i\right) \succsim^n \left(0, \ldots, 0, \sum_{i \in N} v_i\right) \Leftrightarrow \sum_{i \in N} u_i \geq \sum_{i \in N} v_i.$$

■

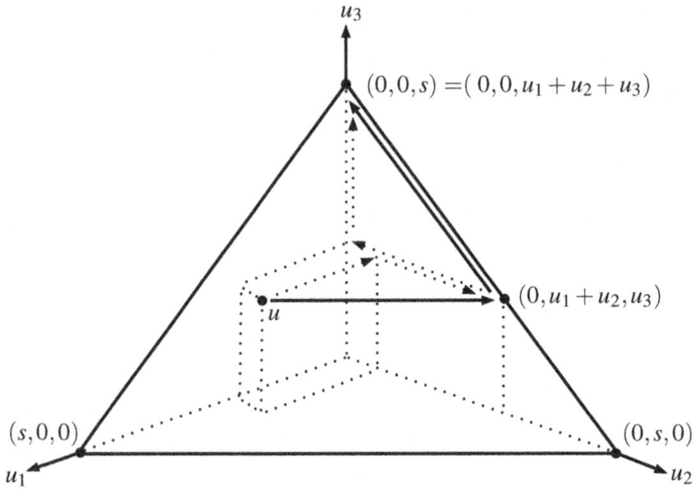


**Fig. 2.1** Implication of incremental equity when $n = 3$

An early axiomatization of the utilitarian social welfare ordering was presented by d'Aspremont and Gevers (1977) using strong Pareto, anonymity, and an informational invariance axiom. An informational invariance axiom formalizes an assumption of the measurability and interpersonal comparability of utilities. For the details on informational invariance axioms, see Blackorby et al. (2005), Bossert and Weymark (2004), and d'Aspremont and Gevers (2002). The invariance axiom that d'Aspremont and Gevers (1977) employed is cardinal unit-comparability, which requires that, for all $u, v, \bar{u}, \bar{v} \in \mathbb{R}^n$, if there exist $\alpha \in \mathbb{R}_{++}$ and $(\beta_1, \ldots, \beta_n) \in \mathbb{R}^n$ such that $\bar{u}_i = \alpha u_i + \beta_i$ and $\bar{v}_i = \alpha v_i + \beta_i$ for all $i \in N$, then $u \succsim^n v$ if and only if $\bar{u} \succsim^n \bar{v}$. As Blackorby et al. (2002, 2005) show, the utilitarian social welfare ordering is also axiomatized using translation-scale invariance instead of cardinal unit-comparability. Translation-scale invariance asserts that utilities are cardinally measurable and utility differences are interpersonally comparable by an absolute unit.

**Translation-scale Invariance**: For all $u, v, \bar{u}, \bar{v} \in \mathbb{R}^n$, if there exists $(\beta_1, \ldots, \beta_n) \in \mathbb{R}^n$ such that $\bar{u}_i = u_i + \beta_i$ and $\bar{v}_i = v_i + \beta_i$ for all $i \in N$, then

$$u \succsim^n v \Leftrightarrow \bar{u} \succsim^n \bar{v}.$$

Translation-scale invariance is logically weaker than cardinal unit-comparability.

The following theorem follows from the stronger result shown by Blackorby et al. (2002, 2005). In Blackorby et al. (2002), they present a stronger result using the weak Pareto principle instead of strong Pareto. Further, in Blackorby et al. (2005), they strengthen the result by weakening weak Pareto to minimal increasingness.

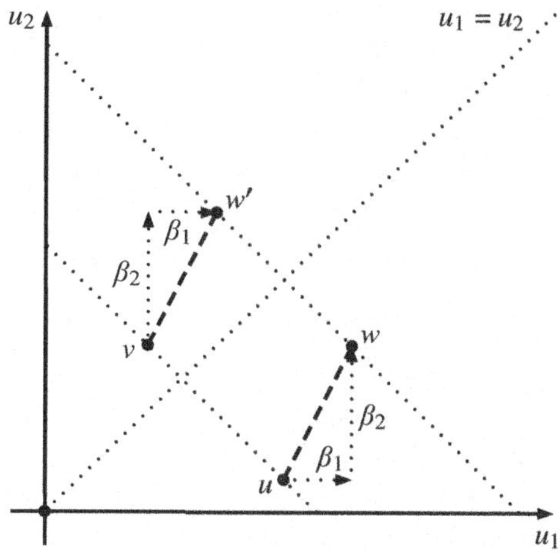


**Fig. 2.2** Diagrammatic proof of Lemma 2.1

**Theorem 2.2** (Blackorby et al. 2002, 2005) *A social welfare quasi-ordering* $\succsim^n$ *on* $\mathbb{R}^n$ *satisfies strong Pareto, anonymity, and translation-scale invariance if and only if* $\succsim^n = \succsim^n_U$.

Theorem 2.2 follows from Theorem 2.1 and the following lemma presented by Blackorby et al. (2002).

**Lemma 2.1** (Blackorby et al. 2002) *If a social welfare quasi-ordering* $\succsim^n$ *on* $\mathbb{R}^n$ *satisfies anonymity and translation-scale invariance, then* $\succsim^n$ *satisfies incremental equity.*

***Proof*** For a formal proof, see Blackorby et al. (2002, Theorem 11). We present a diagrammatic proof for the case where $n = 2$, which visualizes their original proof. Let $u, v \in \mathbb{R}^2$ and suppose that $u_1 - v_1 = v_2 - u_2$ (i.e., $u_1 + u_2 = v_1 + v_2$). Thus, $u$ and $v$ lie on a line with a slope of $-1$. As illustrated in Fig. 2.2, using suitably chosen $\beta_1$ and $\beta_2$ with $\beta_1, \beta_2 > 0$, we can find $w, w' \in \mathbb{R}^2$ that satisfy

$$\begin{aligned}
&w_1 + w_2 = w'_1 + w'_2,\\
&w_1 = w'_2 \text{ and } w_2 = w'_1,\\
&w_1 - w'_1 = u_1 - v_1,\\
&w_i = u_i + \beta_i \text{ and } w'_i = v_i + \beta_i \text{ for each } i = 1, 2.
\end{aligned}$$

The second condition means that $w$ and $w'$ are symmetric with the 45° line. The third condition means that the length of line segment $uv$ is the same as that of line segment $ww'$. From anonymity, $w \sim^n w'$ follows. By translation-scale invariance, we obtain $u \sim^n v$. ■

This diagrammatic proof is easily applicable to the general $n$-person case by setting $\beta_k = 0$ for all $k$ except for $i$ and $j$ considered in the definition of incremental equity. The converse implication of the lemma does not hold. For example, consider the social welfare ordering defined as follows. For all $u, v \in \mathbb{R}^n$, $u \succsim^n v$ if and only if either (i) or (ii) holds:

$$\text{(i)} \sum_{i \in N} u_i \geq \sum_{i \in N} v_i \text{ and } \left[ \sum_{i \in N} u_i \notin [0, 1] \text{ or } \sum_{i \in N} v_i \notin [0, 1] \right],$$

$$\text{(ii)} \sum_{i \in N} u_i \in [0, 1] \text{ and } \sum_{i \in N} v_i \in [0, 1].$$

This ordering satisfies incremental equity (and thus, anonymity) but violates translation-scale invariance.

Another axiomatization of the utilitarian social welfare ordering was provided by Maskin (1978), who used a different informational invariance axiom together with separability and continuity.

Cardinal full comparability corresponds to the assumption that utilities are cardinally measurable and that not only utility differences but also utility levels are interpersonally comparable.

**Cardinal Full Comparability**: For all $u, v, \bar{u}, \bar{v} \in \mathbb{R}^n$, if there exist $\alpha \in \mathbb{R}_{++}$ and $\beta \in \mathbb{R}$ such that $\bar{u}_i = \alpha u_i + \beta$ and $\bar{v}_i = \alpha v_i + \beta$ for all $i \in N$, then

$$u \succsim^n v \Leftrightarrow \bar{u} \succsim^n \bar{v}.$$

Separability asserts that the evaluation is independent of utility-unconcerned individuals.

**Separability**: For $u, v, \bar{u}, \bar{v} \in \mathbb{R}^n$, if there exists $M \subseteq N$ such that $u_i = v_i$ and $\bar{u}_i = \bar{v}_i$ for all $i \in M$ and $u_i = \bar{u}_i$ and $v_i = \bar{v}_i$ for all $i \in N \setminus M$, then

$$u \succsim^n v \Leftrightarrow \bar{u} \succsim^n \bar{v}.$$

Note that separability is implied by translation-scale invariance. This can be verified as follows. Let $u, v, \bar{u}, \bar{v} \in \mathbb{R}^n$ and suppose that there exists $M \subseteq N$ such that $u_i = v_i$ and $\bar{u}_i = \bar{v}_i$ for all $i \in M$ and $u_i = \bar{u}_i$ and $v_i = \bar{v}_i$ for all $i \in N \setminus M$. Then, $(\beta_1, \ldots, \beta_n) \in \mathbb{R}^n$ defined by $\beta_i = \bar{u}_i - u_i$ for all $i \in M$ and $\beta_j = 0$ for all $j \in N \setminus M$ satisfies that $\bar{u}_i = u_i + \beta_i$ and $\bar{v}_i = v_i + \beta_i$ for all $i \in N$. Thus, translation-scale invariance implies that $u \succsim^n v$ if and only if $\bar{u} \succsim^n \bar{v}$.

Continuity asserts that small changes in utilities do not lead to large changes in social welfare. Therefore, it postulates the robustness of the evaluation to small changes in utilities.

**Continuity**: For all $u \in \mathbb{R}^n$, $\{v \in \mathbb{R}^n : v \succsim^n u\}$ and $\{v \in \mathbb{R}^n : u \succsim^n v\}$ are closed in $\mathbb{R}^n$.

Assuming that $n \geq 3$ and a social welfare quasi-ordering is complete (i.e., a social welfare ordering), if we add separability and continuity and replace translation-scale invariance with caridinal full comparability in the list of the axioms of Theorem 2.2, we obtain an alternative axiomatization of the utilitarian social welfare ordering; for a proof, see Maskin (1978).

**Theorem 2.3** (Maskin 1978) *Let $n \geq 3$. A social welfare ordering $\succsim^n$ on $\mathbb{R}^n$ satisfies strong Pareto, anonymity, separability, cardinal full comparability, and continuity if and only if $\succsim^n = \succsim^n_U$.*

If we do not impose cardinal full comparability, a generalized utilitarian social welfare ordering is characterized. This result is a symmetric analogue of the additive separable representation theorem of Debreu (1960); for a proof, see Blackorby et al. (2002, Theorem 5).

**Theorem 2.4** *Let $n \geq 3$. A social welfare ordering $\succsim^n$ on $\mathbb{R}^n$ satisfies strong Pareto, anonymity, separability, and continuity if and only if there exists $g \in G$ such that $\succsim^n = \succsim^n_{U,g}$.*

Next, we present an axiomatization of the leximin social welfare ordering, using a distributional equity axiom. Hammond equity, introduced by Hammond (1976, 1979), asserts that the decrease in utility difference between better-off and worse-off individuals that preserves their relative ranking weakly increases social welfare.

**Hammond Equity**: For all $u, v \in \mathbb{R}^n$, if there exist $i, j \in N$ such that $v_i < u_i \leq u_j < v_j$ and $u_k = v_k$ for all $k \in N \setminus \{i, j\}$, then $u \succsim^n v$.

Note that the leximin social welfare ordering satisfies Hammond equity but violates incremental equity, whereas the utilitarian social welfare ordering satisfies the latter and violates the former.

The following axiomatization was established by Hammond (1979); see also Hammond (1976). It shows that strong Pareto, finite anonymity, and Hammond equity together characterizes the leximin social welfare ordering. The original result in Hammond (1979) assumes the completeness of a social welfare quasi-ordering. However, his proof does not rely on this assumption.

**Theorem 2.5** (Hammond 1979) *A social welfare quasi-ordering $\succsim^n$ on $\mathbb{R}^n$ satisfies strong Pareto, anonymity, and Hammond equity if and only if $\succsim^n = \succsim^n_L$.*

***Proof*** We present a diagrammatic proof for the case where $n = 2$ using Fig. 2.3; for a formal proof, see Hammond (1979), Bossert and Weymark (2004), or Blackorby et al. (2005).

Let $u \in \mathbb{R}^2$. Without loss of generality, we assume $u_1 > u_2 > 0$; if $u_1 = u_2$, then the proof becomes easier because areas $A_1$ and $A'_1$ in Fig. 2.3 disappear. Let $u' = (u_2, u_1)$, that is, the point that is symmetric with the 45° line illustrated by the dotted line in Fig. 2.3. Using the 45° line and the dashed lines passing through $u$ and $u'$, we decompose $\mathbb{R}^2$ into eight areas surrounded by the dashed and dotted lines. Note that areas $A_i$ and $A'_i$ are symmetric with the 45° line for each $i \in \{1, \ldots, 4\}$. We prove that $\succsim^2 = \succsim^2_L$ by showing the ranking for $u$ and an arbitrary point in each of the eight areas. Each area includes its boundary unless otherwise noted.

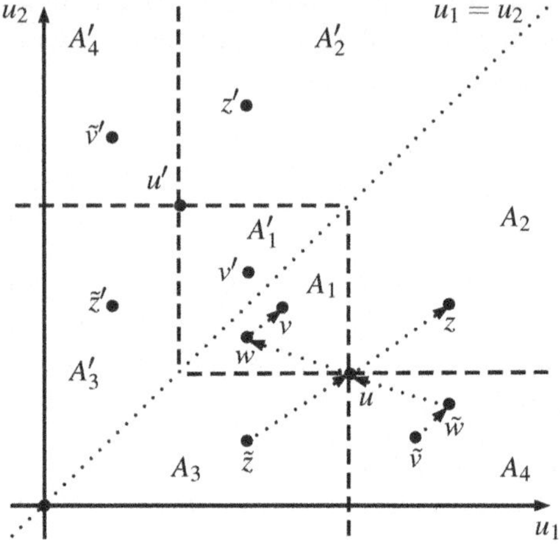


**Fig. 2.3** Diagrammatic proof of Theorem 2.5

First, let $v \in A_1$ and suppose that $v$ does not lie on the horizontal dashed line. Then, we can find $w \in A_1$ that is not on the boundary of $A_1$ and satisfies $v_i > w_i$ for each $i = 1, 2$. Since $\succsim^2$ satisfies strong Pareto, we obtain $v \succ^2 w$. Further, since $u_2 < w_2 < w_1 < u_1$, it follows from Hammond equity that $w \succsim^2 u$. Thus, $v \succ^2 u$ follows from the transitivity of $\succsim^2$. From anonymity and the transitivity of $\succsim^2$, $v' \succ^2 u$ follows for $v' \in A'_1$ that is the symmetric counterpart of $v$.

The analogous argument applies to $\tilde{v} \in A_4$ that is not on the horizontal dashed line and its symmetric counterpart $\tilde{v}' \in A'_4$. Specifically, there exists $\tilde{w} \in A_4$ that is not on the boundary of $A_4$ and satisfies $\tilde{w}_i > \tilde{v}_i$ for each $i = 1, 2$. Thus, from strong Pareto and Hammond equity, we obtain $u \succ^2 \tilde{v}$. Analogously, we obtain $u \succ^2 \tilde{v}'$.

Next, let $z \in A_2$ and $\tilde{z} \in A_3$. Then, from strong Pareto, $z \succ^2 u$ and $u \succ^2 \tilde{z}$ follow. Analogously, we obtain that $z' \succ^2 u$ and $u \succ^2 \tilde{z}'$ for the symmetric counterparts $z' \in A'_2$ and $\tilde{z}' \in A'_3$ of $z$ and $\tilde{z}$, respectively.

Finally, $u \sim^2 u'$ follows from anonymity. Thus, $\succsim^2 = \succsim^2_L$. ■

An alternative axiomatization of the leximin social welfare ordering was presented by d'Aspremont and Gevers (1977) using ordinal full comparability, separability, and minimal equity instead of Hammond equity; see also Gevers (1979) and Ou-Yang (2018).

From Theorems 2.1 and 2.5, the utilitarian and leximin social welfare orderings contrast in their distributional equity properties: The former is characterized by incremental equity, while the latter is compatible with Hammond equity. We now examine possible compromises between them. To this end, we define the property of a social welfare quasi-ordering that has monotonicity with respect to the evaluations of the utilitarian and leximin social welfare orderings. We say that a social welfare quasi-ordering $\succsim^n$ on $\mathbb{R}^n$ is *UL-monotone* if, for all $u, v \in \mathbb{R}^n$,

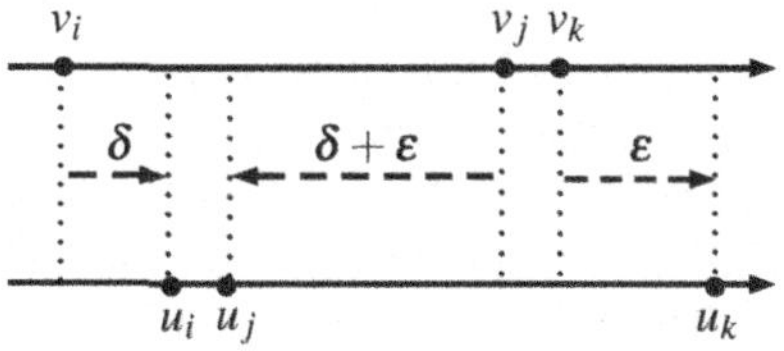


**Fig. 2.4** Transfers in the composite transfer principle

$$u \succ^n v \text{ if } u \succ_U^n v \text{ and } u \succ_L^n v, \tag{2.9a}$$
$$u \succsim^n v \text{ if } u \succsim_U^n v \text{ and } u \succsim_L^n v. \tag{2.9b}$$

Note that (2.9b) is equivalent to requiring that (i) $u \succsim^n v$ if $u \sim_U^n v$ and $u \succ_L^n v$ and (ii) $u \sim v$ if $u \sim_U^n v$ and $u \sim_L^n v$.

To axiomatize a $UL$-monotone social welfare ordering and the intersection $\succsim_\cap^n$ of the utilitarian and leximin social welfare orderings, we consider three transfer principles. First, we present weak and strong versions of the transfer principle of Pigou (1912) and Dalton (1920). The weak version asserts that a progressive utility transfer weakly increases social goodness as long as it maintains the relative ranking of the two individuals involved. The strong version claims that such a transfer increases social welfare.

**Weak Pigou–Dalton Principle**: For all $u, v \in \mathbb{R}^n$, if there exist $i, j \in N$ and $\delta \in \mathbb{R}_{++}$ such that $v_i + \delta = u_i \leq u_j = v_j - \delta$ and $u_k = v_k$ for all $k \in N$, then $u \succsim^n v$.

**Strong Pigou–Dalton Principle**: For all $u, v \in \mathbb{R}^n$, if there exist $i, j \in N$ and $\delta \in \mathbb{R}_{++}$ such that $v_i + \delta = u_i \leq u_j = v_j - \delta$ and $u_k = v_k$ for all $k \in N$, then $u \succ^n v$.

The composite transfer principle was introduced by Kamaga (2018) and used in Bossert and Kamaga (2020). Similarly to the transfer sensitivity axiom of Shorrocks and Foster (1987), it considers a composition of progressive and regressive utility transfers involving three individuals. Specifically, it asserts that the composition of a progressive transfer between the wrost-off and the second worst-off of the three and a regressive transfer between the second worst-off and the best-off of the three weakly increase social welfare (see Fig. 2.4). Its variant is used by Bossert et al. (2020) in the context of inequality measurement.

**Composite Transfer Principle**: For all $u, v \in \mathbb{R}^n$, if there exist $i, j, k \in N$ and $\delta, \varepsilon \in \mathbb{R}_{++}$ such that $u_i = v_i + \delta, u_j = v_j - \delta - \varepsilon, u_k = v_k + \varepsilon, u_i \leq u_j < u_k, v_i < v_j \leq v_k$, and $u_\ell = v_\ell$ for all $\ell \in N \setminus \{i, j, k\}$, then $u \succsim^n v$.

As shown by Bossert and Kamaga (2020), the conjunction of strong Pareto and Hammond equity implies the composite transfer principle. Further, the conjunction of strong Pareto and the composite transfer principle is compatible with continuity, whereas the conjunction of strong Pareto and Hammond equity is not. Bossert and Kamaga (2020) present another justification of the composite transfer principle by referring to Cowell's (1985) argument about a composition of a progressive transfer at the bottom end and a regressive transfer at the top end. As Cowell (1985, p. 568) notes, "some kind of weighting must be imposed on 'top-end' transfers as against 'bottom-end' transfers" to go beyond the implication of the weak or strong Pigou–Dalton transfer principle. In view of this argument, the composite transfer principle is seen to postulate a consistency property asserting that the progressive transfer at the bottom-end never outweighs the regressive transfer at the top-end.

The following theorem shows that a $UL$-monotone social welfare quasi-ordering is axiomatized by adding the weak Pigou–Dalton principle and the composite transfer principle to strong Pareto and anonymity.

**Theorem 2.6** (Kamaga 2018) *A social welfare quasi-ordering $\succsim^n$ on $\mathbb{R}^n$ satisfies strong Pareto, anonymity, the weak Pigou–Dalton principle, and the composite transfer principle if and only if $\succsim^n$ is $UL$-monotone.*

***Proof*** 'If.' Since $\succsim^n_U$ and $\succsim^n_L$ satisfy strong Pareto, it follows from (2.9a) that $\succsim^n$ satisfies strong Pareto. Further, since $\succsim^n_U$ and $\succsim^n_L$ satisfy anonymity, the weak Pigou–Dalton principle, and the composite transfer principle, it follows from (2.9b) that $\succsim^n$ satisfies these axioms.

'Only if.' The proof proceeds in three steps. Let $u, v \in \mathbb{R}^n$.

*Step 1*. We show that $u \sim^n_U v$ and $u \sim^n_L v$ imply $u \sim^n v$. Since $u \sim^n_L v$ and $\succsim^n$ satisfies anonymity, we obtain $u \sim^n v$.

*Step 2*. We show that $u \sim^n_U v$ and $u \succ^n_L v$ imply $u \succsim^n v$. Suppose that $u \sim^n_U v$ and $u \succ^n_L v$. From (2.1) to (2.3a), there exists $m \in N$ with $m < n$ such that $u_{(m)} > v_{(m)}$, $u_{(i)} = v_{(i)}$ for all $i < m$, and $\sum_{i=m}^n u_{(i)} = \sum_{i=m}^n v_{(i)}$. Since $\succsim^n$ satisfies anonymity and transitivity, we can assume that $u_i = u_{(i)}$ and $v_i = v_{(i)}$ for all $i \in N$. We distinguish two cases.

(a) $m = n - 1$. Let $\delta = u_m - v_m$. Then, $u$ and $v$ satisfy that $v_m + \delta = u_m \leq u_n = v_n - \delta$ and $u_k = v_k$ for all $k \in N \setminus \{i, j\}$. Thus, it follows from the weak Pigou–Dalton principle that $u \succsim^n v$.

(b) $m \leq n - 2$. Let $\delta \in \mathbb{R}_{++}$ satisfy

$$\delta < \min\left\{\frac{u_m - v_m}{n - m - 1}, \min\{v_i - u_i : v_i - u_i > 0 \text{ and } i \in \{m + 1, \ldots, n - 1\}\}\right\}.$$

We define the finite sequence $\{w^m, \ldots, w^{n-1}\}$ of vectors in $\mathbb{R}^n$ as follows. Vector $w^m$ is defined by $w^m = v$. For all $t \in \{m + 1, \ldots, n - 1\}$, $w^t$ is defined by

$$\begin{aligned}
w^t_i &= w^{t-1}_i \text{ for all } i \in N \setminus \{m, t, n\},\\
w^t_m &= \begin{cases} w^{t-1}_m & \text{if } u_t \geq v_t \\ w^{t-1}_m + \delta & \text{if } u_t < v_t, \end{cases}\\
w^t_t &= \min\{u_t, v_t\},\\
w^t_n &= \begin{cases} w^{t-1}_n & \text{if } u_t \geq v_t \\ w^{t-1}_n + v_t - u_t - \delta & \text{if } u_t < v_t. \end{cases}
\end{aligned}$$

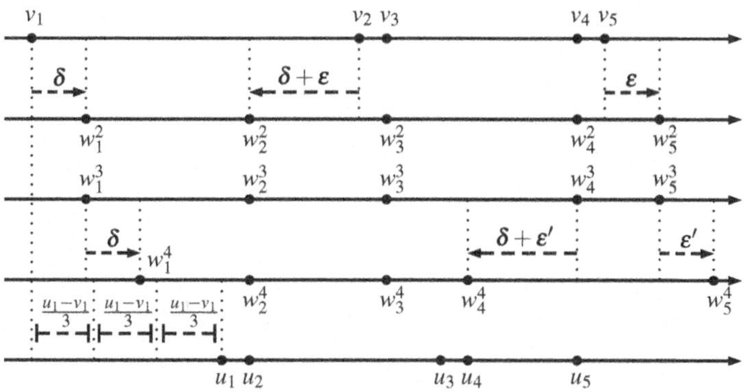


**Fig. 2.5** Construction of the sequence $\{w^2, \ldots, w^4\}$

Figure 2.5 illustrates the construction of sequence $\{w^{m+1}, \ldots, w^{n-1}\}$ where we assume that $m = 1, n = 5, \delta < (u_1 - v_1)/3 < v_2 - u_2 = v_4 - u_4$ and $u_3 > v_3$.

For all $t \in \{m+1, \ldots, n-1\}$, if $u_t \geq v_t$, then it follows from the reflexivity of $\succsim^n$ that

$$w^t \sim^n w^{t-1}$$

and if $u_t < v_t$, then from the composite transfer principle, we obtain

$$w^t \succsim^n w^{t-1}.$$

Since $\succsim^n$ is transitive, we obtain

$$w^{n-1} \succsim^n v.$$

We show that $u \succsim^n w^{n-1}$, which will complete Step 2 since $\succsim$ is transitive. From the definition of sequence $\{w^m, \ldots, w^{n-1}\}$, it follows that $u_i = w_i^{n-1}$ for all $i < m$, $u_m > w_m^{n-1}$, and $u_i \geq w_i^{n-1}$ for all $i \in \{m+1, \ldots, n-1\}$. Further, $u_n < w_n^{n-1}$ holds since $\sum_{i=m}^{n} w_i^{n-1} = \sum_{i=m}^{n} v_i = \sum_{i=m}^{n} u_i$. For all $t \in \{m, \ldots, n-1\}$, let

$$\delta_t = u_t - w_t^{n-1} \geq 0.$$

We define the finite sequence $\{z^n, z^{n-1}, \ldots, z^m\}$ of vectors in $\mathbb{R}^n$ as follows. Vector $z^n$ is defined by $z^n = w^{n-1}$. For all $t \in \{m, \ldots, n-1\}$, $z^t$ is defined by

$$\begin{aligned} z_i^t &= z_i^{t+1} \text{ for all } i \in N \setminus \{t, n\}, \\ z_t^t &= z_t^{t+1} + \delta_t, \\ z_n^t &= z_n^{t+1} - \delta_t. \end{aligned}$$

Note that $z^m = u$ since $\sum_{t=m}^{n-1} \delta_t = w_n^{n-1} - u_n$. Further, for all $t \in \{m, \ldots, n-1\}$,

$$z^{t+1} + \delta_t = z_t^t \leq z_n^t = z_n^{t+1} - \delta_t$$

and $z_i^t = z_i^{t+1}$ for all $i \in N \setminus \{t, n\}$ since $z_t^t = u_t \leq u_n \leq z_n^t$. By the weak Pigou–Dalton principle and the reflexivity of $\succsim^n$, we obtain that for all $t \in \{m+1, \ldots, n-1\}$,

$$z^t \succsim^n z^{t+1}.$$

Moreover, it follows from the weak Pigou–Dalton principle that

$$z^m \succsim^n z^{m+1}.$$

Since $\succsim$ is transitive, we obtain $z^m \succsim^n z^n$, i.e., $u \succsim^n w^{n-1}$.

*Step 3*. We show that $u \succ_U^n v$ and $u \succ_L^n v$ imply $u \succ^n v$. Suppose that $u \succ_U^n v$ and $u \succ_L^n v$. From (2.1) to (2.3a), there exists $m \in N$ such that $u_{(m)} > v_{(m)}$, $u_{(i)} = v_{(i)}$ for all $i < m$, and $\sum_{i=m}^n u_{(i)} > \sum_{i=m}^n v_{(i)}$. Since $\succsim^n$ satisfies anonymity and transitivity, we can assume that $u_i = u_{(i)}$ and $v_i = v_{(i)}$ for all $i \in N$. If $m = n$, then we obtain $u \succ^n v$ by strong Pareto. We now assume that $m < n$. Let $\Delta = \sum_{i=m}^n (u_i - v_i) > 0$ and define $w \in \mathbb{R}^n$ by $w_n = v_n + \Delta$ and $w_i = v_i$ for all $i < n$. Then, we obtain $u \sim_U^n w$ and $u \succ_L^n w$. From Step 2, $u \succsim^n w$ follows. By strong Pareto, we obtain $w \succ^n v$. Since $\succsim^n$ is transitive, $u \succ^n v$ follows. ■

The following theorem shows that if we strengthen the weak Pigou–Dalton principle to the strong version, a permissible social welfare quasi-ordering must respect the evaluation of the intersection of the utilitarian and leximin social welfare orderings.

**Theorem 2.7** (Kamaga 2018) *A social welfare quasi-ordering $\succsim^n$ on $\mathbb{R}^n$ satisfies strong Pareto, anonymity, the strong Pigou–Dalton principle, and the composite transfer principle if and only if $\succsim_\cap^n$ is a subrelation of $\succsim^n$.*

***Proof*** 'If.' Suppose that $\succsim_\cap^n$ is a subrelation of $\succsim^n$. Then, $\succsim^n$ is $UL$-monotone. From Theorem 2.6, $\succsim^n$ satisfies strong Pareto, anonymity, and the composite transfer principle. From (2.5a), $\succsim_\cap^n$ satisfies the strong Pigou–Dalton principle. Thus, $\succsim^n$ also satisfies it.

'Only if.' Let $u, v \in \mathbb{R}^n$. From Theorem 2.6, if $u \succ_U^n v$ and $u \succ_L^n v$ then $u \succ^n v$, and if $u \sim_L^n v$ then $u \sim^n v$. Therefore, from (2.5a) to (2.5b), completing the proof requires only showing that $u \sim_U^n v$ and $u \succ_L^n v$ imply $u \succ^n v$. We can show this by using the strong Pigou–Dalton principle instead of the weak Pigou–Dalton principle in Step 2 of the proof of Theorem 2.6. Specifically, $z^m \succ^n z^{m+1}$ follows from the strong Pigou–Dalton principle; we thus obtain $u \succ^n w^{n-1}$ in Step 2. (We omit its detailed proof.) ■

The classes of social welfare quasi-orderings characterized in Theorems 2.6 and 2.7 contains social welfare orderings. For instance, the class characterized in Theorem 2.7 contains the leximin social welfare ordering and the utilitarianism-first and leximin-second social welfare ordering since, as we noted earlier, they are ordering extensions of $\succsim^n_{\cap}$. In addition to these social welfare orderings, the class characterized in Theorem 2.6 contains the utilitarian social welfare ordering as well. We next examine social welfare orderings in these classes. A closely related result was presented by Deschamps and Gevers (1978) using the minimal equity axiom. Minimal equity is a very weak distributional equity axiom, which is implied by any of incremental equity, Hammond equity, and the weak and strong Pigou–Dalton principles.

**Minimal Equity**: There exist $u, v \in \mathbb{R}^n$ and $i, j \in N$ such that $v_i < u_i < u_j < v_j$, $u_k = v_k$ for all $k \in N \setminus \{i, j\}$, and $u \succsim^n v$.

Assuming that $n \geq 3$ and a social welfare quasi-ordering is complete, Deschamps and Gevers (1978) show that, if we add separability and cardinal full comparability and replace the weak Pigou-Dalton principle and the composite transfer principle with minimal equity, either the leximin social welfare ordering or a weakly utilitarian social welfare ordering is a permissible social welfare ordering; for the proof, see Deschamps and Gevers (1978).

**Theorem 2.8** (Deschamps and Gevers 1978) *Let $n \geq 3$. If a social welfare ordering $\succsim^n$ on $\mathbb{R}^n$ satisfies strong Pareto, anonymity, minimal equity, separability, and cardinal full comparability, then either $\succsim^n = \succsim^n_L$ or $\succsim^n$ is weakly utilitarian.*

In the following theorem, we show the consequence of assuming $n \geq 3$ and the completeness of a social welfare ordering and adding separability and cardinal full comparability in our axiomatization of $UL$-monotone social welfare quasi-orderings (Theorem 2.6). The theorem shows that we obtain a joint characterization of the utilitarian, leximin, and the utilitarianism-first and leximin-second social welfare orderings.

**Theorem 2.9** (Kamaga 2018) *Let $n \geq 3$. A social welfare ordering $\succsim^n$ on $\mathbb{R}^n$ satisfies strong Pareto, anonymity, the weak Pigou–Dalton principle, the composite transfer principle, separability, and cardinal full comparability if and only if any one of the following three holds: $\succsim^n = \succsim^n_U$, $\succsim^n = \succsim^n_{UL}$, and $\succsim^n = \succsim^n_L$.*

To prove the theorem, we use the following lemma. It shows that—assuming anonymity, separability, and cardinal full comparability—if a social welfare ordering satisfies the weak Pigou–Dalton principle, a permissible ordering must satisfy either the strong Pigou–Dalton principle or incremental equity.

**Lemma 2.2** (Kamaga 2018) *Let $n \geq 3$ and suppose that a social welfare ordering $\succsim^n$ on $\mathbb{R}^n$ satisfies anonymity, separability, and cardinal full comparability. Then, $\succsim^n$ satisfies the weak Pigou–Dalton principle if and only if $\succsim^n$ satisfies either the strong Pigou–Dalton principle or incremental equity.*

***Proof*** 'If.' The proof is straightforward, since the strong Pigou–Dalton principle and incremental equity both imply the weak Pigou–Dalton principle.

'Only if.' The proof proceeds in four steps.

*Step 1*. Suppose that there exist $u, v \in \mathbb{R}^n$ and $\delta^* \in \mathbb{R}_{++}$ such that $v_2 + \delta^* = u_2 = u_1 = v_1 - \delta^*$, $u_i = v_i$ for all $i \in N \backslash \{1, 2\}$ and $u \sim^n v$. We show that $\succsim^n$ satisfies incremental equity. By separability, we can assume that $u_i = v_i = u_1$ for all $i \neq 1, 2$. From cardinal full comparability, it follows that

$$(u_1 - u_1, \ldots, u_n - u_1) = (0, 0, 0, \ldots, 0) \sim^n (\delta^*, -\delta^*, 0, \ldots, 0) = (v_1 - u_1, \ldots, v_n - u_1).$$

Further, by cardinal full comparability, we obtain that for any $\alpha \in \mathbb{R}_{++}$,

$$(0, 0, 0, \ldots, 0) \sim^n (\alpha\delta^*, -\alpha\delta^*, 0, \ldots, 0).$$

This means that for all $\delta \in \mathbb{R}_{++}$,

$$(0, 0, 0, \ldots, 0) \sim^n (\delta, -\delta, 0, \ldots, 0). \tag{2.10}$$

Since $\succsim^n$ is transitive and it satisfies anonymity, it follows from (2.10) that for all $\delta \in \mathbb{R}_{++}$,

$$(0, 0, 0, \ldots, 0) \sim^n (-\delta, \delta, 0, \ldots, 0). \tag{2.11}$$

Let $\bar{z} \in \mathbb{R}^n$ and define $D(\bar{z}) \subset \mathbb{R}^n$ by

$$D(\bar{z}) = \{z \in \mathbb{R}^n : z_1 + z_2 = 0 \text{ and } z_i = \bar{z}_i \text{ for all } i \in N \setminus \{1, 2\}\}.$$

Since $\succsim^n$ is transitive and it satisfies separability, it follows from (2.10) to (2.11) that for any $\bar{z} \in \mathbb{R}^n$ and for any $w, z \in D(\bar{z})$,

$$w \sim^n z. \tag{2.12}$$

Now, let $w, z \in \mathbb{R}^n$ and suppose that $w_1 - z_1 = z_2 - w_2$ and $w_i = z_i$ for all $i \in N \setminus \{1, 2\}$. Since $\succsim^n$ satisfies anonymity and transitivity, completing the proof requires only showing that $w \sim^n z$. Note that $w_1 + w_2 = z_1 + z_2$ and $w_i = z_i$ for all $i \neq 1, 2$. Let $\beta \in \mathbb{R}$ with $\beta = (w_1 + w_2)/2$. From cardinal full comparability, it follows that

$$w \succsim^n z \Leftrightarrow (w_1 - \beta, w_2 - \beta, \ldots, w_n - \beta) \succsim^n (z_1 - \beta, z_2 - \beta, \ldots, z_n - \beta). \tag{2.13}$$

Since $w_1 + w_2 - 2\beta = z_1 + z_2 - 2\beta = 0$, $w \sim^n z$ follows from (2.12) to (2.13).

*Step 2*. Suppose that there exist $u, v \in \mathbb{R}^n$ and $\delta^* \in \mathbb{R}_{++}$ such that $v_2 + \delta^* = u_2 < u_1 = v_1 - \delta^*$, $u_k = v_k$ for all $k \in N \setminus \{1, 2\}$ and $u \sim^n v$. We show that for all $w, z \in \mathbb{R}^n$, if there exist $i, j \in N$ such that $w_i - z_i = z_j - w_j$, $w_i \neq w_j$ and $z_i \neq z_j$, then

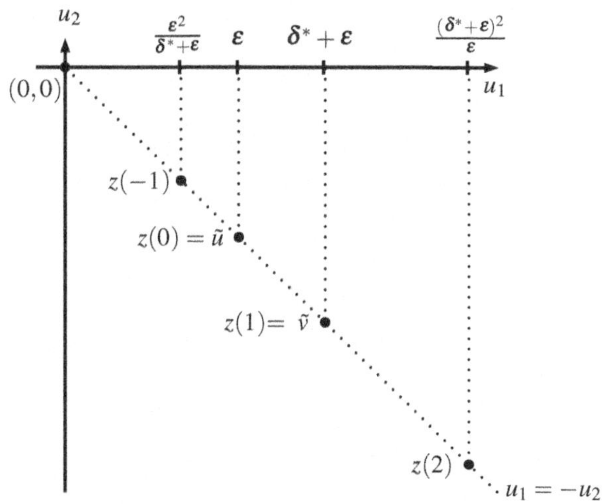


**Fig. 2.6** Construction of $z(m)$ when $(\delta^* + \varepsilon)/\varepsilon = 3/2$

$w \sim^n z$. Let $\varepsilon = (u_1 - u_2)/2$. By separability, we can assume that $u_i = v_i = u_2 + \varepsilon$ for all $i \neq 1, 2$. We define $\tilde{u}, \tilde{v} \in \mathbb{R}^n$ by

$$\tilde{u} = (u_1 - (u_2 + \varepsilon), \dots, u_n - (u_2 + \varepsilon)) = (\varepsilon, -\varepsilon, 0, \dots, 0)$$

and

$$\tilde{v} = (v_1 - (u_2 + \varepsilon), \dots, v_n - (u_2 + \varepsilon)) = (\delta^* + \varepsilon, -(\delta^* + \varepsilon), 0, \dots, 0).$$

From cardinal full comparability, we obtain $\tilde{u} \sim^n \tilde{v}$. For any $m \in \mathbb{Z}$, we define $z(m) \in \mathbb{R}^n$ by

$$z(m) = \left(\frac{\delta^* + \varepsilon}{\varepsilon}\right)^m \tilde{u}.$$

Figure 2.6 illustrates the construction of $z(m)$ assuming that $\varepsilon = 2\delta^*$.

Note that $z(0) = \tilde{u}$ and $z(1) = \tilde{v}$. Further, for all $m \in \mathbb{Z}$, $z(m)_1 = -z(m)_2$ and $z(m)_i = 0$ for all $i \neq 1, 2$. Since $(\delta^* + \varepsilon)/\varepsilon > 1$, we obtain that

$$\lim_{m \to -\infty} z(m)_i = 0 \text{ for each } i = 1, 2$$

and

$$\lim_{m \to \infty} z(m)_1 = \infty, \text{ and } \lim_{m \to \infty} z(m)_2 = -\infty.$$

We show that

$$z(m) \sim^n z(\ell) \text{ for any } m, \ell \in \mathbb{Z}. \tag{2.14}$$

From cardinal full comparability, it follows that for any $m \in \mathbb{Z}$,

$$z(m) \succsim^n z(m+1) \Leftrightarrow z(m+1) \succsim^n z(m+2).$$

Since $z(0) \sim^n z(1)$ and $R$ is reflexive and transitive, it follows that $z(m) \sim^n z(0)$ for any $m \in \mathbb{Z}$. Since $\succsim^n$ is transitive, we obtain (2.14).

Next, let $\bar{z} \in \mathbb{R}^n$. Define $D(\bar{z}) \subset \mathbb{R}^n$ by

$$D(\bar{z}) = \{z \in \mathbb{R}^n : z_1 + z_2 = 0,\ z_1 \neq z_2, \text{ and } z_i = \bar{z}_i \text{ for all } i \neq 1, 2\}.$$

We show that for any $\bar{z} \in \mathbb{R}^n$,

$$w \sim^n z \text{ for any } w, z \in D(\bar{z}). \tag{2.15}$$

We begin by showing that $z \sim^n z(0)$ for any $z \in D(z(0))$. Let $z \in D(z(0))$. Note that $z_1 = -z_2$ and $z_i = 0$ for all $i \neq 1, 2$. Since $\succsim^n$ satisfies anonymity and transitivity, we can assume that $z_2 < 0 < z_1$. By the construction of $z(m)$ (see Fig. 2.6), there exist $\gamma \in (0, 1]$ and $m \in \mathbb{Z}$ such that

$$z = \gamma z(m) + (1-\gamma) z(m+1).$$

If $\gamma = 1$, then by (2.14), we obtain $z \sim^n z(0)$. Now, suppose $\gamma \in (0, 1)$. From the weak Pigou–Dalton principle, it follows that $z(m) \succsim^n z$ and $z \succsim^n z(m+1)$. Since $\succsim^n$ is transitive and $z(m) \sim^n z(m+1)$ by (2.14), it must be the case that $z(m) \sim^n z$. Thus, we obtain $z \sim^n z(0)$ by (2.14) and the transitivity of $\succsim^n$.

We now prove (2.15). Let $\bar{z} \in \mathbb{R}^n$ and $w, z \in D(\bar{z})$. By separability,

$$w \succsim^n z \Leftrightarrow (w_1, w_2, 0, \ldots, 0) \succsim^n (z_1, z_2, 0, \ldots, 0).$$

Since $(w_1, w_2, 0, \ldots, 0), (z_1, z_2, 0, \ldots, 0) \in D(z(0))$ and $\succsim^n$ is transitive, we obtain $(w_1, w_2, 0, \ldots, 0) \sim^n (z_1, z_2, 0, \ldots, 0)$. Thus, $w \sim^n z$ follows.

Finally, let $w, z \in \mathbb{R}^n$ and suppose that $w_1 - z_1 = z_2 - w_2$, $w_1 \neq w_2$, and $z_1 \neq z_2$. Since $\succsim^n$ satisfies anonymity and transitivity, completing the proof requires only showing that $w \sim^n z$. By the same argument as the final part of Step 1, we can show that $w \sim^n z$ using (2.15) instead of (2.12). (We omit its proof.)

*Step 3.* Suppose that there exist $u, v \in \mathbb{R}^n$ and $\delta^* \in \mathbb{R}_{++}$ such that $v_2 + \delta^* = u_2 = u_1 = v_1 - \delta^*$, $u_i = v_i$ for all $i \in N \setminus \{1, 2\}$ and $u \succ^n v$. We show that $\succsim^n$ satisfies the strong Pigou–Dalton principle. Let $w, z \in \mathbb{R}^n$ and suppose that there exist $i, j \in N$ and $\delta \in \mathbb{R}_{++}$ such that $z_i + \delta = w_i \leq w_j = z_j - \delta$ and $w_k = z_k$ for all $k \in N \setminus \{i, j\}$. Since $\succsim^n$ satisfies anonymity and transitivity, we can assume that $i = 2$ and $j = 1$. First, we consider the case that $w_1 = w_2$. By the weak Pigou–Dalton principle, we obtain $w \succsim^n z$. We show $w \succ^n z$ by contradiction. By way of contradiction, suppose $w \sim^n z$. It follows from Step 1 that $\succsim^n$ satisfies incremental equity. However, this is a contradiction since $u \succ^n v$. Thus, $w \succ^n z$ must hold.

Next, suppose that $w_2 < w_1$. By the weak Pigou–Dalton principle, $w \succsim^n z$ holds. We show $w \succ^n z$ by contradiction. Suppose $w \sim^n z$. Since $z_2 < w_2 < w_1 < z_1$, it follows from Step 2 that for all $\tilde{w}, \tilde{z} \in \mathbb{R}^n$, $\tilde{w} \sim^n \tilde{z}$ if there exist $h, k \in N$ such that $\tilde{w}_h - \tilde{z}_h = \tilde{z}_k - \tilde{w}_k$, $\tilde{w}_h \neq \tilde{w}_k$, and $\tilde{z}_h \neq \tilde{z}_k$. Thus, for $\tilde{u}, \tilde{v}, \tilde{w} \in \mathbb{R}^n$ such that $\tilde{u} = (-2, 1, 1, \tilde{u}_4, \ldots, \tilde{u}_n)$, $\tilde{v} = (-1, 0, 1, \tilde{u}_4, \ldots, \tilde{u}_n)$, and $\tilde{w} = (-2, 0, 2, \tilde{u}_4, \ldots, \tilde{u}_n)$, we obtain $\tilde{u} \sim^n \tilde{v}$ and $\tilde{v} \sim^n \tilde{w}$. Since $\succsim^n$ is transitive, $\tilde{u} \sim^n \tilde{w}$ follows. On the other hand, $\tilde{u} \succ^n \tilde{w}$ follows from the above argument for the case where $w_i = w_j$. Thus, we obtain a contradiction, so that $w \succ^n z$ must hold.

*Step 4*. Let $u = (0, 0, u_3, \ldots, u_n), v = (-1, 1, u_3, \ldots, u_n) \in \mathbb{R}^n$. By the weak Pigou–Dalton principle, either $u \succ^n v$ or $u \sim^n v$ holds. If $u \succ^n v$, then it follows from Step 3 that $\succsim^n$ satisfies the strong Pigou–Dalton principle. On the other hand, if $u \sim^n v$, then it follows from Step 1 that $\succsim^n$ satisfies incremental equity. Thus, $\succsim^n$ satisfies either the strong Pigou–Dalton principle or incremental equity. ■

*Proof of Theorem* 2.9. 'If.' Suppose that $\succsim^n$ is $\succsim^n_U$, $\succsim^n_{UL}$, or $\succsim^n_L$. Since $\succsim^n_U$, $\succsim^n_{UL}$, and $\succsim^n_L$ are $UL$-monotone, it follows from Theorem 2.6 that $\succsim$ satisfies strong Pareto, anonymity, the weak Pigou–Dalton principle, and the composite transfer principle. Since $\succsim^n_U$ and $\succsim^n_L$ satisfy separability and cardinal full comparability, $\succsim^n_{UL}$ also satisfies these axioms. Thus, $\succsim^n$ satisfies separability and cardinal full comparability.

'Only if.' Since the weak Pigou–Dalton principle implies minimal equity, it follows from Theorem 2.8 that either $\succsim^n = \succsim^n_L$ or $\succsim^n$ is weakly utilitarian. To complete the proof, suppose $\succsim^n$ is weakly utilitarian, that is, $\succ^n_U \subseteq \succ^n$. We show that either $\succsim^n = \succsim^n_{UL}$ or $\succsim^n = \succsim^n_U$. From Lemma 2.2, it follows that $\succsim^n$ satisfies either the strong Pigou–Dalton principle or incremental equity. If $\succsim^n$ satisfies incremental equity, it follows from Theorem 2.1 that $\succsim^n = \succsim^n_U$. We now assume that $\succsim^n$ satisfies the strong Pigou–Dalton principle. We show that $\succsim^n = \succsim^n_{UL}$. Since $\succsim^n_{UL}$ is complete, it suffices to show that $\succsim^n_{UL}$ is a subrelation of $\succsim^n$. From Theorem 2.7, it follows that $\succsim^n_\cap$ is a subrelation of $\succsim^n$, that is, $\sim^n_\cap \subseteq \sim^n$ and $\succ^n_\cap \subseteq \succ^n$. Thus, we obtain $\sim^n_{UL} \subseteq \sim^n$ since $\sim^n_{UL} = \sim^n_L = \sim^n_\cap$. Further, since $\succsim^n$ is weakly utilitarian, $\succ^n_U \subseteq \succ^n$. Also, from (2.5a), it follows that $\sim^n_U \cap \succ^n_L \subseteq \succ^n_\cap$. Since $\succ^n_{UL} = \succ^n_U \cup (\sim^n_U \cap \succ^n_L)$, we obtain $\succ^n_{UL} \subseteq \succ^n$. ■

Among the three social welfare orderings jointly characterized in Theorem 2.9, only the utilitarian social welfare ordering violates the strong Pigou–Dalton principle. Thus, if we strengthen the weak Pigou–Dalton principle to its strong version in the set of axioms of Theorem 2.9, we immediately obtain a joint characterization of the two lexicographic compositions of the utilitarian and leximin social welfare orderings. We state the following theorem without a proof.

**Theorem 2.10** (Kamaga 2018) *Let $n \geq 3$. A social welfare ordering $\succsim^n$ on $\mathbb{R}^n$ satisfies strong Pareto, anonymity, the strong Pigou–Dalton principle, the composite transfer principle, separability, and cardinal full comparability if and only if either $\succsim^n = \succsim^n_{UL}$ or $\succsim^n = \succsim^n_L$.*

Finally, we present an axiomatization of a mixed utilitarian–maximin social welfare ordering. To this end, we consider the weak form of the grading principle due to

Sen (1970) and Suppes (1966). It requires that the evaluation be efficient and impartial. This axiom was introduced by d'Aspremont and Gevers (2002) and is weaker than the conjunction of strong Pareto and anonymity.

**Weak Suppes–Sen**: For all $u, v \in \mathbb{R}^n$, if $u_{()} \gg v_{()}$, then $u \succ^n v$.

Note that weak Suppes–Sen implies the weak Pareto principle corresponding to the case where $u_{()} = u$ and $v_{()} = v$. Weak Suppes–Sen is weaker than the conjunction of the weak Pareto principle and anonymity.

The following theorem presents an axiomatization of a mixed utilitarian–maximin social welfare ordering. The theorem statement (i) corresponds to Theorem 3 of Bossert and Kamaga (2020). In Bossert and Kamaga (2020), they established the result not only for the domain $\mathbb{R}^n$ but for the restricted domain $\mathbb{R}^n_+ \setminus \{0^n\}$. As discussed by Bossert and Kamaga (2020), if weak Suppes–Sen is replaced with strong Pareto and anonymity, the set of permissible weights $\theta$ becomes the half-closed interval $(0, 1]$; thus, the maximin social welfare ordering is excluded.[1]

**Theorem 2.11** (Bossert and Kamaga 2020)

*(i) A social welfare ordering $\succsim^n$ on $\mathbb{R}^n$ satisfies weak Suppes–Sen, the weak Pigou–Dalton principle, the composite transfer principle, continuity, and cardinal full comparability if and only if there exists $\theta \in [0, 1]$ such that $\succsim = \succsim^n_{UM,\theta}$.*

*(ii) A social welfare ordering $\succsim^n$ on $\mathbb{R}^n$ satisfies strong Pareto, anonymity, the weak Pigou–Dalton principle, the composite transfer principle, continuity, and cardinal full comparability if and only if there exists $\theta \in (0, 1]$ such that $\succsim = \succsim^n_{UM,\theta}$.*

***Proof*** For a proof of (i), see Bossert and Kamaga (2020, Theorems 2 and 3). We prove (ii) using Theorem 2.6.

'If.' Let $\theta \in (0, 1]$. From Theorem 2.11 (i), $\succsim^n_{UM,\theta}$ satisfies the weak Pigou–Dalton principle, the composite transfer principle, continuity and cardinal full comparability. It is straightforward that $\succsim^n_{UM,\theta}$ satisfies anonymity. Further, since $\theta \in (0, 1]$, it satisfies strong Pareto.

'Only if.' The proof proceeds in three steps.

*Step 1*. Define $D \subseteq \mathbb{R}^2$ by

$$D = \{(u_1, u_2) \in \mathbb{R}^2 : u_1 \geq u_2\}.$$

We show that there exists the ordering $\succsim^*$ on $D$ such that for any $u, v \in \mathbb{R}^n$,

$$u \succsim^n v \Leftrightarrow (\mu(u), u_{(1)}) \succsim^* (\mu(v), y_{(1)}). \tag{2.16}$$

From Theorem 2.6, $\succsim^n$ is $UL$-monotone. Thus, for any $u, v \in \mathbb{R}^n$,

$$[\mu(u) > \mu(v) \text{ and } u_{(1)} > v_{(1)}] \Rightarrow u \succ^n v.$$

[1] For an axiomatization of the maximin social welfare ordering, see Bosmans and Ooghe (2013), Miyagishima (2010), and Miyagishima et al. (2014).

Since $\succsim^n$ satisfies continuity, it follows that for all $u, v \in \mathbb{R}^n$,

$$[\mu(u) = \mu(v) \text{ and } u_{(1)} = v_{(1)}] \Rightarrow u \sim^n v. \tag{2.17}$$

We define the binary relation $\succsim^*$ on $D$ as follows. For all $\bar{u}, \bar{v} \in D$, $\bar{u} \succsim^* \bar{v}$ if and only if there exist $u, v \in \mathbb{R}^n$ such that $\bar{u} = (\mu(u), u_{(1)})$, $\bar{v} = (\mu(v), v_{(1)})$ and $u \succsim^n v$. Since $\succsim^n$ is transitive, it follows from (2.17) that $\succsim^*$ satisfies (2.16).

Next, we show that $\succsim^*$ in an ordering on $D$. To show that $\succsim^*$ is complete, let $\bar{u}, \bar{v} \in D$. Then, there exist $u, v \in \mathbb{R}^n$ such that $\bar{u} = (\mu(u), u_{(1)})$ and $\bar{v} = (\mu(v), v_{(1)})$. Since $\succsim^n$ is complete, from (2.16), we obtain $\bar{u} \succsim^* \bar{v}$ or $\bar{v} \succsim^* \bar{u}$. Next, to show that $\succsim^*$ is transitive, let $\bar{u}, \bar{v}, \bar{w} \in D$ and suppose that $\bar{u} \succsim^* \bar{v}$ and $\bar{v} \succsim^* \bar{w}$. Then, there exist $u, v, w \in \mathbb{R}^n$ such that $\bar{u} = (\mu(u), u_{(1)})$, $\bar{v} = (\mu(v), v_{(1)})$ and $\bar{w} = (\mu(w), w_{(1)})$ and it follows from (2.16) that $u \succsim^n v$ and $v \succsim^n w$. Since $\succsim^n$ is transitive, $u \succsim^n w$ follows. From (2.16), we obtain $\bar{u} \succsim^* \bar{w}$.

*Step 2*. We show that $\succsim^*$ is continuous on $D$. Let $\bar{u} \in D$. We show that its upper contour set is closed. To this end, let $\{\bar{v}^m\}_{m \in \mathbb{N}}$ be a sequence in $\{\bar{v} \in D : \bar{v} \succsim^* \bar{u}\}$ that converges to $\bar{v}^* \in D$. We define $u, v^* \in \mathbb{R}^n$ by $u_i = (n\bar{u}_1 - \bar{u}_2)/(n-1)$ and $v_i^* = (n\bar{v}_1^* - \bar{v}_2^*)/(n-1)$ for each $i \in N \setminus \{n\}$, $u_n = \bar{u}_2$ and $v_n^* = \bar{v}_2^*$. Similarly, for each $m \in \mathbb{N}$, define $v^m \in \mathbb{R}^n$ by $v_i^m = (n\bar{v}_1^m - \bar{v}_2^m)/(n-1)$ for each $i \in N \setminus \{n\}$ and $v_n^m = \bar{v}_2^m$. Note that $\bar{u} = (\mu(u), u_{(1)})$, $\bar{v}^* = (\mu(v^*), v_{(1)}^*)$ and $\bar{v}^m = (\mu(v^m), v_{(1)}^m)$ for all $m \in \mathbb{N}$. Further, the sequence $\{v^m\}_{m \in \mathbb{N}}$ converges to $v^*$. From (2.16), it follows that $v^m \succsim^n u$ for all $m \in \mathbb{N}$. Since $\succsim^n$ satisfies continuity, $v^* \succsim^* u$ follows. Thus, we obtain $\bar{v}^* \succsim^* \bar{u}$ from (2.16). The proof that the lower contour set of $\bar{u}$ is closed is analogous.

*Step 3*. We will complete the proof by showing that the level sets of $\succsim^*$ are linear.[2] Since $\succsim^n$ is $UL$-monotone, $\succsim^*$ satisfies that for any $u, v \in D$, if $u_i > v_i$ for all $i \in \{1, 2\}$, then

$$u \succ^* v. \tag{2.18}$$

Furthermore, since $\succsim^n$ satisfies cardinal full comparability, $\succsim^*$ is invariant with respect to common increasing affine transformation, namely, for all $u, v, \bar{u}, \bar{v} \in D$, if there exist $\alpha \in \mathbb{R}_{++}$ and $\beta \in \mathbb{R}$ such that $\bar{u}_i = \alpha u_i + \beta$ and $\bar{v}_i = \alpha v_i + \beta$, then

$$u \succsim^* v \;\Leftrightarrow\; \bar{u} \succsim^* \bar{v}. \tag{2.19}$$

Define $D_+ \subseteq D$ by $D_+ = \{(u_1, u_2) \in D : u_1 > 0 \text{ and } u_2 \geq 0\}$. We show that the level sets of the restriction of $\succsim^*$ to $D_+$ are linear; the proof presented below is illustrated in Fig. 2.7. Since $\succsim^*$ is continuous and it satisfies (2.18), there exists $w \in \{u \in D_+ \setminus \{1^2\} : u_1 \geq 1 \text{ and } u_2 \leq 1\}$ such that $w \sim^* 1^2$. Let $t \in (0, 1)$. We define

---

[2] A shorter proof can be given by applying the argument analogous to that used by Blackorby et al. (1984, pp. 350–352) and Bossert and Weymark (2004, pp. 1131–1132). Their argument is simple and concise, but it crucially relies on the assumption that the origin $0^2$ is included in $D$. Here, we present an argument used by Bossert and Kamaga (2020) that does not rely on this assumption, so that it is applicable to the case where we restrict the domain of $\succsim^n$ to $\mathbb{R}_+^n \setminus \{0^n\}$.

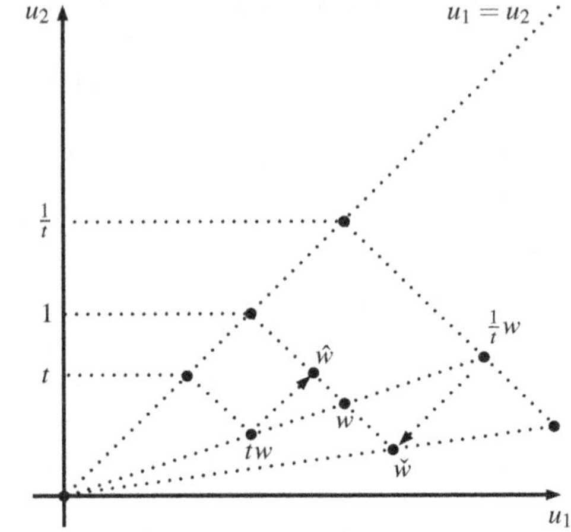


**Fig. 2.7** Geometric exposition of $w$, $tw$, $\frac{1}{t}w$, $\hat{w}$ and $\check{w}$

$\hat{w} = tw + (1-t)1^2$. Since $w \sim^* 1^2$, we obtain by (2.19) that $tw \sim^* t1^2$. Note that $tw_i = \hat{w}_i - (1-t)$ for each $i \in \{1, 2\}$. Furthermore, $t1^2_i = 1^2_i - (1-t)$ for each $i \in \{1, 2\}$. Thus, by (2.19), $tw \sim^* t1^2$ implies $\hat{w} \sim^* 1^2$. Next, we define $\check{w}$ by $w = t\check{w} + (1-t)1^2$. Since $w \sim^* 1^2$, it follows from (2.19) that $(1/t)w \sim^* (1/t)1^2$. Note that $(1/t)w_i = \check{w}_i + (1-t)/t$ and $(1/t)1^2_i = 1 + (1-t)/t$ for all $i \in \{1, 2\}$. Thus, by (2.19), $(1/t)w \sim^* (1/t)1^2$ implies $\check{w} \sim^* 1^2$.

By the transitivity of $\succsim^*$, we obtain $\hat{w} \sim^* \check{w}$. Since $w \in \{u \in D_+ \setminus \{1^2\} : u_1 \geq 1 \text{ and } u_2 \leq 1\}$ and $t \in (0, 1)$ was arbitrarily chosen, there exists $\theta \in [0, 1]$ such that $u \sim^* v$ for all $u, v \in D_+$ with $\theta u_1 + (1-\theta)u_2 = \theta v_1 + (1-\theta)v_2 = 1$. From (2.19), it follows that for all $\alpha \in \mathbb{R}_{++}$, $u \sim^* v$ for all $u, v \in D_+$ with $\theta u_1 + (1-\theta)u_2 = \theta v_1 + (1-\theta)v_2 = \alpha$. By (2.18), we obtain that for all $u, v \in D_+$,

$$u \succsim^* v \;\Leftrightarrow\; \theta u_1 + (1-\theta)u_2 \geq \theta v_1 + (1-\theta)v_2. \tag{2.20}$$

Since $\succsim^n$ satisfies strong Pareto, it follows from (2.16) that $\theta > 0$.

Now, we extend (2.20) to $D$. Let $u, v \in D$. Then, there exist $\bar{u}, \bar{v} \in D_+$ and $\beta \in \mathbb{R}_+$ such that $\bar{u}_i = u_i + \beta$ and $\bar{v}_i = v_i + \beta$ for all $i \in \{1, 2\}$. By (2.19) and (2.20), we obtain

$$\begin{aligned} u \succsim^* v &\Leftrightarrow \tilde{u} \succsim^* \tilde{v} \\ &\Leftrightarrow \theta\tilde{u}_1 + (1-\theta)\tilde{u}_2 \geq \theta\tilde{v}_1 + (1-\theta)\tilde{v}_2 \\ &\Leftrightarrow \theta u_1 + (1-\theta)u_2 \geq \theta v_1 + (1-\theta)v_2. \end{aligned}$$

From (2.16), $\succsim^n = \succsim^n_{UM,\theta}$. ■

## 2.5 Concluding Remarks

We have examined the axiomatic foundations of the utilitarian and leximin or maximin social welfare ordering and their possible compromises. Their axiomatizations presented in this chapter show the contrast between their properties, especially their distributional equity properties. According to the axiomatization results, our choice between the social welfare ordering in evaluating utility distributions or underlying social alternatives boils down to the choice between those equity properties formalized as equity axioms.

While the social welfare orderings and quasi-orderings we considered may serve as a social welfare evaluation criterion for intragenerational utility distributions, they can also be extended to the intergenerational welfare evaluation. This will be analyzed in the next chapter.

## References

Bentham, J. (1776). *A fragment on government*. London: Payne.

Bentham, J. (1789). *An introduction to the principle of morals and legislation*. London: Payne.

Blackorby, C., Bossert, W., & Donaldson, D. (2002). Utilitarianism and the theory of justice. In K. J. Arrow, A. K. Sen, & K. Suzumura (Eds.), *Handbook of social choice and welfare* (Vol. I). Amsterdam: North-Holland.

Blackorby, C., Bossert, W., & Donaldson, D. (2005). *Population issues in social choice theory, welfare economics, and ethics*. Cambridge: Cambridge University Press.

Blackorby, C., & Donaldson, D. (1977). Utility versus equity: Some plausible quasi-orderings. *Journal of Public Economics, 7*, 365–381.

Blackorby, C., Donaldson, D., & Weymark, J. A. (1984). Social choice with interpersonal utility comparisons: A diagrammatic introduction. *International Economic Review, 25*, 327–356

Bosmans, K., & Ooghe, E. (2013). A characterization of maximin. *Economic Theory Bulletin, 1*, 151–156.

Bossert, W., D'Ambrosio, C., & Kamaga, K. (2020). Extreme values, means, and inequality measurement. DSSR Discussion Paper No. 106, Tohoku Univeristy

Bossert, W., & Kamaga, K. (2020). An axiomatization of the mixed utilitarian-maximin social welfare orderings. *Economic Theory, 69*, 451–473. https://doi.org/10.1007/s00199-018-1168-y.

Bossert, W., & Weymark, J. A. (2004). Utility in social choice. In S. Barberà, P. J. Hammond, & C. Seidl (Eds.), *Handbook of utility theory* (vol. 2: Extensions). Dordrecht: Kluwer Academic Publishers.

Cowell, F. A. (1985). 'A fair suck of the sauce bottle' or what do you mean by equality? *Economic Record, 61*, 567–579.

Dalton, H. (1920). The measurement of the inequality of incomes. *Economic Journal, 30*, 348–361.

d'Aspremont, C., & Gevers, L. (1977). Equity and the informational basis of collective choice. *Review of Economic Studies, 44*, 199–209.

d'Aspremont, C., & Gevers, L. (2002). Social welfare functionals and interpersonal comparability. In K. J. Arrow, A. K. Sen, & K. Suzumura (Eds.), *Handbook of social choice and welfare* (Vol. I). Amsterdam: North-Holland.

Debreu, G. (1960). Topological methods in cardinal utility theory. In K. J. Arrow, S. Karlin, & P. Suppes (Eds.), *Mathematical methods in social sciences*. Stanford: Stanford University Press.

Deschamps, R., & Gevers, L. (1978). Leximin and utilitarian rules: A joint characterization. *Journal of Economic Theory, 17*, 143–163.

Gevers, L. (1979). On interpersonal comparability and social welfare orderings. *Econometrica, 47*, 75–89.
Hammond, P. J. (1976). Equity, Arrow's conditions, and Rawls' difference principle. *Econometrica, 44*, 793–804.
Hammond, P. J. (1979). Equity in two person situations: Some consequences. *Econometrica, 47*, 1127–1135.
Kamaga, K. (2018). When do utilitarianism and egalitarianism agree on evaluation? An intersection approach. *Mathematical Social Sciences, 94*, 41–48.
Maskin, E. (1978). A theorem on utilitarianism. *Review of Economic Studies, 45*, 93–96.
Miyagishima, K. (2010). A characterization of the maximin social ordering. *Economics Bulletin, 30*, 1278–1282.
Miyagishima, K., Bosmans, K., & Ooghe, E. (2014). A characterization of maximin: Corrigendum. *Economic Theory Bulletin, 2*, 219–220.
Ou-Yang, K. (2018). Generalized rawlsianism. *Social Choice and Welfare, 50*, 265–279.
Pigou, A. C. (1912). *Wealth and welfare*. London: Macmillan.
Rawls, J. (1971). *A theory of justice*. Cambridge, MA: Harvard University Press.
Roberts, K. W. S. (1980). Interpersonal comparability and social choice theory. *Review of Economic Studies, 47*, 421–439.
Sen, A. K. (1970). *Collective choice and social welfare*. Amsterdam: Holden-Day.
Sen, A. K. (1973). *On economic inequality*. Oxford: Clarendon.
Shorrocks, A. F., & Foster, J. E. (1987). Transfer sensitive inequality measures. *Review of Economic Studies, 54*, 485–497.
Suppes, P. (1966). Some formal model of grading principles. *Synthese, 6*, 284–306.

# Chapter 3
# Intergenerational Social Welfare Evaluation

**Abstract** This chapter analyzes intergenerational social welfare evaluation for infinite utility streams. An infinite utility stream represents an intergenerational utility distribution where each component corresponds to the utility level of each generation. We will establish some general results that show how a social welfare evaluation applied to utilities of the finite number of generations can be extended to a finitely anonymous infinite-horizon social welfare evaluation. Using the general results and axiomatizations of a specific social welfare ordering or quasi-ordering, we will present axiomatic characterizations of specific forms of an infinite-horizon extension of a finite-horizon social welfare evaluation.

**Keywords** Infinite utility stream · Social welfare quasi-ordering · Utilitarianism · Leximin · Overtaking criteria

## 3.1 Introduction

The welfarist analysis of evaluation criteria for intergenerational utility distributions can be traced back to the seminal works of Diamond (1965) and Koopmans (1960). An intergenerational utility distribution is represented by an infinite utility stream, which is an infinite-dimensional vector of a generational utility level. Diamond (1965) and Koopmans (1960) showed that it is impossible to rank infinite utility streams in a way that respects the strong Pareto principle and a weak impartiality requirement called "finite anonymity" if we require the evaluation criterion to be an ordering that satisfies a suitably strong continuity property. Consequently, this chapter focuses on a social welfare quasi-ordering—a reflexive and transitive but not necessarily complete binary relation—for infinite utility streams.

As this chapter makes clear, many social welfare quasi-orderings that satisfy both the strong Pareto principle and the finite anonymity axiom have been proposed and axiomatized. Each of these infinite-horizon evaluation criteria can be seen as an infinite-horizon extension of the specific social welfare ordering or quasi-ordering for utility distributions for fixed and finitely many individuals. The primary purpose of this chapter is to establish general results that show how a social welfare evaluation



K. Kamaga, *Social Welfare Evaluation and Intergenerational Equity*,
Development Bank of Japan Research Series,
https://doi.org/10.1007/978-981-15-4254-1_3

applied to utilities of the finite number of generations can be extended to a finitely anonymous infinite-horizon social welfare evaluation. To this end, we consider a sequence of arbitrary finite-horizon social welfare orderings or quasi-orderings and then analyze a general form of social welfare quasi-ordering associated with that sequence. This approach was first employed by d'Aspremont (2007) and followed by Asheim et al. (2010), Asheim and Banerjee (2010), Kamaga and Kojima (2009, 2010), and Sakai (2010). The main findings present characterization results for a general form of social welfare quasi-ordering associated with a sequence of finite-horizon social welfare orderings or quasi-orderings. Using these general results and the axiomatizations we provided in the previous chapter, we present axiomatizations of specific social welfare quasi-orderings for infinite utility streams, each of which is associated with a sequence of specific finite-horizon social welfare orderings or quasi-orderings.

The next section presents the framework for the analysis of social welfare quasi-orderings for infinite utility streams. Section 3.3 considers a general form of social welfare quasi-ordering that we call "dominance-in-tails criterion" and axiomatizes this general social welfare quasi-ordering. Then, we apply this general result to obtain axiomatizations of a specific social welfare quasi-ordering for infinite utility streams that is associated with a sequence of specific finite-horizon social welfare orderings or quasi-orderings. Sections 3.4 and 3.5 consider general forms of social welfare quasi-ordering, called "overtaking" and "catching-up" criteria, respectively, and establish their axiomatizations. These general results are applied to establish axiomatizations of specific forms of overtaking and catching-up criteria associated with a sequence of specific finite-horizon social welfare orderings or quasi-orderings. Section 3.6 provides concluding remarks.

## 3.2 Preliminaries

### *3.2.1 Basic Framework*

Let $\mathbb{R}$ be the set of all real numbers and $\mathbb{N}$ be the set of all positive integers. In this chapter, we consider the set $\mathbb{R}^{\mathbb{N}}$ of all infinite utility streams $\boldsymbol{u} = (u_1, u_2, \ldots)$. For each $i \in \mathbb{N}$, $u_i$ is the utility level of the $i$th generation. For all $\boldsymbol{u} \in \mathbb{R}^{\mathbb{N}}$ and for all $n \in \mathbb{N}$, we write $\boldsymbol{u}^{-n} = (u_1, \ldots, u_n)$ and $\boldsymbol{u}^{+n} = (u_{n+1}, u_{n+2}, \ldots)$. Thus, $\boldsymbol{u} = (\boldsymbol{u}^{-n}, \boldsymbol{u}^{+n})$. We will refer to $\boldsymbol{u}^{-n}$ and $\boldsymbol{u}^{+n}$ as "$n$-head of stream" and "$n$-tail of stream," respectively. For any $n \in \mathbb{N}$ and $\boldsymbol{w} \in \mathbb{R}^{\mathbb{N}}$, we define $D^n_{\boldsymbol{w}}$ by $D^n_{\boldsymbol{w}} = \{\boldsymbol{u} \in \mathbb{R}^{\mathbb{N}} : \boldsymbol{u}^{+n} = \boldsymbol{w}^{+n}\}$, i.e., the set of all infinite utility streams whose $n$-tails are the same as the $n$-tail of $\boldsymbol{w}$. We assume that $D^n_{\boldsymbol{w}}$ is endowed with the metric $d$ defined by $d(\boldsymbol{u}, \boldsymbol{v}) = \sum_{i \in \mathbb{N}} |u_i - v_i|$ for all $\boldsymbol{u}, \boldsymbol{v} \in D^n_{\boldsymbol{w}}$. For all $\boldsymbol{u} \in \mathbb{R}^{\mathbb{N}}$ and for all $n \in \mathbb{N}$, $(u^{-n}_{(1)}, \ldots, u^{-n}_{(n)})$ denotes a non-decreasing rearrangement of $\boldsymbol{u}^{-n}$, i.e., $u^{-n}_{(1)} \leq \cdots \leq u^{-n}_{(n)}$, ties being broken arbitrarily.

A binary relation $\succsim$ on $\mathbb{R}^{\mathbb{N}}$ is a subset of $\mathbb{R}^{\mathbb{N}} \times \mathbb{R}^{\mathbb{N}}$. For simplicity, we write $\boldsymbol{u} \succsim \boldsymbol{v}$ to mean $(\boldsymbol{u}, \boldsymbol{v}) \in \succsim$. The asymmetric and symmetric parts of $\succsim$ are denoted by $\succ$ and $\sim$, respectively. A social welfare quasi-ordering is a reflexive and transitive binary relation on $\mathbb{R}^{\mathbb{N}}$. A social welfare quasi-ordering is finitely complete if, for all $n \in \mathbb{N}$ and for all $\boldsymbol{u}, \boldsymbol{v} \in \mathbb{R}^{\mathbb{N}}$ with $\boldsymbol{u}^{+n} = \boldsymbol{v}^{+n}$, $\boldsymbol{u} \succsim \boldsymbol{v}$ or $\boldsymbol{v} \succsim \boldsymbol{u}$. A social welfare quasi-ordering $\succsim_A$ is said to be a subrelation of a social welfare quasi-ordering $\succsim_B$ if, for all $\boldsymbol{u}, \boldsymbol{v} \in \mathbb{R}^{\mathbb{N}}$, $\boldsymbol{u} \succ_A \boldsymbol{v}$ implies $\boldsymbol{u} \succ_B \boldsymbol{v}$, and $\boldsymbol{u} \sim_A \boldsymbol{v}$ implies $\boldsymbol{u} \sim_B \boldsymbol{v}$, that is, $\succ_A \subseteq \succ_B$ and $\sim_A \subseteq \sim_B$.

### 3.2.2 *Sequence of Finite-Horizon Quasi-orderings*

A sequence of finite-horizon quasi-orderings (resp. orderings) is a sequence $(\succsim^n)_{n\in\mathbb{N}}$ each of whose components is a quasi-ordering (resp. an ordering) $\succsim^n$ defined on $\mathbb{R}^n$. We say that a sequence $(\succsim^n)_{n\in\mathbb{N}}$ of finite-horizon quasi-orderings is *independent* if for all $n \in \mathbb{N}$ and for all $\boldsymbol{u}, \boldsymbol{v}, \boldsymbol{w} \in \mathbb{R}^{\mathbb{N}}$,

$$\boldsymbol{u}^{-n} \succsim^n \boldsymbol{v}^{-n} \Leftrightarrow (\boldsymbol{u}^{-n}, w_{n+1}) \succsim^{n+1} (\boldsymbol{v}^{-n}, w_{n+1}).$$

An independent sequence of finite-horizon quasi-orderings was considered by Kamaga and Kojima (2009, 2010) and Sakai (2010) in the context of ranking infinite utility streams.

For any $n \in \mathbb{N}$, we say that a finite-horizon quasi-ordering $\succsim^n$ on $\mathbb{R}^n$ is *Paretian* if for all $\boldsymbol{u}^{-n}, \boldsymbol{v}^{-n} \in \mathbb{R}^n$, if $\boldsymbol{u}^{-n} > \boldsymbol{v}^{-n}$ then $\boldsymbol{u}^{-n} \succ^n \boldsymbol{v}^{-n}$. Further, $\succsim^n$ is said to be *anonymous* if for all $\boldsymbol{u}^{-n}, \boldsymbol{v}^{-n} \in \mathbb{R}^n$, if there exist $i, j \in \{1, \ldots, n\}$ such that $u_i = v_j$, $u_j = v_i$, and $u_k = v_k$ for all $k \neq i, j$ then $\boldsymbol{u}^{-n} \sim^n \boldsymbol{v}^{-n}$.

If $(\succsim^n)_{n\in\mathbb{N}}$ is an independent sequence of finite-horizon anonymous quasi-orderings, each component $\succsim^n$ satisfies an additional property. For any $n \in \mathbb{N}$, we say that a finite-horizon quasi-ordering $\succsim^n$ on $\mathbb{R}^n$ is *separable* if for all $\boldsymbol{u}^{-n}, \tilde{\boldsymbol{u}}^{-n}, \boldsymbol{v}^{-n}, \tilde{\boldsymbol{v}}^{-n} \in \mathbb{R}^n$, if there exists $M \subseteq \{1, \ldots, n\}$ such that $u_i = v_i$ and $\tilde{u}_i = \tilde{v}_i$ for all $i \in M$ and $u_i = \tilde{u}_i$ and $v_i = \tilde{v}_i$ for all $i \in \{1, \ldots, n\} \setminus M$, then

$$\boldsymbol{u}^{-n} \succsim^n \boldsymbol{v}^{-n} \Leftrightarrow \tilde{\boldsymbol{u}}^{-n} \succsim^n \tilde{\boldsymbol{v}}^{-n}.$$

**Lemma 3.1** *If $(\succsim^n)_{n\in\mathbb{N}}$ is an independent sequence of finite-horizon anonymous quasi-orderings, then $\succsim^n$ is separable for each $n \in \mathbb{N}$.*

***Proof*** Let $n \in \mathbb{N}$ and $\boldsymbol{u}^{-n}, \tilde{\boldsymbol{u}}^{-n}, \boldsymbol{v}^{-n}, \tilde{\boldsymbol{v}}^{-n} \in \mathbb{R}^n$. Suppose that there exists $M \subseteq \{1, \ldots, n\}$ such that $u_i = v_i$ and $\tilde{u}_i = \tilde{v}_i$ for all $i \in M$ and $u_i = \tilde{u}_i$ and $v_i = \tilde{v}_i$ for all $i \in \{1, \ldots, n\} \setminus M$. Since $(\succsim^n)_{n\in\mathbb{N}}$ is anonymous, we assume $M = \{1, \ldots, |M|\}$ without loss of generality. From the independence and anonymity of $(\succsim^n)_{n\in\mathbb{N}}$, it follows that

$$\begin{aligned} u^{-n} \succsim^n v^{-n} &\Leftrightarrow (u^{-n}, \tilde{u}_1, \ldots, \tilde{u}_{|M|}) \succsim^{n+|M|} (v^{-n}, \tilde{v}_1, \ldots, \tilde{v}_{|M|}) \\ &\Leftrightarrow (\tilde{u}^{-n}, u_1, \ldots, u_{|M|}) \succsim^{n+|M|} (\tilde{v}^{-n}, v_1, \ldots, v_{|M|}) \\ &\Leftrightarrow \tilde{u}^{-n} \succsim^n \tilde{v}^{-n}. \end{aligned}$$

Thus, $\succsim^n$ is separable. ■

We present a property of a social welfare quasi-ordering $\succsim$ on $\mathbb{R}^{\mathbb{N}}$, which formalizes a relationship between $\succsim$ and a sequence $(\succsim^n)_{n\in\mathbb{N}}$ of finite-horizon quasi-orderings. Given a sequence $(\succsim^n)_{n\in\mathbb{N}}$ of finite-horizon quasi-orderings, we say that a social welfare quasi-ordering $\succsim$ on $\mathbb{R}^{\mathbb{N}}$ is an *extension* of $(\succsim^n)_{n\in\mathbb{N}}$ if for any $n \in \mathbb{N}$ and for all $\boldsymbol{u}, \boldsymbol{v}, \boldsymbol{w} \in \mathbb{R}^{\mathbb{N}}$,

$$u^{-n} \succ^n v^{-n} \Rightarrow (u^{-n}, w^{+n}) \succ (v^{-n}, w^{+n}) \tag{3.1a}$$

and

$$u^{-n} \sim^n v^{-n} \Rightarrow (u^{-n}, w^{+n}) \sim (v^{-n}, w^{+n}). \tag{3.1b}$$

The notion of an extension of a sequence of finite-horizon orderings was introduced by Sakai (2010). Note that if $(\succsim^n)_{n\in\mathbb{N}}$ is a sequence of finite-horizon orderings, a social welfare quasi-ordering $\succsim$ on $\mathbb{R}^{\mathbb{N}}$ is an extension of $(\succsim^n)_{n\in\mathbb{N}}$ if and only if, for any $n \in \mathbb{N}$ and for all $\boldsymbol{u}, \boldsymbol{v}, \boldsymbol{w} \in \mathbb{R}^{\mathbb{N}}$,

$$u^{-n} \succsim^n v^{-n} \Leftrightarrow (u^{-n}, w^{+n}) \succsim (v^{-n}, w^{+n}). \tag{3.2}$$

If a social welfare quasi-ordering $\succsim$ on $\mathbb{R}^{\mathbb{N}}$ is an extension of a sequence $(\succsim^n)_{n\in\mathbb{N}}$ of finite-horizon orderings, $(\succsim^n)_{n\in\mathbb{N}}$ must be independent.

**Lemma 3.2** *Let $(\succsim^n)_{n\in\mathbb{N}}$ be a sequence of finite-horizon orderings. If a social welfare quasi-ordering $\succsim$ on $\mathbb{R}^{\mathbb{N}}$ is an extension of $(\succsim^n)_{n\in\mathbb{N}}$, then $(\succsim^n)_{n\in\mathbb{N}}$ is independent.*

***Proof*** Since $\succsim$ is an extension of $(\succsim^n)_{n\in\mathbb{N}}$, it follows that for all $n \in \mathbb{N}$ and for all $\boldsymbol{u}, \boldsymbol{v}, \boldsymbol{w} \in \mathbb{R}^{\mathbb{N}}$,

$$u^{-n} \succsim^n v^{-n} \Leftrightarrow (u^{-n}, w^{+n}) \succsim (v^{-n}, w^{+n}) \Leftrightarrow (u^{-n}, w_{n+1}) \succsim^{n+1} (v^{-n}, w_{n+1}).$$

Thus, $(\succsim^n)_{n\in\mathbb{N}}$ is independent. ■

Among the social welfare quasi-orderings discussed in Chap. 2, the following sequences of finite-horizon quasi-orderings can be used to define a specific example of an independent sequence of finite-horizon Paretian and anonymous quasi-orderings: the sequence $(\succsim_U^n)_{n\in\mathbb{N}}$ of *utilitarian* orderings, the sequence $(\succsim_{U,g}^n)_{n\in\mathbb{N}}$ of *generalized utilitarian* orderings associated with a given transformation $g$, the sequence $(\succsim_L^n)_{n\in\mathbb{N}}$ of *leximin* orderings, the sequence $(\succsim_\cap^n)_{n\in\mathbb{N}}$ of the *intersections of utilitarian and leximin* orderings, the sequence $(\succsim_{UL}^n)_{n\in\mathbb{N}}$ of *utilitarianism-first and leximin-second* orderings; see Sect. 2.3 of Chap. 2 for their definitions. However, a *mixed utilitarian–maximin* ordering $\succsim^n_{UM,\theta}$ associated with $\theta \in (0, 1)$ is not separable, and thus, it follows from Lemma 3.1 that the sequence $(\succsim^n_{UM,\theta})_{n\in\mathbb{N}}$ of the mixed utilitarian–maximin orderings is not independent. Further, from Lemma 3.2, there is no social welfare quasi-ordering that is an extension of the sequence of the mixed utilitarian–maximin orderings.

d'Aspremont (2007) introduced the notion of a *proliferating sequence* of finite-horizon quasi-orderings, a concept similar to the notion of extension of an independent sequence of finite-horizon quasi-orderings. This concept is used in Asheim et al. (2010) and Asheim and Banerjee (2010). While we will consider an independent sequence of finite-horizon quasi-orderings and use the notion of its extension, it is worth discussing our approach to the analysis using a proliferating sequence.

To present the definition of a proliferating sequence, we define a weak notion of the extension of a finite-horizon quasi-ordering. Given $m \in \mathbb{N}$, we say that a social welfare quasi-ordering $\succsim$ on $\mathbb{R}^{\mathbb{N}}$ *extends* a quasi-ordering $\succsim^m$ defined on $\mathbb{R}^m$ if, for all $M \subset \mathbb{N}$ with $|M| = m$ and for all $\boldsymbol{u}, \boldsymbol{v} \in \mathbb{R}^{\mathbb{N}}$ with $u_i = v_i$ for each $i \in \mathbb{N} \setminus M$,

$$(u_i)_{i\in M} \succ^m (v_i)_{i\in M} \Rightarrow \boldsymbol{u} \succ \boldsymbol{v}$$

and

$$(u_i)_{i\in M} \sim^m (v_i)_{i\in M} \Rightarrow \boldsymbol{u} \sim \boldsymbol{v}.$$

A sequence $(\succsim^n)_{n\in\mathbb{N}}$ of finite-horizon quasi-orderings is said to be *proliferating* if any social welfare quasi-ordering $\succsim$ on $\mathbb{R}^{\mathbb{N}}$ that extends $\succsim^2$ also extends $\succsim^m$ for all $m > 2$.

The concept of proliferating sequence includes the weak notion of extension. Still, it is definitely a self-completed property of a sequence of finite-horizon quasi-orderings, not a property of a pair comprising a sequence of finite-horizon quasi-orderings and a social welfare quasi-ordering on $\mathbb{R}^{\mathbb{N}}$. This is because the definition of proliferating sequence requires that *any* social welfare quasi-ordering on $\mathbb{R}^{\mathbb{N}}$ that extends $\succsim^2$ must extend $\succsim^m$ for all $m > 2$. Given this requirement, the concept of proliferating sequence can be used for the analysis of a social welfare quasi-ordering $\succsim$ on $\mathbb{R}^{\mathbb{N}}$ in such a way as to ensure that, given a proliferating sequence $(\succsim^n)_{n\in\mathbb{N}}$, $\succsim$ extends $\succsim^n$ for all $n > 2$ if $\succsim$ is assumed to extend $\succsim^2$.

The following lemma relates the notion of extension of a sequence of finite-horizon quasi-ordering with the concept of proliferating sequence.

**Lemma 3.3** *Let* $\succsim$ *be a social welfare quasi-ordering on* $\mathbb{R}^{\mathbb{N}}$ *and* $(\succsim^n)_{n\in\mathbb{N}}$ *be a sequence of finite-horizon Paretian and anonymous quasi-orderings.*

*(i) If* $(\succsim^n)_{n\in\mathbb{N}}$ *is proliferating and* $\succsim$ *extends* $\succsim^2$*, then* $\succsim$ *is an extension of* $(\succsim^n)_{n\in\mathbb{N}}$.
*(ii) If* $(\succsim^n)_{n\in\mathbb{N}}$ *is independent and* $\succsim$ *is an extension of* $(\succsim^n)_{n\in\mathbb{N}}$*, then* $\succsim$ *extends* $\succsim^n$ *for all* $n \in \mathbb{N}$.

***Proof*** (i) Let $\boldsymbol{u}, \boldsymbol{v}, \boldsymbol{w} \in \mathbb{R}^{\mathbb{N}}$. Since $(\succsim^n)_{n\in\mathbb{N}}$ is proliferating and $\succsim$ extends $\succsim^2$, it follows that for all $n \in \mathbb{N}$ with $n \geq 2$, $\boldsymbol{u}^{-n} \succ^n \boldsymbol{v}^{-n}$ implies $(\boldsymbol{u}^{-n}, \boldsymbol{w}^{+n}) \succ (\boldsymbol{v}^{-n}, \boldsymbol{w}^{+n})$ and $\boldsymbol{u}^{-n} \sim^n \boldsymbol{v}^{-n}$ implies $(\boldsymbol{u}^{-n}, \boldsymbol{w}^{+n}) \sim (\boldsymbol{v}^{-n}, \boldsymbol{w}^{+n})$. We show that the same property holds for $n = 1$. Since $\succsim^1$ is Paretian and reflexive, $u_1 \geq v_1$ if and only if $u_1 \succsim^1 v_1$. Thus, $u_1 \sim^1 v_1$ implies $(u_1, \boldsymbol{w}^{+1}) \sim (v_1, \boldsymbol{w}^{+1})$. Now, assume $u_1 \succ^1 v_1$. Then, $u_1 > v_1$. Since $\succsim^2$ is Paretian, $(u_1, w_2) \succ^2 (v_1, w_2)$ follows. Since $\succsim$ extends $\succsim^2$, we obtain $(u_1, \boldsymbol{w}^{+1}) \succ (v_1, \boldsymbol{w}^{+1})$.

(ii) Let $\boldsymbol{u}, \boldsymbol{v} \in \mathbb{R}^{\mathbb{N}}$ and $M \subset \mathbb{N}$ with $|M| = m \in \mathbb{N}$. Suppose $(u_i)_{i\in M} \succ^m (v_i)_{i\in M}$ and $u_j = v_j$ for all $j \in \mathbb{N} \setminus M$. Let $\bar{m} = \max M$ and $\bar{M} = \{1, \ldots, \bar{m}\}$. Note that $M \subseteq \bar{M}$. Since $(\succsim^n)_{n\in\mathbb{N}}$ is independent, it follows that

$$((u_i)_{i\in M}, (u_j)_{j\in\bar{M}\setminus M}) \succ^{\bar{m}} ((v_i)_{i\in M}, (v_j)_{j\in\bar{M}\setminus M})$$

Since $\succsim^{\bar{m}}$ is anonymous and transitive, we obtain

$$\boldsymbol{u}^{-\bar{m}} \succ^{\bar{m}} \boldsymbol{v}^{-\bar{m}}.$$

Since $\succsim$ is an extension of $(\succsim^n)_{n\in\mathbb{N}}$, $\boldsymbol{u} \succ \boldsymbol{v}$ follows. The proof that $(u_i)_{i\in M} \sim^m (v_i)_{i\in M}$ implies $\boldsymbol{u} \sim \boldsymbol{v}$ is analogous. ■

From part (i) of Lemma 3.3, the analysis of a social welfare ordering $\succsim$ on $\mathbb{R}^{\mathbb{N}}$ using the notion of extension of a sequence $(\succsim^n)_{n\in\mathbb{N}}$ of finite-horizon Paretian and anonymous quasi-orderings can be replicated using a profilerating sequence of Paretian and anonymous quasi-orderings. Further, as part (ii) of the lemma shows, if $\succsim$ is an extension of an independent sequence $(\succsim^n)_{n\in\mathbb{N}}$ of finite-horizon Paretian and anonymous quasi-orderings, $\succsim$ extends not only $\succsim^2$ but also $\succsim^n$ for all $n \in \mathbb{N}$. As noted, this implication is an essential and sufficient property of a proliferating sequence for the analysis of a social welfare ordering on $\mathbb{R}^{\mathbb{N}}$. Thus, the analysis using a proliferating sequence can be also replicated using the notion of extending an independent sequence of finite-horizon Paretian and anonymous quasi-orderings.

## 3.3 Dominance-in-Tails Criteria

### *3.3.1 Generalized Definition and Characterizations*

There are several ways to rank infinite utility streams applying a sequence of finite-horizon quasi-orderings. One of them is to apply a finite-horizon quasi-ordering $\succsim^n$ to heads of streams and check the Pareto dominance-in-tails of streams. We call this generalized criterion *dominance-in-tails criterion*.[1] Formally, given an independent sequence $(\succsim^n)_{n\in\mathbb{N}}$ of finite-horizon Paretian and anonymous quasi-orderings, the

---

[1]This generalized criterion is called *simplified criterion* in d'Aspremont (2007) because it is a simplified reformulation of his generalized overtaking criterion.

dominance-in-tails criterion associated with $(\succsim^n)_{n\in\mathbb{N}}$ is defined as the following binary relation $\succsim^D$ on $\mathbb{R}^{\mathbb{N}}$. For all $\boldsymbol{u}, \boldsymbol{v} \in \mathbb{R}^{\mathbb{N}}$,

$$\boldsymbol{u} \succsim^D \boldsymbol{v} \Leftrightarrow \text{there exists } n \in \mathbb{N} \text{ such that } \boldsymbol{u}^{-n} \succsim^n \boldsymbol{v}^{-n} \text{ and } \boldsymbol{u}^{+n} \geq \boldsymbol{v}^{+n}. \quad (3.3)$$

Note that $\succsim^D$ is an extension of $(\succsim^n)_{n\in\mathbb{N}}$.

As the following lemma shows, $\succsim^D$ associated with an independent sequence $(\succsim^n)_{n\in\mathbb{N}}$ of finite-horizon Paretian and anonymous quasi-orderings is well-defined as a quasi-ordering on $\mathbb{R}^{\mathbb{N}}$. The lemma also presents a characterization of the asymmetric and symmetric parts of $\succsim^D$.

**Lemma 3.4** *Let $(\succsim^n)_{n\in\mathbb{N}}$ be an independent sequence of finite-horizon Paretian quasi-orderings.*

*(i) $\succsim^D$ associated with $(\succsim^n)_{n\in\mathbb{N}}$ is a social welfare quasi-ordering on $\mathbb{R}^{\mathbb{N}}$. Further, if $\succsim^n$ is an ordering for each $n \in \mathbb{N}$, $\succsim^D$ is finitely complete.*
*(ii) The asymmetric and symmetric parts of $\succsim^D$ associated with $(\succsim^n)_{n\in\mathbb{N}}$ are characterized as follows: for all $\boldsymbol{u}, \boldsymbol{v} \in \mathbb{R}^{\mathbb{N}}$,*

$$\boldsymbol{u} \succ^D \boldsymbol{v} \Leftrightarrow \text{there exists } n \in \mathbb{N} \text{ such that } \boldsymbol{u}^{-n} \succ^n \boldsymbol{v}^{-n} \text{ and } \boldsymbol{u}^{+n} \geq \boldsymbol{v}^{+n}, \quad (3.4a)$$

$$\boldsymbol{u} \sim^D \boldsymbol{v} \Leftrightarrow \text{there exists } n \in \mathbb{N} \text{ such that } \boldsymbol{u}^{-n} \sim^n \boldsymbol{v}^{-n} \text{ and } \boldsymbol{u}^{+n} = \boldsymbol{v}^{+n}. \quad (3.4b)$$

***Proof*** (i) Since $\succsim^n$ is reflexive for each $n \in \mathbb{N}$, it is straightforward that $\succsim^D$ is reflexive. To show that $\succsim^D$ is transitive, let $\boldsymbol{u}, \boldsymbol{v}, \boldsymbol{w} \in \mathbb{R}^{\mathbb{N}}$ and suppose that $\boldsymbol{u} \succsim^D \boldsymbol{v}$ and $\boldsymbol{v} \succsim^D \boldsymbol{w}$. From (3.3), there exists $m \in \mathbb{N}$ such that $\boldsymbol{u}^{-m} \succsim^m \boldsymbol{v}^{-m}$ and $\boldsymbol{u}^{-m} \geq \boldsymbol{v}^{-m}$ and there exists $n \in \mathbb{N}$ such that $\boldsymbol{v}^{-n} \succsim^n \boldsymbol{w}^{-n}$ and $\boldsymbol{v}^{-n} \geq \boldsymbol{w}^{-n}$. Let $\overline{n} = \max\{m, n\}$. Since $(\succsim^n)_{n\in\mathbb{N}}$ is independent and $\succsim^n$ is Paretian and transitive for each $n \in \mathbb{N}$, it follows that $\boldsymbol{u}^{-\overline{n}} \succsim^{\overline{n}} \boldsymbol{w}^{-\overline{n}}$ and $\boldsymbol{u}^{-\overline{n}} \geq \boldsymbol{w}^{-\overline{n}}$. By (3.3), we obtain $\boldsymbol{u} \succsim^D \boldsymbol{v}$. Finally, suppose that $\succsim^n$ is an ordering for each $n \in \mathbb{N}$. To show that $\succsim^D$ is finitely complete, let $\boldsymbol{u}, \boldsymbol{v} \in \mathbb{R}^{\mathbb{N}}$ and suppose $\boldsymbol{u}^{+n} = \boldsymbol{v}^{+n}$ for some $n \in \mathbb{N}$. Since $\succsim^n$ is complete, we obtain $\boldsymbol{u}^{-n} \succsim^n \boldsymbol{v}^{-n}$ or $\boldsymbol{v}^{-n} \succsim^n \boldsymbol{u}^{-n}$. From (3.3), it follows that $\boldsymbol{u} \succsim^D \boldsymbol{v}$ or $\boldsymbol{v} \succsim^D \boldsymbol{u}$.

(ii) We begin by proving (3.4b). From (3.3), the "if" part of (3.4b) is straightforward. We prove the "only if" part. Let $\boldsymbol{u}, \boldsymbol{v} \in \mathbb{N}$ and suppose $\boldsymbol{u} \sim^D \boldsymbol{v}$. From (3.3), there exist $m \in \mathbb{N}$ such that $\boldsymbol{u}^{-m} \succsim^m \boldsymbol{v}^{-m}$ and $\boldsymbol{u}^{+m} \geq \boldsymbol{v}^{+m}$, and there exists $n \in \mathbb{N}$ such that $\boldsymbol{v}^{-n} \succsim^n \boldsymbol{u}^{-n}$ and $\boldsymbol{v}^{+n} \geq \boldsymbol{u}^{+n}$. Without loss of generality, we assume $m \leq n$. Since $(\succsim^n)_{n\in\mathbb{N}}$ is independent and $\succsim^{n'}$ is Paretian and transitive for each $n' \in \mathbb{N}$, it follows that $\boldsymbol{u}^{-n} \succsim^n \boldsymbol{v}^{-n}$ and $\boldsymbol{u}^{+n} \geq \boldsymbol{v}^{+n}$. Thus, we obtain $\boldsymbol{u} \sim^D \boldsymbol{v}$ by (3.3).

Next, we prove (3.4a). Let $\boldsymbol{u}, \boldsymbol{v} \in \mathbb{R}^{\mathbb{N}}$. First, suppose $\boldsymbol{u} \succ^D \boldsymbol{v}$. From (3.3), there exists $n \in \mathbb{N}$ such that $\boldsymbol{u}^{-n} \succsim^n \boldsymbol{v}^{-n}$ and $\boldsymbol{u}^{+n} \geq \boldsymbol{v}^{+n}$. We distinguish two cases: (a) $\boldsymbol{u}^{+n} = \boldsymbol{v}^{+n}$ and (b) $u_m > v_m$ for some $m \geq n$. In case (a), $\boldsymbol{u}^{-n} \succ^n \boldsymbol{v}^{-n}$ must hold since if $\boldsymbol{v}^{-n} \sim^n \boldsymbol{u}^{-n}$ holds, we obtain a contradiction with (3.4b). In case (b), $\boldsymbol{u}^{-m} \succ^m \boldsymbol{v}^{-m}$ follows since $(\succsim^n)_{n\in\mathbb{N}}$ is independent and $\succsim^n$ is Paretian and transitive for each $n \in \mathbb{N}$. Thus, there exists $n \in \mathbb{N}$ such that $\boldsymbol{u}^{-n} \succ^n \boldsymbol{v}^{-n}$ and $\boldsymbol{u}^{+n} \geq \boldsymbol{v}^{+n}$. Finally, suppose that there exists $n \in \mathbb{N}$ such that $\boldsymbol{u}^{-n} \succ^n \boldsymbol{v}^{-n}$ and $\boldsymbol{u}^{+n} \geq \boldsymbol{v}^{+n}$. By (3.3), $\boldsymbol{u} \succsim^D \boldsymbol{v}$ follows. By way of contradiction, suppose $\boldsymbol{v} \succsim^D \boldsymbol{u}$. It follows from (3.4b) that there exists $m \in \mathbb{N}$ such that $\boldsymbol{u}^{-m} \sim^m \boldsymbol{v}^{-m}$ and $\boldsymbol{u}^{+m} = \boldsymbol{v}^{+m}$. Let $\overline{n} = \max\{m, n\}$. Since $(\succsim^n)_{n\in\mathbb{N}}$ is independent and $\succsim^n$ is Paretian and transitive for each $n \in \mathbb{N}$, we obtain $\boldsymbol{u}^{-\overline{n}} \succ^{\overline{n}} \boldsymbol{v}^{-\overline{n}}$ and $\boldsymbol{u}^{-\overline{n}} \sim^{\overline{n}} \boldsymbol{v}^{-\overline{n}}$. This is a contradiction. Thus, $\boldsymbol{u} \succ^D \boldsymbol{v}$ must hold. ■

We present a characterization of the dominance-in-tails criterion associated with an independent sequence of finite-horizon Paretian and anonymous quasi-orderings using the extension notion and the strong Pareto principle. Strong Pareto requires that the evaluation be positively sensitive to generations' utilities.

**Strong Pareto**: For all $\boldsymbol{u}, \boldsymbol{v} \in \mathbb{R}^{\mathbb{N}}$, if $\boldsymbol{u} > \boldsymbol{v}$ then $\boldsymbol{u} \succ \boldsymbol{v}$.

The following theorem is a restatement of the result obtained by d'Aspremont (2007, Theorems 3 and 4). His original result was established using a proliferating sequence of finite-horizon Paretian and anonymous quasi-orderings.

**Theorem 3.1** *Let $(\succsim^n)_{n\in\mathbb{N}}$ be an independent sequence of finite-horizon Paretian and anonymous quasi-orderings. A social welfare quasi-ordering $\succsim$ on $\mathbb{R}^{\mathbb{N}}$ is an extension of $(\succsim^n)_{n\in\mathbb{N}}$ and satisfies strong Pareto if and only if $\succsim^D$ associated with $(\succsim^n)_{n\in\mathbb{N}}$ is a subrelation of $\succsim$.*

***Proof*** 'If.' Suppose that $\succsim^D$ associated with $(\succsim^n)_{n\in\mathbb{N}}$ is a subrelation of $\succsim$. First, we show that $\succsim$ is an extension of $(\succsim^n)_{n\in\mathbb{N}}$. Let $n \in \mathbb{N}$ and $\boldsymbol{u}, \boldsymbol{v}, \boldsymbol{w} \in \mathbb{R}^{\mathbb{N}}$. From (3.4a), $\boldsymbol{u}^{-n} \succ^n \boldsymbol{v}^{-n}$ implies $(\boldsymbol{u}^{-n}, \boldsymbol{w}^{+n}) \succ (\boldsymbol{v}^{-n}, \boldsymbol{w}^{+n})$. Analogously, it follows from (3.4b) that $\boldsymbol{u}^{-n} \sim^n \boldsymbol{v}^{-n}$ implies $(\boldsymbol{u}^{-n}, \boldsymbol{w}^{+n}) \sim (\boldsymbol{v}^{-n}, \boldsymbol{w}^{+n})$. Next, to show that $\succsim$ satisfies strong Pareto, let $\boldsymbol{u}, \boldsymbol{v} \in \mathbb{R}^{\mathbb{N}}$ and suppose $\boldsymbol{u} > \boldsymbol{v}$. Then, there exists $n \in \mathbb{N}$ such that $\boldsymbol{u}^{-n} > \boldsymbol{v}^{-n}$. Since $\succsim^n$ is Paretian, we obtain $\boldsymbol{u}^{-n} \succ^n \boldsymbol{v}^{-n}$. From (3.4a), $\boldsymbol{u} \succ \boldsymbol{v}$ follows.

'Only if.' Suppose that $\succsim$ is an extension of $(\succsim^n)_{n\in\mathbb{N}}$ and satisfies strong Pareto. To show that $\succsim^D$ associated with $(\succsim^n)_{n\in\mathbb{N}}$ is a subrelation of $\succsim$, let $\boldsymbol{u}, \boldsymbol{v} \in \mathbb{R}^{\mathbb{N}}$ and suppose $\boldsymbol{u} \succ^D \boldsymbol{v}$. From (3.4a), there exists $n \in \mathbb{N}$ such that $\boldsymbol{u}^{-n} \succ^n \boldsymbol{v}^{-n}$ and $\boldsymbol{u}^{+n} \geq \boldsymbol{v}^{+n}$. Define $\boldsymbol{w} \in \mathbb{R}^{\mathbb{N}}$ by $\boldsymbol{w} = (\boldsymbol{u}^{-n}, \boldsymbol{v}^{+n})$. Since $\succsim$ is an extension of $(\succsim^n)_{n\in\mathbb{N}}$, it follows that $\boldsymbol{w} \succ \boldsymbol{v}$. Since $\succsim$ is reflexive and satisfies strong Pareto, we obtain $\boldsymbol{u} \succsim \boldsymbol{w}$. By the transitivity of $\succsim$, we obtain $\boldsymbol{u} \succ \boldsymbol{v}$. Finally, since $\succsim$ is an extension of $(\succsim^n)_{n\in\mathbb{N}}$, it follows from (3.1b) to (3.4b) that $\boldsymbol{u} \sim^D \boldsymbol{v}$ implies $\boldsymbol{u} \sim \boldsymbol{v}$. ■

Next, we axiomatize the dominance-in-tails criterion associated with an independent sequence of finite-horizon Paretian and anonymous orderings. To this end, we use two additional axioms. Finite anonymity formalizes the equal treatment of finitely many generations, asserting that any two utility streams must be declared equally good if they coincide with each other through a transposition of two generations.

**Finite Anonymity**: For all $\boldsymbol{u}, \boldsymbol{v} \in \mathbb{R}^{\mathbb{N}}$, if there exist $i, j \in \mathbb{N}$ such that $u_i = v_j$, $u_j = v_i$, and $u_k = v_k$ for all $k \neq i, j$, then $\boldsymbol{u} \sim \boldsymbol{v}$.

The axiom of separable present asserts that the evaluation of infinite utility streams must be independent of common tails. This property was first discussed by Asheim and Banerjee (2010, Proposition 1) regarding the examination of a proliferating

sequence. It is stronger than postulate 3a in Koopmans (1960), which is obtained by setting $n = 1$ in the following definition.
**Separable Present**: For all $n \in \mathbb{N}$ and all $\boldsymbol{u}, \boldsymbol{v} \in \mathbb{R}^{\mathbb{N}}$,

$$\boldsymbol{u} \succsim (\boldsymbol{v}^{-n}, \boldsymbol{u}^{+n}) \Leftrightarrow (\boldsymbol{u}^{-n}, \boldsymbol{v}^{+n}) \succsim \boldsymbol{v}.$$

Assuming that a social welfare quasi-ordering is finitely complete, the following theorem shows that the three axioms presented above characterize the dominance-in-tails criterion associated with an independent sequence of finite-horizon Paretian and anonymous orderings.

**Theorem 3.2** *A finitely complete social welfare quasi-ordering $\succsim$ on $\mathbb{R}^{\mathbb{N}}$ satisfies strong Pareto, finite anonymity, and separable present if and only if there exists an independent sequence $(\succsim^n)_{n\in\mathbb{N}}$ of finite-horizon Paretian and anonymous orderings such that $\succsim^D$ associated with $(\succsim^n)_{n\in\mathbb{N}}$ is a subrelation of $\succsim$.*

To prove Theorem 3.2, we use the following lemma.

**Lemma 3.5** *A finitely complete social welfare quasi-ordering $\succsim$ on $\mathbb{R}^{\mathbb{N}}$ satisfies separable present if and only if there exists an independent sequence $(\succsim^n)_{n\in\mathbb{N}}$ of finite-horizon orderings such that $\succsim$ is an extension of $(\succsim^n)_{n\in\mathbb{N}}$.*

***Proof*** 'If.' The proof is straightforward and we omit its proof.

'Only if.' Let $n \in \mathbb{N}$ and $\boldsymbol{w} \in \mathbb{R}^{\mathbb{N}}$. Since there exists a bijection from $\mathbb{R}^n$ to $D^n_{\boldsymbol{w}}$, we can define the ordering $\succsim^n$ on $\mathbb{R}^n$ as follows: for all $\boldsymbol{u}, \boldsymbol{v} \in D^n_{\boldsymbol{w}}$,

$$\boldsymbol{u}^{-n} \succsim^n \boldsymbol{v}^{-n} \Leftrightarrow \boldsymbol{u} \succsim \boldsymbol{v}.$$

Since $\succsim$ satisfies separable present, it follows that for any $\boldsymbol{u}^{-n}, \boldsymbol{v}^{-n} \in \mathbb{R}^n$ and any $\tilde{\boldsymbol{w}} \in \mathbb{R}^{\mathbb{N}}$,

$$(\boldsymbol{u}^{-n}, \boldsymbol{w}^{+n}) \succsim (\boldsymbol{v}^{-n}, \boldsymbol{w}^{+n}) \Leftrightarrow (\boldsymbol{u}^{-n}, \tilde{\boldsymbol{w}}^{+n}) \succsim (\boldsymbol{v}^{-n}, \tilde{\boldsymbol{w}}^{+n}).$$

Thus, $\succsim^n$ satisfies that for any $\boldsymbol{u}, \boldsymbol{v} \in \mathbb{R}^{\mathbb{N}}$ with $\boldsymbol{u}^{+n} = \boldsymbol{v}^{+n}$,

$$\boldsymbol{u}^{-n} \succsim^n \boldsymbol{v}^{-n} \Leftrightarrow \boldsymbol{u} \succsim \boldsymbol{v}.$$

Since $n$ was chosen arbitrarily, $\succsim$ is an extension of $(\succsim^n)_{n\in\mathbb{N}}$. From Lemma 3.2, $(\succsim^n)_{n\in\mathbb{N}}$ is independent. ■

*Proof of Theorem* 3.2. 'If.' From Theorem 3.1, $\succsim$ is an extension of $(\succsim^n)_{n\in\mathbb{N}}$ and satisfies strong Pareto. From Lemma 3.5, $\succsim$ satisfies separable present. Further, since $\succsim^n$ is anonymous for each $n \in \mathbb{N}$, it follows from (3.2) that $\succsim$ satisfies finite anonymity.

'Only if.' From Lemma 3.5, there exists an independent sequence $(\succsim^n)_{n\in\mathbb{N}}$ of finite-horizon orderings such that $\succsim$ is an extension of $(\succsim^n)_{n\in\mathbb{N}}$. Since $\succsim$ satisfies strong Pareto and finite anonymity, $\succsim^n$ is Paretian and anonymous for each $n \in \mathbb{N}$.

We show that $\succsim^D$ associated with $(\succsim^n)_{n\in\mathbb{N}}$ is a subrelation of $\succsim$. Let $\boldsymbol{u}, \boldsymbol{v} \in \mathbb{R}^{\mathbb{N}}$. First, suppose $\boldsymbol{u} \succ^D \boldsymbol{v}$. From (3.4a) in Lemma 3.4 (ii), there exists $n \in \mathbb{N}$ such that $\boldsymbol{u}^{-n} \succ^n \boldsymbol{v}^{-n}$ and $\boldsymbol{u}^{+n} \geq \boldsymbol{v}^{+n}$. Define $\boldsymbol{w} \in \mathbb{R}^{\mathbb{N}}$ by $\boldsymbol{w} = (\boldsymbol{u}^{-n}, \boldsymbol{v}^{+n})$. Since $\succsim$ is an extension of $(\succsim^n)_{n\in\mathbb{N}}$, it follows that $\boldsymbol{w} \succ \boldsymbol{v}$. Since $\succsim$ is reflexive and satisfies strong Pareto, we obtain $\boldsymbol{u} \succsim \boldsymbol{w}$. By the transitivity of $\succsim$, $\boldsymbol{u} \succ \boldsymbol{v}$ follows. Next, suppose $\boldsymbol{u} \sim^D \boldsymbol{v}$. From (3.4b) in Lemma 3.4 (ii), there exists $n \in \mathbb{N}$ such that $\boldsymbol{u}^{-n} \sim^n \boldsymbol{v}^{-n}$ and $\boldsymbol{u}^{+n} = \boldsymbol{v}^{+}$. Since $\succsim$ is an extension of $(\succsim^n)_{n\in\mathbb{N}}$, we obtain $\boldsymbol{u} \sim \boldsymbol{v}$. ■

### 3.3.2 Dominance-in-tails Criteria Associated with Specific Sequences

We consider several specific forms of the dominance-in-tails criterion associated with a specific sequence of finite-horizon Paretian and anonymous quasi-orderings. Their axiomatizations are established by applying the general results—Theorems 3.1 and 3.2—combined with the axiomatizations of finite-horizon quasi-orderings provided in Chap. 2.

The *utilitarian* social welfare quasi-ordering $\succsim_U^D$ on $\mathbb{R}^{\mathbb{N}}$ is the dominance-in-tails criterion associated with the sequence $(\succsim_U^n)$ of finite-horizon utilitarian orderings, which was introduced by Basu and Mitra (2007). It is defined as follows. For all $\boldsymbol{u}, \boldsymbol{v} \in \mathbb{R}^{\mathbb{N}}$,

$$\boldsymbol{u} \succsim_U^D \boldsymbol{v} \Leftrightarrow \text{there exists } n \in \mathbb{N} \text{ such that } \boldsymbol{u}^{-n} \succsim_U^n \boldsymbol{v}^{-n} \text{ and } \boldsymbol{u}^{+n} \geq \boldsymbol{v}^{+n}.$$

To present its axiomatizations, we consider four additional axioms, each of which is an infinite-horizon extension of the corresponding axiom defined for a finite-horizon quasi-ordering in Chap. 2. Incremental equity requires that the evaluation be neutral with respect to a utility transfer between generations.

**Incremental Equity**: For all $\boldsymbol{u}, \boldsymbol{v} \in \mathbb{R}^{\mathbb{N}}$, if there exist $i, j \in N$ such that $u_i - v_i = v_j - u_j$ and $u_k = v_k$ for all $k \in \mathbb{N} \setminus \{i, j\}$, then $\boldsymbol{u} \sim \boldsymbol{v}$.

Note that incremental equity implies finite anonymity.

We present two informational invariance axioms, which are defined for streams with a common tail. Translation-scale invariance asserts that the utilities of generations are cardinally measurable and utility differences are intergenerationally comparable by an absolute unit. On the other hand, cardinal full comparability corresponds to the assumption that the utilities of generations are cardinally measurable and intergenerationally comparable.

**Translation-scale Invariance**: For all $n \in \mathbb{N}$ and all $\boldsymbol{u}, \tilde{\boldsymbol{u}}, \boldsymbol{v}, \tilde{\boldsymbol{v}} \in \mathbb{R}^{\mathbb{N}}$ with $\boldsymbol{u}^{+n} = \boldsymbol{v}^{+n}$ and $\tilde{\boldsymbol{u}}^{+n} = \tilde{\boldsymbol{v}}^{+n}$, if there exists $\boldsymbol{\beta} \in \mathbb{R}^{\mathbb{N}}$ such that $u_i = \tilde{u}_i + \beta_i$ and $v_i = \tilde{v}_i + \beta_i$ for all $i \in \mathbb{N}$, then

$$\boldsymbol{u} \succsim \boldsymbol{v} \Leftrightarrow \tilde{\boldsymbol{u}} \succsim \tilde{\boldsymbol{v}}$$

**Cardinal Full Comparability**: For all $n \in \mathbb{N}$ and all $\boldsymbol{u}, \tilde{\boldsymbol{u}}, \boldsymbol{v}, \tilde{\boldsymbol{v}} \in \mathbb{R}^{\mathbb{N}}$ with $\boldsymbol{u}^{+n} = \boldsymbol{v}^{+n}$ and $\tilde{\boldsymbol{u}}^{+n} = \tilde{\boldsymbol{v}}^{+n}$, if there exist $\alpha \in \mathbb{R}_{++}$ and $\beta \in \mathbb{R}$ such that $u_i = \alpha\tilde{u}_i + \beta$ and $v_i = \alpha\tilde{v}_i + \beta$ for all $i \in \mathbb{N}$, then

$$\boldsymbol{u} \succsim \boldsymbol{v} \;\Leftrightarrow\; \tilde{\boldsymbol{u}} \succsim \tilde{\boldsymbol{v}}$$

Translation-scale invariance was introduced by Basu and Mitra (2007) under the name of partial translation-scale invariance; see also Banerjee (2006). Note that translation-scale invariance implies separable present.

Restricted continuity postulates the robustness of the evaluation to small changes in the utilities of generations. It requires the property only for the evaluation of streams with a common tail.

**Restricted Continuity**: For all $n \in \mathbb{N}$, there exists $\boldsymbol{w} \in \mathbb{R}^{\mathbb{N}}$ such that for all $\boldsymbol{u} \in D^n_{\boldsymbol{w}}$, $\{\boldsymbol{v} \in D^n_{\boldsymbol{w}} : \boldsymbol{v} \succsim \boldsymbol{u}\}$ and $\{\boldsymbol{v} \in D^n_{\boldsymbol{w}} : \boldsymbol{u} \succsim \boldsymbol{v}\}$ are closed in $D^n_{\boldsymbol{w}}$.

A similar axiom that is defined by setting $\boldsymbol{w} = (0, 0, \ldots)$ was introduced by Mitra (2005).

The following theorem shows that the utilitarian social welfare quasi-ordering is axiomatized by strong Pareto and incremental equity. This result was established by Kamaga and Kojima (2009) and is the infinite-horizon counterpart of Theorem 2.1.

**Theorem 3.3** (Kamaga and Kojima 2009) *A social welfare quasi-ordering $\succsim$ on $\mathbb{R}^{\mathbb{N}}$ satisfies strong Pareto and incremental equity if and only if $\succsim^D_U$ is a subrelation of $\succsim$.*

***Proof*** 'If.' Since $(\succsim^n_U)_{n\in\mathbb{N}}$ is an independent sequence of finite-horizon Paretian and anonymous orderings, it follows from Theorem 3.1 that $\succsim$ is an extension of $(\succsim^n_U)_{n\in\mathbb{N}}$ and satisfies strong Pareto. It is straightforward from (3.4b) that $\succsim^D_U$ satisfies incremental equity. Since $\succsim^D_U$ is a subrelation of $\succsim$, $\succsim$ satisfies incremental equity.

'Only if.' We show that $\succsim$ is an extension of $(\succsim^n_U)_{n\in\mathbb{N}}$. Let $n \in \mathbb{N}$ and $\boldsymbol{w} \in \mathbb{R}^{\mathbb{N}}$. We define the quasi-ordering $\succsim^n$ on $\mathbb{R}^n$ as follows. For all $\boldsymbol{u}, \boldsymbol{v} \in D^n_{\boldsymbol{w}}$, $\boldsymbol{u}^{-n} \succsim^n \boldsymbol{v}^{-n}$ if and only if $\boldsymbol{u} \succsim \boldsymbol{v}$. Since $\succsim$ satisfies strong Pareto, $\succsim^n$ is Paretian. Further, since $\succsim$ satisfies incremental equity, $\succsim^n$ satisfies the following corresponding property. For all $\boldsymbol{u}^{-n}, \boldsymbol{v}^{-n} \in \mathbb{R}^n$, if there exist $i, j \in \{1, \ldots, n\}$ such that $u_i - v_i = v_j - u_j$ and $u_k = v_k$ for all $k \neq i, j$, then $\boldsymbol{u}^{-n} \sim^n \boldsymbol{v}^{-n}$. From Theorem 2.1, it follows that $\succsim^n = \succsim^n_U$. Since $n$ and $\boldsymbol{w}$ were arbitrarily chosen, $\succsim$ is an extension of $(\succsim^n_U)_{n\in\mathbb{N}}$. From Theorem 3.1, $\succsim^D_U$ is a subrelation of $\succsim$. ■

Another axiomatization of the utilitarian social welfare quasi-ordering was presented by Basu and Mitra (2007) using translation-scale invariance, which corresponds to Theorem 2.2 in Chap. 2.

**Theorem 3.4** (Basu and Mitra 2007) *A social welfare quasi-ordering $\succsim$ on $\mathbb{R}^{\mathbb{N}}$ satisfies strong Pareto, finite anonymity, and translation-scale invariance if and only if $\succsim^D_U$ is a subrelation of $\succsim$.*

***Proof*** 'If.' From Theorem 3.3, $\succsim$ satisfies strong Pareto. Since $\succsim$ is an extension of $(\succsim_U^n)_{n\in\mathbb{N}}$, it follows from (3.2) that $\succsim$ satisfies finite anonymity and translation-scale invariance.

'Only if.' We show that $\succsim$ is an extension of $(\succsim_U^n)_{n\in\mathbb{N}}$. Let $n \in \mathbb{N}$ and $\boldsymbol{w} \in \mathbb{R}^{\mathbb{N}}$. We define the quasi-ordering $\succsim^n$ on $\mathbb{R}^n$ as follows. For all $\boldsymbol{u}, \boldsymbol{v} \in D_{\boldsymbol{w}}^n$,

$$\boldsymbol{u}^{-n} \succsim^n \boldsymbol{v}^{-n} \Leftrightarrow \boldsymbol{u} \succsim \boldsymbol{v}. \tag{3.5}$$

Since translation-scale invariance implies separable present, $\succsim^n$ satisfies (3.5) for all $\boldsymbol{u}, \boldsymbol{v} \in \mathbb{R}^n$ with $\boldsymbol{u}^{+n} = \boldsymbol{v}^{+n}$. Since $\succsim$ satisfies strong Pareto and finite anonymity, $\succsim^n$ is Paretian and anonymous. Further, since $\succsim$ satisfies translation-scale invariance, $\succsim^n$ satisfies the following corresponding property.

For all $\boldsymbol{u}^{-n}, \boldsymbol{v}^{-n}, \tilde{\boldsymbol{u}}^{-n}, \tilde{\boldsymbol{v}}^{-n} \in \mathbb{R}^n$, if there exists $(\beta_1, \ldots, \beta_n) \in \mathbb{R}^n$ such that $u_i = \tilde{u}_i + \beta_i$ and $v_i = \tilde{v}_i + \beta_i$ for all $i \in \{1, \ldots, n\}$, then

$$\boldsymbol{u}^{-n} \succsim^n \boldsymbol{v}^{-n} \Leftrightarrow \tilde{\boldsymbol{u}}^{-n} \succsim^n \tilde{\boldsymbol{v}}^{-n}.$$

Thus, it follows from Theorem 2.2 that $\succsim^n = \succsim_U^n$; this follows from strong Pareto if $n = 1$. Since $n$ was arbitrarily chosen, $\succsim$ is an extension of $(\succsim_U^n)_{n\in\mathbb{N}}$. From Theorem 3.1, $\succsim_U^D$ is a subrelation of $\succsim$. ■

Assuming that a social welfare quasi-ordering on $\mathbb{R}^{\mathbb{N}}$ is finitely complete, we obtain the axiomatization of the utilitarian social welfare quasi-ordering with separable present, cardinal full comparability, and restricted continuity. This result is an infinite-horizon counterpart of Maskin's (1978) characterization of a finite-horizon utilitarian social welfare ordering (Theorem 2.3 in Chap. 2).

**Theorem 3.5** *A finitely complete social welfare quasi-ordering $\succsim$ on $\mathbb{R}^{\mathbb{N}}$ satisfies strong Pareto, finite anonymity, separable present, cardinal full comparability, and restricted continuity if and only if $\succsim_U^D$ is a subrelation of $\succsim$.*

***Proof*** 'If.' Suppose that $\succsim_U^D$ is a subrelation of $\succsim$. From Theorem 3.2, it suffices to show that $\succsim$ satisfies cardinal full comparability and restricted continuity. From Theorem 3.1, $\succsim$ is an extension of $(\succsim_U^n)_{n\in\mathbb{N}}$. Thus, from (3.2), $\succsim$ satisfies cardinal full comparability and restricted continuity.

'Only if.' From Theorem 3.2, there exists an independent sequence $(\succsim^n)_{n\in\mathbb{N}}$ of finite-horizon Paretian and anonymous orderings such that $\succsim^D$ associated with $(\succsim^n)_{n\in\mathbb{N}}$ is a subrelation of $\succsim$. We show that $(\succsim^n)_{n\in\mathbb{N}} = (\succsim_U^n)_{n\in\mathbb{N}}$. From Lemma 3.1, $\succsim^n$ is separable for each $n \in \mathbb{N}$. Further, from Theorem 3.1, $\succsim$ is an extension of $(\succsim^n)_{n\in\mathbb{N}}$. Since $\succsim$ satisfies cardinal full comparability and restricted continuity, it follows that, for any $n \in \mathbb{N}$, $\succsim^n$ satisfies the following corresponding properties.

(i) For all $\boldsymbol{u}^{-n}, \tilde{\boldsymbol{u}}^{-n}, \boldsymbol{v}^{-n}, \tilde{\boldsymbol{v}}^{-n} \in \mathbb{R}^n$, if there exist $\alpha \in \mathbb{R}_{++}$ and $\beta \in \mathbb{R}$ such that $u_i = \alpha\tilde{u}_i + \beta$ and $v_i = \alpha\tilde{v}_i + \beta$ for all $i \in \{1, \ldots, n\}$, then

$$\boldsymbol{u}^{-n} \succsim^n \boldsymbol{v}^{-n} \Leftrightarrow \tilde{\boldsymbol{u}}^{-n} \succsim^n \tilde{\boldsymbol{v}}^{-n}.$$

(ii) For any $\boldsymbol{u}^{-n} \in \mathbb{R}^n$, $\{\boldsymbol{v}^{-n} \in \mathbb{R}^n : \boldsymbol{v}^{-n} \succsim^n \boldsymbol{u}^{-n}\}$ and $\{\boldsymbol{v}^{-n} \in \mathbb{R}^n : \boldsymbol{u}^{-n} \succsim^n \boldsymbol{v}^{-n}\}$ are closed in $\mathbb{R}^n$.

Therefore, it follows from Theorem 2.3 that for each $n \in \mathbb{N}$ with $n \geq 3$, $\succsim^n = \succsim^n_U$. Let $m \in \{1, 2\}$ and $\boldsymbol{u}, \boldsymbol{v} \in \mathbb{R}^{\mathbb{N}}$ with $\boldsymbol{u}^{+m} = \boldsymbol{v}^{+m}$. Since $(\succsim^n_U)_{n\in\mathbb{N}}$ is independent, it follows that

$$\boldsymbol{u}^{-m} \succsim^m_U \boldsymbol{v}^{-m} \;\Leftrightarrow\; \boldsymbol{u}^{-3} \succsim^3_U \boldsymbol{v}^{-3}.$$

Since $\succsim$ is an extension of $(\succsim^n)_{n\in\mathbb{N}}$, we obtain

$$\boldsymbol{u}^{-3} \succsim^3_U \boldsymbol{v}^{-3} \;\Leftrightarrow\; \boldsymbol{u} \succsim \boldsymbol{v} \;\Leftrightarrow\; \boldsymbol{u}^{-m} \succsim^m \boldsymbol{v}^{-m}.$$

Thus, combining the above equivalence assertions, we obtain $\succsim^m = \succsim^m_U$. ∎

Let $G$ be the set of all continuous and increasing functions $g : \mathbb{R} \to \mathbb{R}$ satisfying $g(0) = 0$. Given $g \in G$, the *generalized utilitarian* social welfare quasi-ordering $\succsim^D_{U,g}$ on $\mathbb{R}^{\mathbb{N}}$ associated with $g$ is the dominance-in-tails criterion associated with the sequence $(\succsim^n_{U,g})_{n\in\mathbb{N}}$ of finite-horizon generalized utilitarian orderings associated with $g$. Formally, for all $\boldsymbol{u}, \boldsymbol{v} \in \mathbb{R}^{\mathbb{N}}$,

$$\boldsymbol{u} \succsim^D_{U,g} \boldsymbol{v} \;\Leftrightarrow\; \text{there exists } n \in \mathbb{N} \text{ such that } \boldsymbol{u}^{-n} \succsim^n_{U,g} \boldsymbol{v}^{-n} \text{ and } \boldsymbol{u}^{+n} \geq \boldsymbol{v}^{+n},$$

The class of generalized utilitarian quasi-orderings on $\mathbb{R}^{\mathbb{N}}$ was introduced by d'Aspremont (2007).

Dropping cardinal full comparability from Theorem 3.5, we obtain the axiomatization of the generalized utilitarian social welfare quasi-ordering that corresponds to Theorem 2.4 in Chap. 2.

**Theorem 3.6** *A finitely complete social welfare quasi-ordering $\succsim$ on $\mathbb{R}^{\mathbb{N}}$ satisfies strong Pareto, finite anonymity, separable present, and restricted continuity if and only if there exists $g \in G$ such that $\succsim^D_{U,g}$ is a subrelation of $\succsim$.*

***Proof*** Using Theorem 2.4 instead of Theorem 2.3, the proof is analogous to the proof of Theorem 3.5. ∎

We only outline the proof of the only-if part. To prove it, we need to show that there exists $g \in G$ such that $(\succsim^n)_{n\in\mathbb{N}} = (\succsim^n_{U,g})_{n\in\mathbb{N}}$. From Theorem 2.9, it follows that, for each $n \in \mathbb{N}$ with $n \geq 3$, there exists $g^n \in G$ such that $\succsim^n = \succsim^n_{U,g^n}$. Since $g^n$ is unique up to a positive affine transformation and $(\succsim^n)_{n\in\mathbb{N}}$ is independent, it can be shown that we can assume $g^n = g^{n'}$ for all $n, n' \geq 3$. This can be extended to $n = 1, 2$.

We now consider an infinite-horizon extension of the leximin principle. The *leximin* social welfare quasi-ordering $\succsim^D_L$ on $\mathbb{R}^{\mathbb{N}}$ is the dominance-in-tails criterion associated with the sequence $(\succsim^n_L)$ of finite-horizon leximin orderings, which was introduced by Bossert et al. (2007). Formally, for all $\boldsymbol{u}, \boldsymbol{v} \in \mathbb{R}^{\mathbb{N}}$,

$$\boldsymbol{u} \succsim^D_L \boldsymbol{v} \;\Leftrightarrow\; \text{there exists } n \in \mathbb{N} \text{ such that } \boldsymbol{u}^{-n} \succsim^n_L \boldsymbol{v}^{-n} \text{ and } \boldsymbol{u}^{+n} \geq \boldsymbol{v}^{+n},$$

The infinite-horizon reformulation of Hammond's (1976, 1979) equity axiom can be defined in an analogous manner to the infinite-horizon reformulation of incremental equity. It asserts that the decrease in utility difference between better-off and worse-off generations that preserves their relative ranking is deemed weakly better. This axiom appeared in Lauwers (1997); see also Asheim and Tungodden (2004) and Bossert et al. (2007).

**Hammond Equity**: For all $\boldsymbol{u}, \boldsymbol{v} \in \mathbb{R}^{\mathbb{N}}$, if there exist $i, j \in N$ such that $v_i < u_i \leq u_j < v_j$ and $u_k = v_k$ for all $k \neq i, j$, then $\boldsymbol{u} \succsim \boldsymbol{v}$.

Bossert et al. (2007) axiomatized the leximin social welfare quasi-ordering using Hammond equity.

**Theorem 3.7** (Bossert et al. 2007) *A social welfare quasi-ordering* $\succsim$ *on* $\mathbb{R}^{\mathbb{N}}$ *satisfies strong Pareto, finite anonymity, and Hammond equity if and only if* $\succsim_L^D$ *is a subrelation of* $\succsim$.

***Proof*** Using Theorem 2.5 instead of Theorem 2.1, the proof is analogous to the proof of Theorem 3.3. ■

As we have seen, the axiomatic foundations of the (generalized) utilitarian and leximin social welfare quasi-orderings for infinite utility streams are established analogously to what we have seen in the analysis of the finite-horizon intragenerational social welfare evaluation. We now examine compromises between the utilitarian and leximin social welfare quasi-orderings.

The *intersection* of utilitarian and leximin social welfare quasi-orderings $\succsim_\cap^D$ on $\mathbb{R}^{\mathbb{N}}$ is defined as the dominance-in-tails criterion associated with the sequence $(\succsim_\cap^n)_{n\in\mathbb{N}}$ of the intersections of finite-horizon utilitarian and leximin orderings. For all $\boldsymbol{u}, \boldsymbol{v} \in \mathbb{R}^{\mathbb{N}}$,

$$\boldsymbol{u} \succsim_\cap^D \boldsymbol{v} \;\Leftrightarrow\; \text{there exists } n \in \mathbb{N} \text{ such that } \boldsymbol{u}^{-n} \succsim_\cap^n \boldsymbol{v}^{-n} \text{ and } \boldsymbol{u}^{+n} \geq \boldsymbol{v}^{+n}.$$

As the following lemma shows, $\succsim_\cap^D$ is actually the intersection of the utilitarian and leximin social welfare quasi-orderings.

**Lemma 3.6** $\succsim_\cap^D = \succsim_U^D \cap \succsim_L^D$.

***Proof*** It is straightforward that $\succsim_U^D \cap \succsim_L^D \subseteq \succsim_\cap^D$. To show that $\succsim_\cap^D \subseteq \succsim_U^D \cap \succsim_L^D$, let $\boldsymbol{u}, \boldsymbol{v} \in \mathbb{R}^{\mathbb{N}}$, and suppose that $\boldsymbol{u} \succsim_\cap^D \boldsymbol{v}$. Then, $\boldsymbol{u} \succsim_U^D \boldsymbol{v}$ and $\boldsymbol{u} \succsim_L^D \boldsymbol{v}$. Thus, there exist $m, n \in \mathbb{N}$ such that $\boldsymbol{u}^{-m} \succsim_U^m \boldsymbol{v}^{-m}$, $\boldsymbol{u}^{-n} \succsim_L^n \boldsymbol{v}^{-n}$, $\boldsymbol{u}^{+m} \geq \boldsymbol{v}^{+m}$, and $\boldsymbol{u}^{+n} \geq \boldsymbol{v}^{+n}$. Assume $m \leq n$. Since $(\succsim_U^n)_{n\in\mathbb{N}}$ is an independent sequence of Paretian orderings, it follows that $\boldsymbol{u}^{-n} \succsim_U^n \boldsymbol{v}^{-n}$ and $\boldsymbol{u}^{+n} \geq \boldsymbol{v}^{+n}$. Thus, $\boldsymbol{u}^{-n} \succsim_\cap^n \boldsymbol{v}^{-n}$ holds. The proof for the case where $m > n$ is analogous since $(\succsim_L^n)_{n\in\mathbb{N}}$ is an independent sequence of Paretian orderings. ■

The *utilitarianism-first and leximin-second* social welfare quasi-ordering $\succsim_{UL}^D$ on $\mathbb{R}^{\mathbb{N}}$ is the dominance-in-tails criterion associated with the sequence $(\succsim_{UL}^n)_{n\in\mathbb{N}}$ of finite-horizon utilitarinism-first and leximin-second orderings. That is, for all $\boldsymbol{u}, \boldsymbol{v} \in \mathbb{R}^{\mathbb{N}}$,

$$\boldsymbol{u} \succsim_{UL}^{D} \boldsymbol{v} \Leftrightarrow \text{ there exists } n \in \mathbb{N} \text{ such that } \boldsymbol{u}^{-n} \succsim_{UL}^{n} \boldsymbol{v}^{-n} \text{ and } \boldsymbol{u}^{+n} \geq \boldsymbol{v}^{+n}.$$

The following lemma shows that $\succsim_{UL}^{D}$ applies the utilitarian social welfare quasi-ordering $\succsim_{U}^{D}$ first and the leximin social welfare quasi-ordering $\succsim_{L}^{D}$ second.

**Lemma 3.7** *For all* $\boldsymbol{u}, \boldsymbol{v} \in \mathbb{R}^{\mathbb{N}}$,

$$\boldsymbol{u} \succsim_{UL}^{D} \boldsymbol{v} \Leftrightarrow \boldsymbol{u} \succ_{U}^{D} \boldsymbol{v} \text{ or } [\boldsymbol{u} \sim_{U}^{D} \boldsymbol{v} \text{ and } \boldsymbol{u} \succsim_{L}^{D} \boldsymbol{v}].$$

***Proof*** 'If.' Let $\boldsymbol{u}, \boldsymbol{v} \in \mathbb{R}^{\mathbb{N}}$. First, suppose that $\boldsymbol{u} \succ_{U}^{D} \boldsymbol{v}$. From (3.4a), there exists $n \in \mathbb{N}$ such that $\boldsymbol{u}^{-n} \succ_{U}^{n} \boldsymbol{v}^{-n}$ and $\boldsymbol{u}^{+n} \geq \boldsymbol{v}^{+n}$. Thus, $\boldsymbol{u} \succsim_{UL}^{D} \boldsymbol{v}$ follows. Next, we suppose that $\boldsymbol{u} \sim_{U}^{D} \boldsymbol{v}$ and $\boldsymbol{u} \succsim_{L}^{D} \boldsymbol{v}$. Then, there exist $n, m \in \mathbb{N}$ such that $\boldsymbol{u}^{-n} \sim_{U}^{n} \boldsymbol{v}^{-n}$, $\boldsymbol{u}^{-m} \succsim_{L}^{m} \boldsymbol{v}^{-m}$, $\boldsymbol{u}^{+n} = \boldsymbol{v}^{+n}$, and $\boldsymbol{u}^{+m} \geq \boldsymbol{v}^{+m}$. Let $k = \max\{n, m\}$. Then, $\boldsymbol{u}^{+k} = \boldsymbol{v}^{+k}$. Further, since both $(\succsim_{U}^{n})_{n \in \mathbb{N}}$ and $(\succsim_{L}^{n})_{n \in \mathbb{N}}$ are an independent sequence of finite-horizon Paretian orderings, it follows that $\boldsymbol{u}^{-k} \sim_{U}^{k} \boldsymbol{v}^{-k}$ and $\boldsymbol{u}^{-k} \succsim_{L}^{k} \boldsymbol{v}^{-k}$, which means that $\boldsymbol{u}^{-k} \succsim_{UL}^{k} \boldsymbol{v}^{-k}$. Thus, we obtain $\boldsymbol{u} \succsim_{UL}^{D} \boldsymbol{v}$.

'Only if.' Let $\boldsymbol{u}, \boldsymbol{v} \in \mathbb{R}^{\mathbb{N}}$ and suppose that $\boldsymbol{u} \succsim_{UL}^{D} \boldsymbol{v}$. Then, there exists $n \in \mathbb{N}$ such that $\boldsymbol{u}^{-n} \succsim_{UL}^{n} \boldsymbol{v}^{-n}$ and $\boldsymbol{u}^{+n} \geq \boldsymbol{v}^{+n}$. By the definition of $\boldsymbol{u}^{-n} \succsim_{UL}^{n} \boldsymbol{v}^{-n}$, it must be the case that $\boldsymbol{u}^{-n} \succ_{U}^{n} \boldsymbol{v}^{-n}$ or $[\boldsymbol{u}^{-n} \sim_{U}^{n} \boldsymbol{v}^{-n}$ and $\boldsymbol{u}^{-n} \succsim_{L}^{n} \boldsymbol{v}^{-n}]$. If $\boldsymbol{u}^{-n} \succ_{U}^{n} \boldsymbol{v}^{-n}$ holds, then $\boldsymbol{u} \succ_{U}^{D} \boldsymbol{v}$ follows. Now, suppose that $\boldsymbol{u}^{-n} \sim_{U}^{n} \boldsymbol{v}^{-n}$ and $\boldsymbol{u}^{-n} \succsim_{L}^{n} \boldsymbol{v}^{-n}$. We distinguish two cases. First, consider the case that there exists $m > n$ such that $u_m > v_m$. Since $(\succsim_{U}^{n})_{n \in \mathbb{N}}$ is an independent sequence of finite-horizon Paretian orderings, we obtain $\boldsymbol{u}^{-m} \succ_{U}^{m} \boldsymbol{v}^{-m}$, which together with $\boldsymbol{u}^{+n} \geq \boldsymbol{v}^{+n}$ imply that $\boldsymbol{u} \succ_{U}^{D} \boldsymbol{v}$. Next, consider the case that $\boldsymbol{u}^{+n} = \boldsymbol{v}^{+n}$. By (3.4b), we obtain that $\boldsymbol{u} \sim_{U}^{D} \boldsymbol{v}$ and $\boldsymbol{u} \succsim_{L}^{D} \boldsymbol{v}$. ∎

Note that, from Lemmas 3.6 and 3.7, $\succsim_{\cap}^{D}$ is a subrelation of both $\succsim_{L}^{D}$ and $\succsim_{UL}^{D}$.

We consider three axioms regarding utility transfer between generations. Infinite-horizon reformulations of the transfer principle of Pigou (1912) and Dalton (1920) are defined as follows.

**Weak Pigou–Dalton Principle**: For all $\boldsymbol{u}, \boldsymbol{v} \in \mathbb{R}^{\mathbb{N}}$, if there exist $i, j \in \mathbb{N}$ and $\delta \in \mathbb{R}_{++}$ such that $v_i + \delta = u_i \leq u_j = v_j - \delta$ and $u_k = v_k$ for all $k \in \mathbb{N} \setminus \{i, j\}$, then $\boldsymbol{u} \succsim \boldsymbol{v}$.

**Strong Pigou–Dalton Principle**: For all $\boldsymbol{u}, \boldsymbol{v} \in \mathbb{R}^{\mathbb{N}}$, if there exist $i, j \in \mathbb{N}$ and $\delta \in \mathbb{R}_{++}$ such that $v_i + \delta = u_i \leq u_j = v_j - \delta$ and $u_k = v_k$ for all $k \in \mathbb{N} \setminus \{i, j\}$, then $\boldsymbol{u} \succ \boldsymbol{v}$.

Hammond equity implies the weak Pigou–Dalton principle. Further, if a social welfare quasi-ordering satisfies strong Pareto and Hammond equity, it also satisfies the strong Pigou–Dalton principle.

The infinite-horizon reformulation of the composite transfer principle in Kamaga (2018) is defined as follows.

**Composite Transfer Principle**: For all $\boldsymbol{u}, \boldsymbol{v} \in \mathbb{R}^{\mathbb{N}}$, if there exist $i, j, k \in \mathbb{N}$ and $\delta, \varepsilon \in \mathbb{R}_{++}$ such that $u_i = v_i + \delta$, $u_j = v_j - \delta - \varepsilon$, $u_k = v_k + \varepsilon$, $u_\ell = v_\ell$ for all $\ell \in \mathbb{N} \setminus \{i, j, k\}$, $u_i \le u_j < u_k$, and $v_i < v_j \le v_k$, then $\boldsymbol{u} \succsim \boldsymbol{v}$.

If a social welfare quasi-ordering satisfies strong Pareto and Hammond equity, it also satisfies the composite transfer principle.

The following theorem presents the axiomatization of the intersection of utilitarian and leximin social welfare quasi-orderings using the strong Pigou–Dalton principle and the composite transfer principle. This axiomatization corresponds to Theorem 2.7 in Chap. 2.

**Theorem 3.8** *A social welfare quasi-ordering $\succsim$ on $\mathbb{R}^{\mathbb{N}}$ satisfies strong Pareto, finite anonymity, the strong Pigou–Dalton principle, and the composite transfer principle if and only if $\succsim_{\cap}$ is a subrelation of $\succsim$.*

***Proof*** 'If.' The proof is analogous to the proof of Theorem 3.3.

'Only if.' We show that $\succsim$ is an extension of $(\succsim_{\cap}^{n})_{n \in \mathbb{N}}$. Let $n \in \mathbb{N}$ and $\boldsymbol{w} \in \mathbb{R}^{\mathbb{N}}$. We define the quasi-ordering $\succsim^n$ on $\mathbb{R}^n$ as follows. For all $\boldsymbol{u}, \boldsymbol{v} \in D_{\boldsymbol{w}}^n$, $\boldsymbol{u}^{-n} \succsim^n \boldsymbol{v}^{-n}$ if and only if $\boldsymbol{u} \succsim \boldsymbol{v}$. Since $\succsim$ satisfies strong Pareto and finite anonymity, $\succsim^n$ is Paretian and anonymous. Further, since $\succsim$ satisfies the strong Pigou–Dalton principle and the composite transfer principle, $\succsim^n$ satisfies the following corresponding properties.

(iii) For all $\boldsymbol{u}^{-n}, \boldsymbol{v}^{-n} \in \mathbb{R}^n$, if there exist $i, j \in \{1, \ldots, n\}$ and $\delta \in \mathbb{R}_{++}$ such that $v_i + \delta = u_i \le u_j = v_j - \delta$ and $u_k = v_k$ for all $k \ne i, j$, then $\boldsymbol{u}^{-n} \succ^n \boldsymbol{v}^{-n}$.

(iv) For all $\boldsymbol{u}^{-n}, \boldsymbol{v}^{-n} \in \mathbb{R}^n$, if there exist $i, j, k \in \{1, \ldots, n\}$ and $\delta, \varepsilon \in \mathbb{R}_{++}$ such that $u_i = v_i + \delta$, $u_j = v_j - \delta - \varepsilon$, $u_k = v_k + \varepsilon$, $u_i \le u_j < u_k$, $v_i < v_j \le v_k$, and $u_\ell = v_\ell$ for all $\ell \ne i, j, k$, then $\boldsymbol{u}^{-n} \succsim^n \boldsymbol{v}^{-n}$.

From Theorem 2.7, it follows that $\succsim_{\cap}^{n}$ is a subrelation of $\succsim^n$—that is, for all $\boldsymbol{u}^{-n}, \boldsymbol{v}^{-n} \in \mathbb{R}^n$,

$$\boldsymbol{u}^{-n} \succ_{\cap}^{n} \boldsymbol{v}^{-n} \Rightarrow \boldsymbol{u}^{-n} \succ^{n} \boldsymbol{v}^{-n} \quad \text{and} \quad \boldsymbol{u}^{-n} \sim_{\cap}^{n} \boldsymbol{v}^{-n} \Rightarrow \boldsymbol{u}^{-n} \sim^{n} \boldsymbol{v}^{-n}.$$

Since $n$ and $\boldsymbol{w}$ were arbitrarily chosen, $\succsim$ is an extension of $(\succsim_{\cap}^{n})_{n \in \mathbb{N}}$. From Theorem 3.1, $\succsim_{\cap}^{D}$ is a subrelation of $\succsim$. ■

Bossert et al. (2007) showed that if the strong Pigou–Dalton principle is retained and the composite transfer principle is dropped from Theorem 3.8, the generalized-Lorenz social welfare quasi-ordering is characterized; see their Theorem 3.1.

Assuming the finite completeness of a social welfare quasi-ordering, we jointly axiomatize the utilitarian and leximin social welfare quasi-orderings and the utilitarianism-first and leximin-second social welfare quasi-ordering by weakening the Pigou–Dalton principle and adding separable present and cardinal full comparability. This result is the infinite-horizon counterpart of Theorem 2.9 in Chap. 2.

**Theorem 3.9** *A finitely complete social welfare quasi-ordering $\succsim$ on $\mathbb{R}^{\mathbb{N}}$ satisfies strong Pareto, finite anonymity, the weak Pigou–Dalton principle, the composite transfer principle, separable present, and cardinal full comparability if and only if any one of $\succsim_{U}^{D}$, $\succsim_{UL}^{D}$, and $\succsim_{L}^{D}$ is a subrelation of $\succsim$.*

***Proof*** 'If.' Note that each of $(\succsim_U^n)_{n\in\mathbb{N}}$, $(\succsim_{UL}^n)_{n\in\mathbb{N}}$, and $(\succsim_L^n)_{n\in\mathbb{N}}$ is an independent sequence of finite-horizon Paretian and anonymous orderings. From Theorem 3.2, $\succsim$ satisfies strong Pareto, finite anonymity, and separable present. Further, from Theorem 3.1, $\succsim$ is an extension of $(\succsim_U^n)_{n\in\mathbb{N}}$, $(\succsim_{UL}^n)_{n\in\mathbb{N}}$, or $(\succsim_L^n)_{n\in\mathbb{N}}$. Thus, it follows from (3.2) that $\succsim$ satisfies the weak Pigou–Dalton principle, the composite transfer principle, and cardinal full comparability.

'Only if.' From Theorem 3.2, there exists an independent sequence $(\succsim^n)_{n\in\mathbb{N}}$ of finite-horizon Paretian and anonymous orderings such that $\succsim^D$ associated with $(\succsim^n)_{n\in\mathbb{N}}$ is a subrelation of $\succsim$. Therefore, it suffices to show that $(\succsim^n)_{n\in\mathbb{N}}$ is any one of $(\succsim_U^n)_{n\in\mathbb{N}}$, $(\succsim_{UL}^n)_{n\in\mathbb{N}}$, and $(\succsim_L^n)_{n\in\mathbb{N}}$. From Theorem 3.1, $\succsim$ is an extension of $(\succsim^n)_{n\in\mathbb{N}}$. Since $\succsim$ satisfies cardinal full comparability and the composite transfer principle, $\succsim$ satisfies properties (i) and (iv) presented in the proofs of Theorems 3.5 and 3.8, respectively. Further, since $\succsim$ satisfies the weak Pigou–Dalton principle, it follows that, for each $n \in \mathbb{N}$, $\succsim^n$ satisfies the following corresponding property.

For all $\boldsymbol{u}^{-n}, \boldsymbol{v}^{-n} \in \mathbb{R}^n$, if there exist $i, j \in \{1, \ldots, n\}$ and $\delta \in \mathbb{R}_{++}$ such that $v_i + \delta = u_i \leq u_j = v_j - \delta$ and $u_k = v_k$ for all $k \neq i, j$, then $\boldsymbol{u}^{-n} \succsim^n \boldsymbol{v}^{-n}$.

Further, it follows from Lemma 3.1 that $\succsim^n$ is separable for each $n \in \mathbb{N}$. Therefore, from Theorem 2.9, it follows that for each $n \in \mathbb{N}$ with $n \geq 3$, $\succsim^n$ is $\succsim_U^n$, $\succsim_{UL}^n$, or $\succsim_L^n$.

To complete the proof, let $n \geq 3$ and we distinguish three cases: (i) $\succsim^n = \succsim_U^n$, (ii) $\succsim^n = \succsim_{UL}^n$, and (iii) $\succsim^n = \succsim_L^n$. First, we consider case (i) and show that $(\succsim^n)_{n\in\mathbb{N}} = (\succsim_U^n)_{n\in\mathbb{N}}$. Let $m \in \mathbb{N}\setminus\{n\}$. We first assume that $m > n$. Let $\boldsymbol{u}, \boldsymbol{v} \in \mathbb{R}^{\mathbb{N}}$ with $\boldsymbol{u}^{+n} = \boldsymbol{v}^{+}$. Since $\boldsymbol{u}^{-n}$ and $\boldsymbol{v}^{-n}$ were chosen arbitrarily, this equivalence assertion must hold for $\boldsymbol{u}, \boldsymbol{v} \in \mathbb{R}^{\mathbb{N}}$ such that $\boldsymbol{u}^{-n} \sim_U^n \boldsymbol{v}^{-n}$ and $\boldsymbol{u}^{-n} \succ_L^n \boldsymbol{v}^{-n}$ (thus, $\boldsymbol{u}^{-n} \succ_{UL}^n \boldsymbol{v}^{-n}$). Since $(\succsim_{UL}^n)_{n\in\mathbb{N}}$ and $(\succsim_L^n)_{n\in\mathbb{N}}$ are independent, $\succsim^m = \succsim_U^m$ must hold. The proof that $\succsim^m = \succsim_U^m$ for any $m < n$ is analogous to the proof of Theorem 3.5; we omit its proof.

The proof that $(\succsim^n)_{n\in\mathbb{N}} = (\succsim_{UL}^n)_{n\in\mathbb{N}}$ in case (ii) and $(\succsim^n)_{n\in\mathbb{N}} = (\succsim_L^n)_{n\in\mathbb{N}}$ in case (iii) is analogous. ∎

Among the three social welfare quasi-orderings jointly characterized in Theorem 3.9, only $\succsim_U^D$ satisfies restricted continuity. Thus, adding restricted continuity to the list of axioms in Theorem 3.9 produces an alternative characterization of $\succsim_U^D$. However, as we saw in Theorem 3.5, the weak Pigou–Dalton principle and the composite transfer principle are redundant.

The lexicographic composition of the utilitarian and leximin social welfare quasi-orderings—$\succsim_U^D$ and $\succsim_L^D$—that applies the leximin first is the leximin social welfare quasi-ordering. Thus, the following theorem presents a joint characterization of the lexicographic compositions of the utilitarian and leximin social welfare quasi-orderings by strengthening the Pigou–Dalton principle. This is an infinite-horizon counterpart of Theorem 2.10 in Chap. 2.

**Theorem 3.10** *A finitely complete social welfare quasi-ordering $\succsim$ on $\mathbb{R}^{\mathbb{N}}$ satisfies strong Pareto, finite anonymity, the strong Pigou–Dalton principle, the composite transfer principle, separable present, and cardinal full comparability if and only if either $\succsim_{UL}^D$ or $\succsim_L^D$ is a subrelation of $\succsim$.*

***Proof*** 'If.' The proof is analogous to the proof of Theorem 3.9.

'Only if.' From Theorem 3.9, any one of $\succsim_U^D$, $\succsim_{UL}^D$, and $\succsim_L^D$ is a subrelation of $\succsim$. If $\succsim_U^D$ is a subrelation of $\succsim$, $\succsim$ violates the strong Pigou–Dalton principle since $\boldsymbol{u} \sim_U^D \boldsymbol{v}$ holds (and thus, $\boldsymbol{u} \sim \boldsymbol{v}$ follows) for any $\boldsymbol{u}, \boldsymbol{v} \in \mathbb{R}^{\mathbb{N}}$ satisfying the condition of the strong Pigou–Dalton principle. Thus, either $\succsim_{UL}^D$ or $\succsim_L^D$ is a subrelation of $\succsim$. ■

## 3.4 Overtaking Criteria

### *3.4.1 Generalized Definition and Characterizations*

In this section, we consider a generalized overtaking criterion for ranking infinite utility streams. Given an independent sequence $(\succsim^n)_{n\in\mathbb{N}}$ of finite-horizon orderings, the *overtaking criterion* associated with $(\succsim^n)_{n\in\mathbb{N}}$ is defined as the following binary relation $\succsim^O$ on $\mathbb{R}^{\mathbb{N}}$. For all $\boldsymbol{u}, \boldsymbol{v} \in \mathbb{R}^{\mathbb{N}}$,

$$\boldsymbol{u} \succ^O \boldsymbol{v} \Leftrightarrow \text{there exists } \bar{n} \in \mathbb{N} \text{ such that } \boldsymbol{u}^{-n} \succ^n \boldsymbol{v}^{-n} \text{ for all } n \geq \bar{n}, \tag{3.6a}$$

$$\boldsymbol{u} \sim^O \boldsymbol{v} \Leftrightarrow \text{there exists } \bar{n} \in \mathbb{N} \text{ such that } \boldsymbol{u}^{-n} \sim^n \boldsymbol{v}^{-n} \text{ for all } n \geq \bar{n}. \tag{3.6b}$$

The generalized overtaking criterion was analyzed by Asheim and Banerjee (2010) using a proliferating sequence of finite-horizon Paretian and anonymous orderings.

The following lemma shows that the overtaking criterion associated with an independent sequence $(\succsim^n)_{n\in\mathbb{N}}$ of finite-horizon orderings is well-defined as a finitely complete social welfare quasi-ordering. Moreover, it relates its symmetric part and that of the dominance-in-tails criterion.

**Lemma 3.8** *Let $(\succsim^n)_{n\in\mathbb{N}}$ be an independent sequence of finite-horizon orderings and suppose that $\succsim^O$ is associated with $(\succsim^n)_{n\in\mathbb{N}}$.*

*(i) $\succsim^O$ is a finitely complete social welfare quasi-ordering.*
*(ii) If $\succsim^n$ is Paretian for each $n \in \mathbb{N}$, then for all $\boldsymbol{u}, \boldsymbol{v} \in \mathbb{R}^{\mathbb{N}}$,*

$$\boldsymbol{u} \sim^O \boldsymbol{v} \Leftrightarrow \boldsymbol{u} \sim^D \boldsymbol{v}$$

*where $\succsim^D$ is the dominance-in-tails criterion associated with $(\succsim^n)_{n\in\mathbb{N}}$.*

***Proof*** (i) First, we show that $\succsim^O$ is well-defined as a binary relation on $\mathbb{R}^{\mathbb{N}}$. To this end, let $\succsim = \succ^O \cup \sim^O$. We show that $\succ = \succ^O$ and $\sim = \sim^O$. Note that it suffices to show that (i) $\succ^O \cap \sim^O = \varnothing$, (ii) $\succ^O$ is an asymmetric binary relation, and $\sim^O$ is a symmetric binary relation. To show that $\succ^O \cap \sim^O = \varnothing$, let $\boldsymbol{u}, \boldsymbol{v} \in \mathbb{R}^{\mathbb{N}}$. By way of contradiction, suppose $\boldsymbol{u} \succ^O \boldsymbol{v}$ and $\boldsymbol{u} \sim^O \boldsymbol{v}$. From (3.6a) to (3.6b), there exists $\bar{n}_1 \in \mathbb{N}$ such that $\boldsymbol{u}^{-n} \succ^n \boldsymbol{v}^{-n}$ for all $n \geq \bar{n}_1$ and there exists $\bar{n}_2 \in \mathbb{N}$ such that $\boldsymbol{u}^{-n} \sim^n \boldsymbol{v}^{-n}$ for all $n \geq \bar{n}_2$. Let $\bar{n} = \max\{\bar{n}_1, \bar{n}_2\}$. Then, it follows that $\boldsymbol{u}^{-\bar{n}} \succ^{\bar{n}} \boldsymbol{v}^{-\bar{n}}$ and $\boldsymbol{u}^{-\bar{n}} \sim^{\bar{n}} \boldsymbol{v}^{-\bar{n}}$.

This is a contradiction. Thus, $\succ^O \cap \sim^O = \varnothing$. Next, to show that $\succ^O$ is asymmetric, suppose $\boldsymbol{u} \succ^O \boldsymbol{v}$. From (3.6a), there exists $\bar{n} \in \mathbb{N}$ such that $\boldsymbol{u}^{-n} \succ^n \boldsymbol{v}^{-n}$ for all $n \geq \bar{n}$. This implies that there is no $\bar{n} \in \mathbb{N}$ such that $\boldsymbol{v}^{-n} \succ^n \boldsymbol{u}^{-n}$ for all $n \geq \bar{n}$. From (3.6a), $\neg \boldsymbol{v} \succ^O \boldsymbol{u}$ follows. Thus, $\succ^O$ is asymmetric. We can analogously prove that $\sim^O$ is a symmetric binary relation; we omit its proof. Finally, we show that $\succsim^O$ is a finitely complete social welfare quasi-ordering. It is straightforward that $\succsim^O$ is a quasi-ordering. Thus, we show only that $\succsim^O$ is finitely complete. Let $\boldsymbol{u}, \boldsymbol{v} \in \mathbb{R}^{\mathbb{N}}$ and suppose that there exists $\bar{n} \in \mathbb{N}$ such that $\boldsymbol{u}^{+\bar{n}} = \boldsymbol{v}^{+\bar{n}}$. Since $\succsim^n$ is an ordering for each $n \in \mathbb{N}$, any one of the following three holds: $\boldsymbol{u}^{-\bar{n}} \succ^{-\bar{n}} \boldsymbol{v}^{-\bar{n}}$, $\boldsymbol{u}^{-\bar{n}} \sim^{-\bar{n}} \boldsymbol{v}^{-\bar{n}}$, and $\boldsymbol{v}^{-\bar{n}} \succ^{-\bar{n}} \boldsymbol{u}^{-\bar{n}}$. Since $(\succsim^n)_{n\in\mathbb{N}}$ is independent, it follows that any one of the following three holds: $\boldsymbol{u} \succ^O \boldsymbol{v}$, $\boldsymbol{u} \sim^O \boldsymbol{v}$, and $\boldsymbol{v} \succ^O \boldsymbol{u}$.

(ii) 'If.' Let $\boldsymbol{u}, \boldsymbol{v} \in \mathbb{R}^{\mathbb{N}}$ and suppose $\boldsymbol{u} \sim^D \boldsymbol{v}$. From (3.4b) in Lemma 3.4, there exists $\bar{n} \in \mathbb{N}$ such that $\boldsymbol{u}^{-\bar{n}} \sim^{\bar{n}} \boldsymbol{v}^{-\bar{n}}$ and $\boldsymbol{u}^{+\bar{n}} = \boldsymbol{v}^{-\bar{n}}$. Since $(\succsim^n)_{n\in\mathbb{N}}$ is independent, it follows that for all $n \in \mathbb{N}$ with $n \geq \bar{n}$, $\boldsymbol{u}^{-n} \sim^n \boldsymbol{v}^{-n}$. By (3.6b), we obtain $\boldsymbol{u} \sim^O \boldsymbol{v}$.

'Only if.' Let $\boldsymbol{u}, \boldsymbol{v} \in \mathbb{R}^{\mathbb{N}}$ and suppose $\boldsymbol{u} \succ^O \boldsymbol{v}$ From (3.6b), there exists $\bar{n} \in \mathbb{N}$ such that for all $n \geq \bar{n}$, $\boldsymbol{u}^{-n} \sim^n \boldsymbol{v}^{-n}$. We show that $u_n = v_n$ for all $n > \bar{n}$. By way of contradiction, suppose that there exists $n \in \mathbb{N}$ with $n > \bar{n}$ such that $u_n \neq v_n$. Define $n^* \in \mathbb{N}$ by $n^* = \min\{n \in \mathbb{N} : n > \bar{n} \text{ and } u_n \neq v_n\}$. Without loss of generality, we assume $u_{n^*} > v_{n^*}$. Since $(\succsim^n)_{n\in\mathbb{N}}$ is independent and $\succsim^{n^*}$ is Paretian and transitive, it follows that $\boldsymbol{u}^{-n^*} \succ^{n^*} \boldsymbol{v}^{-n^*}$. However, this is a contradiction since $\boldsymbol{u}^{-n^*} \sim^{n^*} \boldsymbol{v}^{-n^*}$. Thus, $u_n = v_n$ for all $n > \bar{n}$. From (3.4b) in Lemma 3.4, $\boldsymbol{u} \sim^D \boldsymbol{v}$ follows. ■

From Lemmas 3.4 and 3.8, given an independent sequence $(\succsim^n)_{n\in\mathbb{N}}$ of finite-horizon Paretian orderings, the symmetric part of the dominance-in-tails criterion $\succsim^D$ associated with $(\succsim^n)_{n\in\mathbb{N}}$ and that of the overtaking criterion $\succsim^O$ associated with $(\succsim^n)_{n\in\mathbb{N}}$ coincide with each other. Further, using (3.4a) and (3.4b) in Lemma 3.4, (3.6a) and (3.6b), it can be verified that $\succsim^D$ associated with $(\succsim^n)_{n\in\mathbb{N}}$ is a subrelation of $\succsim^O$ associated with $(\succsim^n)_{n\in\mathbb{N}}$. Thus, the following relationship holds between them; we omit an easy proof.

**Lemma 3.9** *Let $(\succsim^n)_{n\in\mathbb{N}}$ be an independent sequence of finite-horizon Paretian orderings and $\succsim$ be a social welfare quasi-ordering on $\mathbb{R}^{\mathbb{N}}$. If $\succsim^O$ associated with $(\succsim^n)_{n\in\mathbb{N}}$ is a subrelation of $\succsim$, then $\succsim^D$ associated with $(\succsim^n)_{n\in\mathbb{N}}$ is a subrelation of $\succsim$.*

We present characterizations of the generalized notion of overtaking criterion. To this end, we use the following axiom, which was presented by Kamaga and Kojima (2010). It asserts that the evaluation of two streams must be consistent with the evaluations obtained when their tails are replaced with an arbitrary common tail. Similar and slightly stronger axioms are presented by Asheim and Banerjee (2010), Asheim and Tungodden (2004), and Basu and Mitra (2007).

**Weak Preference Consistency**: For all $\boldsymbol{u}, \boldsymbol{v} \in \mathbb{R}^{\mathbb{N}}$, if $(\boldsymbol{u}^{-n}, \boldsymbol{w}^{+n}) \succ (\boldsymbol{v}^{-n}, \boldsymbol{w}^{+n})$ for all $n \in \mathbb{N}$ and all $\boldsymbol{w} \in \mathbb{R}^{\mathbb{N}}$, then $\boldsymbol{u} \succ \boldsymbol{v}$.

We first present a characterization of the overtaking criterion associated with an independent sequence of finite-horizon Paretian and anonymous orderings. The following theorem shows that its characterization is obtained by replacing strong Pareto with weak preference consistency in Theorem 3.1 where we characterized the dominance-in-tails criterion. This result is a restatement of the characterization of $\succsim^O$ presented by Asheim and Banerjee(2010, Proposition 3). Their original result was established by using a proliferating sequence $(\succsim^n)_{n\in\mathbb{N}}$ of finite-horizon Paretian and anonymous orderings and an axiom that is slightly stronger than weak preference consistency.

**Theorem 3.11** *Let $(\succsim^n)_{n\in\mathbb{N}}$ be an independent sequence of finite-horizon Paretian and anonymous orderings. A social welfare quasi-ordering $\succsim$ on $\mathbb{R}^{\mathbb{N}}$ is an extension of $(\succsim^n)_{n\in\mathbb{N}}$ and satisfies weak preference consistency if and only if $\succsim^O$ associated with $(\succsim^n)_{n\in\mathbb{N}}$ is a subrelation of $\succsim$.*

***Proof*** 'If.' Suppose that $\succsim^O$ associated with $(\succsim^n)_{n\in\mathbb{N}}$ is a subrelation of $\succsim$. From Lemma 3.9, $\succsim^D$ associated with $(\succsim^n)_{n\in\mathbb{N}}$ is a subrelation of $\succsim$. From Theorem 3.1, $\succsim$ is an extension of $(\succsim^n)_{n\in\mathbb{N}}$. To show that $\succsim$ satisfies weak preference consistency, let $\boldsymbol{u}, \boldsymbol{v} \in \mathbb{R}^{\mathbb{N}}$ and suppose that $(\boldsymbol{u}^{-n}, \boldsymbol{w}^{+n}) \succ (\boldsymbol{v}^{-n}, \boldsymbol{w}^{+n})$ for all $n \in \mathbb{N}$ and all $\boldsymbol{w} \in \mathbb{R}^{\mathbb{N}}$. Since $\succsim$ is an extension of $(\succsim^n)_{n\in\mathbb{N}}$, it follows from (3.2) that $\boldsymbol{u}^{-n} \succ^n \boldsymbol{v}^{-n}$ for all $n \in \mathbb{N}$. From (3.6a), $\boldsymbol{u} \succ^O \boldsymbol{v}$. Since $\succsim^O$ is a subrelation of $\succsim$, we obtain $\boldsymbol{u} \succ \boldsymbol{v}$.

'Only if.' Let $\boldsymbol{u}, \boldsymbol{v} \in \mathbb{R}^{\mathbb{N}}$. To show that $\succsim^O$ associated with $(\succsim^n)_{n\in\mathbb{N}}$ is a subrelation of $\succsim$, suppose $\boldsymbol{u} \succ^O \boldsymbol{v}$. From (3.6a), there exists $n \in \mathbb{N}$ such that for all $n' \geq n$, $\boldsymbol{u}^{-n'} \succ^{n'} \boldsymbol{v}^{-n'}$. Employing an argument analogous to that used by Asheim and Banerjee (2010, Lemma 4 and Proposition 3), we show that $\boldsymbol{u} \succ \boldsymbol{v}$. Define $\hat{\boldsymbol{u}}, \check{\boldsymbol{v}} \in \mathbb{R}^{\mathbb{N}}$ as follows:

$$\hat{\boldsymbol{u}} = (u^{-n}_{(n)}, u^{-n}_{(n-1)}, \ldots, u^{-n}_{(1)}, \boldsymbol{u}^{+n}) \text{ and } \check{\boldsymbol{v}} = (v^{-n}_{(1)}, v^{-n}_{(2)}, \ldots\ldots, v^{-n}_{(n)}, \boldsymbol{v}^{+n}).$$

Note that

$$\hat{u}_1 - \check{v}_1 \geq \hat{u}_2 - \check{v}_2 \geq \cdots \geq \hat{u}_n - \check{v}_n.$$

Further, $\hat{u}_1 - \check{v}_1 > 0$; otherwise, $\check{\boldsymbol{v}} \succsim^n \hat{\boldsymbol{u}}$ follows since $(\succsim^n)_{n\in\mathbb{N}}$ is independent and $\succsim^n$ is Paretian for each $n \in \mathbb{N}$; thus, we obtain a contradiction since it follows from the transitivity and anonymity of $\succsim^n$ that $\boldsymbol{u}^{-n} \succ^n \boldsymbol{v}^{-n}$ implies $\hat{\boldsymbol{u}}^{-n} \succ^n \check{\boldsymbol{v}}^{-n}$.

Since $\succsim^m$ is transitive and anonymous for each $m \in \mathbb{N}$, it follows from the definitions of $\hat{\boldsymbol{u}}$ and $\check{\boldsymbol{v}}$ that, for all $m \in \mathbb{N}$ with $m > n$, $\hat{\boldsymbol{u}}^{-m} \succ^m \check{\boldsymbol{v}}^{-m}$. We show that, for all $m \leq n$, $\hat{\boldsymbol{u}}^{-m} \succ^m \check{\boldsymbol{v}}^{-m}$. If $\hat{u}_n - \check{v}_n \geq 0$, then it follows that $\hat{\boldsymbol{u}}^{-m} \succ^m \check{\boldsymbol{v}}^{-m}$ for all $m \leq n$ since $(\succsim^n)_{n\in\mathbb{N}}$ is an independent sequence of Paretian and anonymous orderings. We now assume that $\{m \in \{2, \ldots, n\} : \hat{u}_m - \check{v}_m < 0\} \neq \varnothing$. Let $\underline{m} = \min\{m \in \{2, \ldots, n\} : \hat{u}_m - \check{v}_m < 0\}$. Note that $\hat{u}_m - \check{v}_m < 0$ for all $m \in \{\underline{m}, \ldots, n\}$. Since $(\succsim^n)_{n\in\mathbb{N}}$ is an independent sequence of Paretian and anonymous orderings, it follows that $\hat{\boldsymbol{u}}^{-m} \succ^m \check{\boldsymbol{v}}^{-m}$ for each $m < \underline{m}$. We show that $\hat{\boldsymbol{u}}^{-m} \succ^m \check{\boldsymbol{v}}^{-m}$ for all $m \in \{\underline{m}, \ldots, n\}$. Since $\succsim^m$ is complete for each $m \in \mathbb{N}$, by way of contradiction, we suppose that $\check{\boldsymbol{v}}^{-m} \succsim^m \hat{\boldsymbol{u}}^{-m}$ for some $m \in \{\underline{m}, \ldots, n\}$. Since $(\succsim^n)_{n\in\mathbb{N}}$ is an independent sequence of Paretian and anonymous orderings, it follows that $\check{\boldsymbol{v}} \succ^n \hat{\boldsymbol{u}}$. This is a contradiction since $\boldsymbol{u}^{-n} \succ^n \boldsymbol{v}^{-n}$ implies $\hat{\boldsymbol{u}}^{-n} \succ^n \check{\boldsymbol{v}}^{-n}$.

Since $\succsim$ is an extension of $(\succsim^n)_{n\in\mathbb{N}}$, it follows that for all $n \in \mathbb{N}$ and for all $\boldsymbol{w} \in \mathbb{R}^{\mathbb{N}}$, $(\hat{\boldsymbol{u}}^{-n}, \boldsymbol{w}^{+n}) \succ (\check{\boldsymbol{v}}^{-n}, \boldsymbol{w}^{+n})$. By weak preference consistency, we obtain $\hat{\boldsymbol{u}} \succ \check{\boldsymbol{v}}$. Since $\succsim$ is an extension of $(\succsim^n)_{n\in\mathbb{N}}$ and $\succsim^n$ is anonymous for each $n \in \mathbb{N}$, $\succsim$ satisfies finite anonymity. From finite anonymity, it follows that $\hat{\boldsymbol{u}} \sim \boldsymbol{u}$ and $\check{\boldsymbol{v}} \sim \boldsymbol{v}$. Since $\succsim$ is transitive, we obtain $\boldsymbol{u} \succ \boldsymbol{v}$.

Next, we suppose $\boldsymbol{u} \sim^O \boldsymbol{v}$. From Lemmas 3.4 and 3.8, there exists $n \in \mathbb{N}$ such that $\boldsymbol{u}^{-n} \sim^n \boldsymbol{v}^{-n}$ and $\boldsymbol{u}^{+n} = \boldsymbol{v}^{+n}$. Since $\succsim$ is an extension of $(\succsim^n)_{n\in\mathbb{N}}$, we obtain $\boldsymbol{u} \sim \boldsymbol{v}$. ■

Next, we assume finite completeness of a social welfare quasi-ordering and present an axiomatization of the overtaking criterion associated with an independent sequence of finite-horizon Paretian and anonymous orderings. The following theorem shows that we obtain its axiomatization adding weak preference consistency to the three axioms we used to characterize the dominance-in-tails criterion in Theorem 3.2.

**Theorem 3.12** *A finitely complete social welfare quasi-ordering $\succsim$ on $\mathbb{R}^{\mathbb{N}}$ satisfies strong Pareto, finite anonymity, separable present, and weak preference consistency if and only if there exists an independent sequence $(\succsim^n)_{n\in\mathbb{N}}$ of finite-horizon Paretian and anonymous orderings such that $\succsim^O$ associated with $(\succsim^n)_{n\in\mathbb{N}}$ is a subrelation of $\succsim$.*

***Proof*** 'If.' Suppose that there exists an independent sequence $(\succsim^n)_{n\in\mathbb{N}}$ of finite-horizon Paretian and anonymous orderings such that $\succsim^O$ associated with $(\succsim^n)_{n\in\mathbb{N}}$ is a subrelation of $\succsim$. Since $\succsim^D$ associated with $(\succsim^n)_{n\in\mathbb{N}}$ is a subrelation of $\succsim^O$ associated with $(\succsim^n)_{n\in\mathbb{N}}$, $\succsim^D$ associated with $(\succsim^n)_{n\in\mathbb{N}}$ is a subrelation of $\succsim$. From Theorem 3.2, $\succsim$ satisfies strong Pareto, finite anonymity, and separable present. Further, from Theorem 3.11, $\succsim$ satisfies weak preference consistency.

'Only if.' From Theorem 3.2, there exists an independent sequence $(\succsim^n)_{n\in\mathbb{N}}$ of finite-horizon Paretian and anonymous orderings such that $\succsim^D$ associated with $(\succsim^n)_{n\in\mathbb{N}}$ is a subrelation of $\succsim$. From Theorem 3.1, it follows that $\succsim$ is an extension of $(\succsim^n)_{n\in\mathbb{N}}$. From Theorem 3.11, $\succsim^O$ associated with $(\succsim^n)_{n\in\mathbb{N}}$ is a subrelation of $\succsim$. ■

### 3.4.2 Overtaking Criteria Associated with Specific Sequences

We present overtaking criteria associated with specific sequences of finite-horizon orderings. The orderings we consider are utilitarian, leximin, utilitarianism-first and leximin-second, and generalized utilitarian orderings. We will show that axiomatizations of the specific forms of overtaking criterion are obtained by combining the general results in the previous section with the axiomatizations of specific forms of dominance-in-tails criterion.

The *utilitarian overtaking* social welfare quasi-ordering $\succsim_U^O$ on $\mathbb{R}^{\mathbb{N}}$, introduced by von Weizsäcker (1965), is the overtaking criterion associated with the sequence $(\succsim_U^n)_{n\in\mathbb{N}}$ of finite-horizon utilitarian orderings. Formally, for all $\boldsymbol{u}, \boldsymbol{v} \in \mathbb{R}^{\mathbb{N}}$,

$$\boldsymbol{u} \succ_U^O \boldsymbol{v} \Leftrightarrow \text{there exists } \bar{n} \in \mathbb{N} \text{ such that } \boldsymbol{u}^{-n} \succ_U^n \boldsymbol{v}^{-n} \text{ for all } n \geq \bar{n},$$
$$\boldsymbol{u} \sim_U^O \boldsymbol{v} \Leftrightarrow \text{there exists } \bar{n} \in \mathbb{N} \text{ such that } \boldsymbol{u}^{-n} \sim_U^n \boldsymbol{v}^{-n} \text{ for all } n \geq \bar{n}.$$

The following theorem presents axiomatizations of $\succsim_U^O$, which shows the consequence of adding weak preference consistency to the axioms of Theorems 3.3 and 3.4. In the theorem, the equivalence between the theorem statements (i) and (ii) was presented by Basu and Mitra (2007) using an axiom that is stronger than weak preference consistency. See also the axiomatization presented by Asheim and Tungodden (2004) using a different invariance axiom and an axiom that is stronger than weak preference consistency.

**Theorem 3.13** *Let $\succsim$ be a social welfare quasi-ordering $\succsim$ on $\mathbb{R}^{\mathbb{N}}$. The following three statements are equivalent:*

*(i) $\succsim_U^O$ is a subrelation of $\succsim$;*
*(ii) $\succsim$ satisfies strong Pareto, incremental equity, and weak preference consistency;*
*(iii) $\succsim$ satisfies strong Pareto, finite anonymity, translation-scale invariance, and weak preference consistency.*

***Proof*** (i) $\Rightarrow$ (iii). Since $(\succsim_U^n)_{n\in\mathbb{N}}$ is an independent sequence of finite-horizon Paretian and anonymous orderings, it follows from Theorem 3.11 that $\succsim$ satisfies weak preference consistency. From Lemma 3.9, $\succsim_U^D$ is a subrelation of $\succsim$. Thus, from Theorem 3.4, $\succsim$ satisfies strong Pareto, finite anonymity, and translation-scale invariance.

(iii) $\Rightarrow$ (ii). Applying Lemma 2.1, it is easy to verify that finite anonymity and translation-scale invariance together imply incremental equity.

(ii) $\Rightarrow$ (i). From Theorem 3.3, $\succsim_U^D$ is a subrelation of $\succsim$. Since $(\succsim_U^n)$ is an independent sequence of finite-horizon Paretian and anonymous orderings, it follows from Theorem 3.1 that $\succsim$ is an extension of $(\succsim_U^n)_{n\in\mathbb{N}}$. From Theorem 3.11, $\succsim_U^O$ is a subrelation of $\succsim$. ■

Assuming that a social welfare quasi-ordering is finitely complete, another axiomatization of $\succsim_U^O$ is given by adding weak preference consistency to the axioms in Theorem 3.5.

**Theorem 3.14** *A finitely complete social welfare quasi-ordering $\succsim$ on $\mathbb{R}^{\mathbb{N}}$ satisfies strong Pareto, finite anonymity, separable present, cardinal full comparability, restricted continuity, and weak preference consistency if and only if $\succsim_U^O$ is a subrelation of $\succsim$.*

***Proof*** 'If.' From Theorem 3.12, $\succsim$ satisfies strong Pareto, finite anonymity, separable present, and weak preference consistency. From Lemma 3.9, $\succsim_U^D$ is a subrelation of $\succsim$. Thus, from Theorem 3.5, $\succsim$ satisfies cardinal full comparability and restricted continuity.

'Only if.' From Theorem 3.5, $\succsim_U^D$ is a subrelation of $\succsim$. From Theorem 3.1, $\succsim$ is an extension of $(\succsim_U^n)_{n\in\mathbb{N}}$. Therefore, from Theorem 3.11, $\succsim_U^O$ is a subrelation of $\succsim$. ■

Given $g \in G$, the *generalized utilitarian overtaking* social welfare quasi-ordering $\succsim_{U,g}^{O}$ associated with $g$ on $\mathbb{R}^{\mathbb{N}}$ is the overtaking criterion associated with the sequence $(\succsim_{U,g}^{n})_{n\in\mathbb{N}}$ of finite-horizon generalized utilitarian orderings associated with $g$. Formally, for all $\boldsymbol{u}, \boldsymbol{v} \in \mathbb{R}^{\mathbb{N}}$,

$$\boldsymbol{u} \succ_{U,g}^{O} \boldsymbol{v} \Leftrightarrow \text{there exists } \bar{n} \in \mathbb{N} \text{ such that } \boldsymbol{u}^{-n} \succ_{U,g}^{n} \boldsymbol{v}^{-n} \text{ for all } n \geq \bar{n},$$
$$\boldsymbol{u} \sim_{U,g}^{O} \boldsymbol{v} \Leftrightarrow \text{there exists } \bar{n} \in \mathbb{N} \text{ such that } \boldsymbol{u}^{-n} \sim_{U,g}^{n} \boldsymbol{v}^{-n} \text{ for all } n \geq \bar{n}.$$

The following theorem axiomatizes a generalized utilitarian overtaking social welfare quasi-ordering by dropping cardinal full comparability from the set of axioms of Theorem 3.14.

**Theorem 3.15** *A finitely complete social welfare quasi-ordering $\succsim$ on $\mathbb{R}^{\mathbb{N}}$ satisfies strong Pareto, finite anonymity, separable present, restricted continuity, and weak preference consistency if and only if there exists $g \in G$ such that $\succsim_{U,g}^{O}$ is a subrelation of $\succsim$.*

***Proof*** Using Theorem 3.6 instead of Theorem 3.5, the proof is analogous to that of Theorem 3.14. ■

The *leximin overtaking* social welfare quasi-ordering $\succsim_{L}^{O}$ on $\mathbb{R}^{\mathbb{N}}$ is the overtaking criterion associated with the sequence $(\succsim_{L}^{n})_{n\in\mathbb{N}}$ of finite-horizon leximin orderings. That is, for all $\boldsymbol{u}, \boldsymbol{v} \in \mathbb{R}^{\mathbb{N}}$,

$$\boldsymbol{u} \succ_{L}^{O} \boldsymbol{v} \Leftrightarrow \text{there exists } \bar{n} \in \mathbb{N} \text{ such that } \boldsymbol{u}^{-n} \succ_{L}^{n} \boldsymbol{v}^{-n} \text{ for all } n \geq \bar{n},$$
$$\boldsymbol{u} \sim_{L}^{O} \boldsymbol{v} \Leftrightarrow \text{there exists } \bar{n} \in \mathbb{N} \text{ such that } \boldsymbol{u}^{-n} \sim_{L}^{n} \boldsymbol{v}^{-n} \text{ for all } n \geq \bar{n}.$$

The leximin overtaking social welfare quasi-ordering was introduced by Asheim and Tungodden (2004).

The following theorem shows that replacing translation-scale invariance with Hammond equity in Theorem 3.13 (iii) produces an axiomatization of $\succsim_{L}^{O}$. This result is a restatement of the axiomatization provided by Asheim and Tungodden (2004), which uses an axiom that is stronger than weak preference consistency.

**Theorem 3.16** *A social welfare quasi-ordering $\succsim$ on $\mathbb{R}^{\mathbb{N}}$ satisfies strong Pareto, finite anonymity, Hammond equity, and weak preference consistency if and only if $\succsim_{L}^{O}$ is a subrelation of $\succsim$.*

***Proof*** 'If.' From Theorem 3.11, $\succsim$ satisfies weak preference consistency. From Lemma 3.9, $\succsim_{L}^{D}$ is a subrelation of $\succsim$. Thus, from Theorem 3.7, $\succsim$ satisfies the other axioms.

'Only if.' From Theorem 3.7, $\succsim_{L}^{D}$ is a subrelation of $\succsim$. From Theorem 3.1, $\succsim$ is an extension of $(\succsim_{L}^{n})_{n\in\mathbb{N}}$. Therefore, from Theorem 3.11, $\succsim_{L}^{O}$ is a subrelation of $\succsim$. ■

The *utilitarianism-first and leximin-second overtaking* social welfare quasi-ordering $\succsim^O_{UL}$ on $\mathbb{R}^{\mathbb{N}}$ is defined as the overtaking criterion associated with the sequence $(\succsim^n_{UL})_{n\in\mathbb{N}}$ of finite-horizon utilitarianism-first and leximin-second orderings. For all $\boldsymbol{u}, \boldsymbol{v} \in \mathbb{R}^{\mathbb{N}}$,

$$\boldsymbol{u} \succ^O_{UL} \boldsymbol{v} \Leftrightarrow \text{there exists } \bar{n} \in \mathbb{N} \text{ such that } \boldsymbol{u}^{-n} \succ^n_{UL} \boldsymbol{v}^{-n} \text{ for all } n \geq \bar{n},$$
$$\boldsymbol{u} \sim^O_{UL} \boldsymbol{v} \Leftrightarrow \text{there exists } \bar{n} \in \mathbb{N} \text{ such that } \boldsymbol{u}^{-n} \sim^n_{UL} \boldsymbol{v}^{-n} \text{ for all } n \geq \bar{n}.$$

In the following theorem, we assume the finite completeness of a social welfare quasi-ordering and jointly characterize the three specific forms of overtaking criterion presented above. It show the consequence of adding weak preference consistency to the axioms of Theorem 3.9.

**Theorem 3.17** *A finitely complete social welfare quasi-ordering $\succsim$ on $\mathbb{R}^{\mathbb{N}}$ satisfies strong Pareto, finite anonymity, the weak Pigou–Dalton principle, the composite transfer principle, separable present, cardinal full comparability, and weak preference consistency if and only if any one of $\succsim^O_U$, $\succsim^O_{UL}$, and $\succsim^O_L$ is a subrelation of $\succsim$.*

***Proof*** 'If.' From Theorem 3.12, $\succsim$ satisfies strong Pareto, finite anonymity, separable present, and weak preference consistency. From Lemma 3.9, any one of $\succsim^D_U$, $\succsim^D_{UL}$, and $\succsim^D_L$ is a subrelation of $\succsim$. Thus, from Theorem 3.9, $\succsim$ satisfies the weak Pigou–Dalton principle, the composite transfer principle, and cardinal full comparability.

'Only if.' From Theorem 3.9, any one of $\succsim^D_U$, $\succsim^D_{UL}$, and $\succsim^D_L$ is a subrelation of $\succsim$. From Theorem 3.1, $\succsim$ is an extension of $(\succsim^n_U)_{n\in\mathbb{N}}$, $(\succsim^n_{UL})_{n\in\mathbb{N}}$, or $(\succsim^n_L)_{n\in\mathbb{N}}$. Therefore, from Theorem 3.11, any one of $\succsim^O_U$, $\succsim^O_{UL}$, and $\succsim^O_L$ is a subrelation of $\succsim$. ■

Among the three overtaking criteria characterized in Theorem 3.17, only the utilitarian overtaking criteria violates the strong Pigou–Dalton principle. Thus, strengthening the weak Pigou–Dalton principle to the strong Pigou–Dalton principle in the theorem, we obtain a joint axiomatization of the other two overtaking criteria. We state the following theorem without a proof.

**Theorem 3.18** *A finitely complete social welfare quasi-ordering $\succsim$ on $\mathbb{R}^{\mathbb{N}}$ satisfies strong Pareto, finite anonymity, the strong Pigou–Dalton principle, the composite transfer principle, separable present, cardinal full comparability, and weak preference consistency if and only if either $\succsim^O_{UL}$ or $\succsim^O_L$ is a subrelation of $\succsim$.*

## 3.5 Catching-Up Criteria

### *3.5.1 Generalized Definition and Characterizations*

Given an independent sequence $(\succsim^n)_{n\in\mathbb{N}}$ of finite-horizon orderings, the *catching-up criterion* associated with $(\succsim^n)_{n\in\mathbb{N}}$ is defined as the following binary relation $\succsim^C$ on $\mathbb{R}^{\mathbb{N}}$. For all $\boldsymbol{u}, \boldsymbol{v} \in \mathbb{R}^{\mathbb{N}}$,

$$\boldsymbol{u} \succsim^C \boldsymbol{v} \Leftrightarrow \text{there exists } \bar{n} \in \mathbb{N} \text{ such that } \boldsymbol{u}^{-n} \succsim^n \boldsymbol{v}^{-n} \text{ for all } n \geq \bar{n}. \tag{3.7}$$

The generalized catching-up criterion was analyzed by Asheim and Banerjee (2010) using a proliferating sequence of finite-horizon Paretian and anonymous orderings.

The following theorem shows that the catching-up criterion associated with an independent sequence of finite-horizon orderings is a finitely complete social welfare quasi-ordering. It also characterizes the asymmetric and symmetric parts of it.

**Lemma 3.10** *Let* $(\succsim^n)_{n\in\mathbb{N}}$ *be an independent sequence of finite-horizon orderings.* $\succsim^C$ *associated with* $(\succsim^n)_{n\in\mathbb{N}}$ *is a finitely complete quasi-ordering on* $\mathbb{R}^{\mathbb{N}}$. *For any* $\boldsymbol{u}, \boldsymbol{v} \in \mathbb{R}^{\mathbb{N}}$,

$$\begin{aligned} \boldsymbol{u} \succ^C \boldsymbol{v} \Leftrightarrow\ & \text{there exists } \bar{n} \in \mathbb{N} \text{ such that } \boldsymbol{u}^{-n} \succsim^n \boldsymbol{v}^{-n} \text{ for all } n \geq \bar{n}, \text{ and} \\ & \text{for all } n' \in \mathbb{N}, \text{ there exists } n \geq n' \text{ such that } \boldsymbol{u}^{-n} \succ^n \boldsymbol{v}^{-n}, \end{aligned} \tag{3.8a}$$

$$\boldsymbol{u} \sim^C \boldsymbol{v} \Leftrightarrow \text{there exists } \bar{n} \in \mathbb{N} \text{ such that } \boldsymbol{u}^{-n} \sim^n \boldsymbol{v}^{-n} \text{ for all } n \geq \bar{n}. \tag{3.8b}$$

***Proof*** First, we show that $\succsim^C$ associated with $(\succsim^n)_{n\in\mathbb{N}}$ is a finitely complete quasi-ordering on $\mathbb{R}^{\mathbb{N}}$. Since the proof of the reflexivity and transitivity of $\succsim^C$ is easy, we show only that $\succsim^C$ is finitely complete. Let $\boldsymbol{u}, \boldsymbol{v} \in \mathbb{R}^{\mathbb{N}}$ and suppose that $\boldsymbol{u}^{+n} = \boldsymbol{v}^{+n}$ for some $n \in \mathbb{N}$. Since $\succsim^n$ is complete for each $n \in \mathbb{N}$, it follows that $\boldsymbol{u}^{-n} \succsim^n \boldsymbol{v}^{-n}$ or $\boldsymbol{v}^{-n} \succsim^n \boldsymbol{u}^{-n}$. Since $(\succsim^n)_{n\in\mathbb{N}}$ is independent, it follows that $\boldsymbol{u} \succsim^C$ or $\boldsymbol{v} \succsim^C \boldsymbol{u}$.

From (3.7), it is straightforward that (3.8b) holds; thus, we omit the detailed proof of (3.8b). To prove (3.8a), suppose $\boldsymbol{u} \succ^C \boldsymbol{v}$. From (3.7), there exists $\bar{n} \in \mathbb{N}$ such that $\boldsymbol{u}^{-n} \succsim^n \boldsymbol{v}^{-n}$ for all $n \geq \bar{n}$. By way of contradiction, suppose that there exists $n'$ such that for all $n \geq n'$, $\boldsymbol{v}^{-n} \succsim^n \boldsymbol{u}^{-n}$. Let $\tilde{n} = \max\{\bar{n}, n'\}$. Then, we obtain that $\boldsymbol{u}^{-n} \sim^n \boldsymbol{v}^{-n}$ for all $n \geq \tilde{n}$. From (3.8b), $\boldsymbol{u} \sim^C \boldsymbol{v}$. This is a contradiction with $\boldsymbol{u} \succ^C \boldsymbol{v}$. Thus, for any $n' \in \mathbb{N}$, there exists $n \geq n'$ such that $\boldsymbol{u}^{-n} \succ^n \boldsymbol{v}^{-n}$. Next, suppose that there exists $\bar{n} \in \mathbb{N}$ such that $\boldsymbol{u}^{-n} \succsim^n \boldsymbol{v}^{-n}$ for all $n \geq \bar{n}$, and for all $n' \in \mathbb{N}$, there exists $n \geq n'$ such that $\boldsymbol{u}^{-n} \succ^n \boldsymbol{v}^{-n}$. From (3.7), $\boldsymbol{u} \succsim^C \boldsymbol{v}$ follows. By way of contradiction, suppose that $\boldsymbol{v} \succsim^C \boldsymbol{u}$ holds. From (3.8b), there exists $\bar{n} \in \mathbb{N}$ such that $\boldsymbol{u}^{-n} \sim^n \boldsymbol{v}^{-n}$ for all $n \geq \bar{n}$. This is a contradiction since, for all $n' \in \mathbb{N}$, there exists $n \geq n'$ such that $\boldsymbol{u}^{-n} \succ^n \boldsymbol{v}^{-n}$. Thus, $\boldsymbol{u} \succ^C \boldsymbol{v}$ must hold. ■

From Lemma 3.10 and (3.6b), given an independent sequence $(\succsim^n)_{n\in\mathbb{N}}$ of finite-horizon orderings, the symmetric part of the overtaking criterion $\succsim^O$ associated with $(\succsim^n)_{n\in\mathbb{N}}$ and that of the catching-up criterion $\succsim^C$ associated with $(\succsim^n)_{n\in\mathbb{N}}$ coincide with each other. Further, from (3.6a), $\succsim^O$ associated with $(\succsim^n)_{n\in\mathbb{N}}$ is a subrelation of $\succsim^C$ associated with $(\succsim^n)_{n\in\mathbb{N}}$. Consequently, if $\succsim^n$ is Paretian for each $n \in \mathbb{N}$, $\succsim^D$ associated with $(\succsim^n)_{n\in\mathbb{N}}$ is a subrelation of $\succsim^C$ associated with $(\succsim^n)_{n\in\mathbb{N}}$.

We now characterize the catching-up criterion associated with an independent sequence of finite-horizon Paretian and anonymous orderings. We use the following stronger version of weak preference consistency, which was presented by Kamaga and Kojima (2010). For similar axioms, see also Asheim and Banerjee (2010), Asheim and Tungodden (2004), and Basu and Mitra (2007).

**Strong Preference Consistency**: For all $\boldsymbol{u}, \boldsymbol{v} \in \mathbb{R}^{\mathbb{N}}$, if, for all $\boldsymbol{w} \in \mathbb{R}^{\mathbb{N}}$, $(\boldsymbol{u}^{-n}, \boldsymbol{w}^{+n}) \succsim (\boldsymbol{v}^{-n}, \boldsymbol{w}^{+n})$ for all $n \in \mathbb{N}$, and for all $n \in \mathbb{N}$, there exists $n' \geq n$ such that $(\boldsymbol{u}^{-n'}, \boldsymbol{w}^{+n'}) \succ (\boldsymbol{v}^{-n'}, \boldsymbol{w}^{+n'})$, then $\boldsymbol{u} \succ \boldsymbol{v}$.

The following theorem characterizes the catching-up criterion associated with an independent sequence of finite-horizon Paretian and anonymous orderings by strengthening weak preference consistency to strong preference consistency in Theorem 3.11. This result is a restatement of the result of Asheim and Banerjee (2010, Proposition 4) that was established using a proliferating sequence $(\succsim^n)_{n \in \mathbb{N}}$ of finite-horizon Paretian and anonymous orderings and an axiom that is slightly stronger than strong preference consistency.

**Theorem 3.19** *Let $(\succsim^n)_{n \in \mathbb{N}}$ be an independent sequence of finite-horizon Paretian and anonymous orderings. A social welfare quasi-ordering $\succsim$ on $\mathbb{R}^{\mathbb{N}}$ is an extension of $(\succsim^n)_{n \in \mathbb{N}}$ and satisfies strong preference consistency if and only if $\succsim^C$ associated with $(\succsim^n)_{n \in \mathbb{N}}$ is a subrelation of $\succsim$.*

***Proof*** 'If.' From Theorem 3.11, $\succsim$ is an extension of $(\succsim^n)_{n \in \mathbb{N}}$. To show that $\succsim$ satisfies strong preference consistency, let $\boldsymbol{u}, \boldsymbol{v} \in \mathbb{R}^{\mathbb{N}}$ and suppose that for all $\boldsymbol{w} \in \mathbb{R}^{\mathbb{N}}$, $(\boldsymbol{u}^{-n}, \boldsymbol{w}^{+n}) \succsim (\boldsymbol{v}^{-n}, \boldsymbol{w}^{+n})$ for all $n \in \mathbb{N}$, and for all $n \in \mathbb{N}$, there exists $n' \geq n$ such that $(\boldsymbol{u}^{-n'}, \boldsymbol{w}^{+n'}) \succ (\boldsymbol{v}^{-n'}, \boldsymbol{w}^{+n'})$. Since $\succsim$ is an extension of $(\succsim^n)_{n \in \mathbb{N}}$, it follows that for all $n \in \mathbb{N}$, $\boldsymbol{u}^{-n} \succsim^n \boldsymbol{v}^{-n}$, and for all $n \in \mathbb{N}$, there exists $n' \geq n$ such that $\boldsymbol{u}^{-n} \succ^n \boldsymbol{v}^{-n}$. From (3.8a) in Lemma 3.10, $\boldsymbol{u} \succ^C \boldsymbol{v}$. Since $\succsim^C$ is a subrelation of $\succsim$, we obtain $\boldsymbol{u} \succ \boldsymbol{v}$.

'Only if.' Let $\boldsymbol{u}, \boldsymbol{v} \in \mathbb{R}^{\mathbb{N}}$. From Lemma 3.10, the symmetric parts of $\succsim^O$ associated with $(\succsim^n)_{n \in \mathbb{N}}$ and $\succsim^C$ associated with $(\succsim^n)_{n \in \mathbb{N}}$ coincide. Thus, from Theorem 3.11, $\boldsymbol{u} \sim^C \boldsymbol{v}$ implies $\boldsymbol{u} \sim \boldsymbol{v}$. Now suppose $\boldsymbol{u} \succ^C \boldsymbol{v}$. From Lemma 3.10, there exists $\bar{n} \in \mathbb{N}$ such that $\boldsymbol{u}^{-n} \succsim^n \boldsymbol{v}^{-n}$ for all $n \geq \bar{n}$, and for all $n \in \mathbb{N}$, there exists $n' \geq n$ such that $\boldsymbol{u}^{-n'} \succ^{n'} \boldsymbol{v}^{-n'}$. Let $n^* = \min\{n \in \mathbb{N} : n \geq \bar{n} \text{ and } \boldsymbol{u}^{-n} \succ^n \boldsymbol{v}^{-n}\}$. Define $\hat{\boldsymbol{u}}, \check{\boldsymbol{v}} \in \mathbb{R}^{\mathbb{N}}$ by

$$\hat{\boldsymbol{u}} = (u_{(n^*)}^{-n^*}, u_{(n^*-1)}^{-n^*}, \ldots, u_{(1)}^{-n^*}, \boldsymbol{u}^{+n^*}) \text{ and } \check{\boldsymbol{v}} = (v_{(1)}^{-n^*}, v_{(2)}^{-n^*}, \ldots\ldots, v_{(n^*)}^{-n^*}, \boldsymbol{v}^{+n^*}).$$

Then, using (3.8a) and employing an argument analogous to that of the proof of Theorem 3.11, we obtain $\boldsymbol{u} \succ \boldsymbol{v}$. ■

We present an axiomatization of the catching-up criterion associated with an independent sequence of finite-horizon Paretian and anonymous orderings strengthening weak preference consistency to strong preference consistency in Theorem 3.12.

**Theorem 3.20** *A finitely complete social welfare quasi-ordering $\succsim$ on $\mathbb{R}^{\mathbb{N}}$ satisfies strong Pareto, finite anonymity, separable present, and strong preference consistency if and only if there exists an independent sequence $(\succsim^n)_{n \in \mathbb{N}}$ of finite-horizon Paretian and anonymous orderings such that $\succsim^C$ associated with $(\succsim^n)_{n \in \mathbb{N}}$ is a subrelation of $\succsim$.*

***Proof*** The proof is analogous to the proof of Theorem 3.12 using Theorem 3.19 instead of Theorem 3.11. ■

### 3.5.2 Catching-Up Criteria Associated with Specific Sequences

We present specific forms of the catching-up criterion, which are counterparts of the specific forms of the overtaking criterion we considered in Sect. 3.4.2. We also axiomatize them using strong preference consistency. The axiomatization theorems we present below can be proved using Theorems 3.19 and 3.20 instead of Theorems 3.11 and 3.12 and by employing an analogous argument to the proofs of Theorems 3.13–3.15; thus, we omit their proofs.

The *utilitarian catching-up* social welfare quasi-ordering $\succsim_U^C$ on $\mathbb{R}^{\mathbb{N}}$ is the catching-up criterion associated with the sequence $(\succsim_U^n)$ of finite-horizon utilitarian orderings. Formally, for all $\boldsymbol{u}, \boldsymbol{v} \in \mathbb{R}^{\mathbb{N}}$,

$$\boldsymbol{u} \succsim_U^C \boldsymbol{v} \Leftrightarrow \text{there exists } \bar{n} \in \mathbb{N} \text{ such that } \boldsymbol{u}^{-n} \succsim_U^n \boldsymbol{v}^{-n} \text{ for all } n \geq \bar{n}.$$

It was considered in Atsumi (1965) and von Weizsäcker (1965) and first presented by Svensson (1980) in the form of social welfare quasi-ordering. See also Asheim and Tungodden (2004) and Basu and Mitra (2007).

In the following theorem, we present axiomatizations of $\succsim_U^C$ strengthening weak preference consistency to strong preference consistency in Theorem 3.13. The equivalence between the theorem statements (i) and (iii) was presented by Basu and Mitra (2007) using an axiom that is stronger than strong preference consistency; see also Asheim and Tungodden (2004) for a similar result.

**Theorem 3.21** *Let $\succsim$ be a social welfare quasi-ordering $\succsim$ on $\mathbb{R}^{\mathbb{N}}$. The following three statements are equivalent:*

*(i) $\succsim_U^C$ is a subrelation of $\succsim$;*
*(ii) $\succsim$ satisfies strong Pareto, incremental equity, and strong preference consistency;*
*(iii) $\succsim$ satisfies strong Pareto, finite anonymity, translation-scale invariance, and strong preference consistency.*

Assuming that a social welfare quasi-ordering is finitely complete, we obtain the following axiomatization of $\succsim_U^C$.

**Theorem 3.22** *A finitely complete social welfare quasi-ordering $\succsim$ on $\mathbb{R}^{\mathbb{N}}$ satisfies strong Pareto, finite anonymity, separable present, cardinal full comparability, restricted continuity, and strong preference consistency if and only if $\succsim_U^C$ is a subrelation of $\succsim$.*

Given $g \in G$, the *generalized utilitarian catching-up* social welfare quasi-ordering $\succsim_{U,g}^C$ associated with $g$ on $\mathbb{R}^{\mathbb{N}}$ is the catching-up criterion associated with the sequence $(\succsim_{U,g}^n)_{n\in\mathbb{N}}$ of finite-horizon generalized utilitarian orderings associated with $g$. Formally, for all $\boldsymbol{u}, \boldsymbol{v} \in \mathbb{R}^{\mathbb{N}}$,

$$u \succsim_{U,g}^{C} v \Leftrightarrow \text{there exists } \bar{n} \in \mathbb{N} \text{ such that } u^{-n} \succsim_{U,g}^{n} v^{-n} \text{ for all } n \geq \bar{n}.$$

This was first presented by Mitra (2005).

The following theorem presents an axiomatization of a generalized utilitarian catching-up social welfare quasi-ordering. See a similar result by Mitra (2005, Theorem 3) .

**Theorem 3.23** *A finitely complete social welfare quasi-ordering* $\succsim$ *on* $\mathbb{R}^{\mathbb{N}}$ *satisfies strong Pareto, finite anonymity, separable present, restricted continuity, and strong preference consistency if and only if there exists* $g \in G$ *such that* $\succsim_{U,g}^{C}$ *is a subrelation of* $\succsim$.

The *leximin catching-up* social welfare quasi-ordering $\succsim_{L}^{C}$ on $\mathbb{R}^{\mathbb{N}}$ is the catching-up criterion associated with the sequence $(\succsim_{L}^{n})$ of finite-horizon leximin orderings. Formally, for all $u, v \in \mathbb{R}^{\mathbb{N}}$,

$$u \succsim_{L}^{C} v \Leftrightarrow \text{there exists } \bar{n} \in \mathbb{N} \text{ such that } u^{-n} \succsim_{L}^{n} v^{-n} \text{ for all } n \geq \bar{n}.$$

This was introduced by Asheim and Tungodden (2004).

The following axiomatization of the leximin catching-up social welfare quasi-ordering is a restatement of the axiomatization provided by Asheim and Tungodden (2004, Proposition 2) who used an axiom stronger than strong preference consistency.

**Theorem 3.24** *A social welfare quasi-ordering* $\succsim$ *on* $\mathbb{R}^{\mathbb{N}}$ *satisfies strong Pareto, finite anonymity, Hammond equity, and strong preference consistency if and only if* $\succsim_{L}^{C}$ *is a subrelation of* $\succsim$.

Finally, the *utilitarianism-first and leximin-second catching-up* social welfare quasi-ordering $\succsim_{UL}^{C}$ on $\mathbb{R}^{\mathbb{N}}$ is defined as the catching-up criterion associated with the sequence $(\succsim_{UL}^{n})$ of finite-horizon utilitarianism-first and leximin-second orderings. For all $u, v \in \mathbb{R}^{\mathbb{N}}$,

$$u \succsim_{UL}^{C} v \Leftrightarrow \text{there exists } \bar{n} \in \mathbb{N} \text{ such that } u^{-n} \succsim_{UL}^{n} v^{-n} \text{ for all } n \geq \bar{n}.$$

Strengthening weak preference consistency in Theorems 3.17 and 3.18, we obtain the following two joint characterization results.

**Theorem 3.25** *A finitely complete social welfare quasi-ordering* $\succsim$ *on* $\mathbb{R}^{\mathbb{N}}$ *satisfies strong Pareto, finite anonymity, the weak Pigou–Dalton principle, the composite transfer principle, separable present, cardinal full comparability, and strong preference consistency if and only if any one of* $\succsim_{U}^{C}$, $\succsim_{UL}^{C}$, *and* $\succsim_{L}^{C}$ *is a subrelation of* $\succsim$.

**Theorem 3.26** *A finitely complete social welfare quasi-ordering* $\succsim$ *on* $\mathbb{R}^{\mathbb{N}}$ *satisfies strong Pareto, finite anonymity, the strong Pigou–Dalton principle, the composite transfer principle, separable present, cardinal full comparability, and strong preference consistency if and only if either* $\succsim_{UL}^{C}$ *or* $\succsim_{L}^{C}$ *is a subrelation of* $\succsim$.

## 3.6 Concluding Remarks

We considered general forms of social welfare quasi-orderings for infinite utility streams—namely, the dominance-in-tails criterion, the overtaking criterion, and the catching-up criterion. They can represent a specific social welfare quasi-ordering using a sequence of specific finite-horizon social welfare orderings or quasi-orderings. Our general results on the three versions of general social welfare quasi-orderings can be used to obtain axiomatizations of specific social welfare quasi-orderings associated with a sequence of specific finite-horizon social welfare orderings or quasi-orderings.

All the quasi-orderings considered in this chapter satisfy finite anonymity. However, finite anonymity is the weakest formalization of the equal treatment of generations. Extended anonymity axioms and social welfare quasi-orderings that satisfy them will be explored in the next chapter.

## References


Asheim, G. B., d'Aspremont, C., & Banerjee, K. (2010). Generalized time-invariant overtaking. *Journal of Mathematical Economics*, *46*, 519–533.

Asheim, G. B., & Banerjee, K. (2010). Fixed-step anonymous overtaking and catching-up. *International Journal of Economic Theory*, *6*, 149–165.

Asheim, G. B., & Tungodden, B. (2004). Resolving distributional conflicts between generations. *Economic Theory*, *24*, 221–230.

d'Aspremont, C. (2007). Formal welfarism and intergenerational equity. In J. E. Roemer & K. Suzumura (Eds.), *Intergenerational equity and sustainability*. Basingstoke: Palgrave-Macmillan.

Atsumi, H. (1965). Neoclassical growth and the efficient program of capital accumulation. *Review of Economic Studies*, *32*, 127–136.

Banerjee, K. (2006). On the extension of the utilitarian and Suppes-Sen social welfare relations to infinite utility streams. *Social Choice and Welfare*, *27*, 327–339.

Basu, K., & Mitra, T. (2007). Utilitarianism for infinite utility streams: A new welfare criterion and its axiomatic characterization. *Journal of Economic Theory*, *133*, 350–373.

Bossert, W., Sprumont, Y., & Suzumura, K. (2007). Ordering infinite utility streams. *Journal of Economic Theory*, *135*, 579–589.

Dalton, H. (1920). The measurement of the inequality of incomes. *Economic Journal*, *30*, 348–361

Diamond, P. (1965). The evaluation of infinite utility streams. *Econometrica*, *33*, 170–177.

Hammond, P. J. (1976). Equity, Arrow's conditions, and Rawls' difference principle. *Econometrica*, *44*, 793–804.

Hammond, P. J. (1979). Equity in two person situations: Some consequences. *Econometrica*, *47*, 1127–1135.

Kamaga, K. (2018). When do utilitarianism and egalitarianism agree on evaluation? An intersection approach. *Mathematical Social Sciences*, *94*, 41–48.

Kamaga, K., & Kojima, T. (2009). $\mathcal{Q}$-anonymous social welfare relations on infinite utility streams. *Social Choice and Welfare*, *33*, 405–413.

Kamaga, K., & Kojima, T. (2010). On the leximin and utilitarian overtaking criteria with extended anonymity. *Social Choice and Welfare*, *35*, 377–392.

Koopmans, T. C. (1960). Stationary ordinal utility and impatience. *Econometrica*, *28*, 287–309.

Lauwers, L. (1997). Rawlsian equity and generalized utilitarianism with and infinite population. *Economic Theory*, *9*, 143–150.
Maskin, E. (1978). A theorem on utilitarianism. *Review of Economic Studies*, *45*(1), 93–96.
Mitra, T. (2005). Intergenerational equity and the forest management problem. In S. Kant & R. A. Berry (Eds.), *Economics sustainability, and natural resources: Economics of sustainable forest management*. Dordrecht: Springer.
Pigou, A. C. (1912). *Wealth and welfare*. London: Macmillan.
Sakai, T. (2010). Intertemporal equity and an explicit construction of welfare criteria. *Social Choice and Welfare*, *35*, 393–414.
Svensson, L.-G. (1980). Equity among generations. *Econometrica*, *48*, 1251–1256.
von Weizsäcker, C. C. (1965). Existence of optimal programs of accumulation for an infinite time horizon. *Review of Economic Studies*, *32*, 85–104.

# Chapter 4
# Extended Anonymity and Intergenerational Social Welfare Evaluation

**Abstract** This chapter examines an extended anonymity axiom that is compatible with a strongly Paretian relation for infinite utility streams. It is well-known that the cyclicity of a permutation and the group structure of a set of permutations are both necessary and sufficient for the resulting anonymity axiom to be compatible with a Paretian social welfare quasi-ordering. The set of fixed-step permutations is an example of a group of cyclic permutations. Using the same analytical framework as that used in the previous chapter, we first examine an algebraic structure of a set of permutations that can be used to define a Pareto-compatible anonymity axiom. Then, using anonymity axioms defined by a group of cyclic permutations or the set of fixed-step permutations, we will consider general forms of a social welfare quasi-ordering that satisfy the extended anonymity axioms. Our main results are general characterizations of those general social welfare quasi-orderings. Using the general results, we will present axiomatizations of specific social welfare quasi-orderings that are associated with a sequence of specific finite-horizon social welfare orderings or quasi-orderings.

**Keywords** Extended anonymity · Fixed-step anonymity · Utilitarianism · Leximin · Generalized Pareto axiom

## 4.1 Introduction

Finite anonymity is a very weak representation of the equal treatment of generations since it can realize only the equal treatment of the finite number of generations. In ranking infinite utility streams that represent intergenerational utility distributions, finite anonymity seems insufficiently strong to represent the equal treatment of generations. It is well-known that the strong anonymity axiom that is defined by the set of all permutations of generations is incompatible with the strong Pareto principle (Lauwers 1997a; van Liedekerke 1995). Several extended anonymity axioms have been proposed to realize the equal treatment of infinitely many generations. Lauwers (1997b) introduced fixed-step anonymity, defined as the set of so-called "fixed-step permutations." It yields the equal treatment of infinitely many generations in a



K. Kamaga, *Social Welfare Evaluation and Intergenerational Equity*,
Development Bank of Japan Research Series,
https://doi.org/10.1007/978-981-15-4254-1_4

specific way. Mitra and Basu (2007) presented a systematic analysis of the structure of a set of permutations that can be used to define a Pareto-compatible anonymity axiom. Using the group notion in algebra, they provided a necessary and sufficient condition for a set of permutations to define an anonymity axiom which is compatible with a Paretian social welfare quasi-ordering.

This chapter begins by analyzing an algebraic restriction for a set of permutations to define an anonymity axiom that is compatible with a social welfare relation satisfying coherence properties weaker than transitivity. Then, we present general forms of social welfare quasi-orderings associated with an arbitrary sequence of finite-horizon social welfare orderings or quasi-orderings. Our main purpose is to establish general results that show how a social welfare evaluation applied to utilities of the finite number of generations can be extended to an infinite-horizon social welfare evaluation that satisfies an extended anonymity axiom. Then, utilizing the general results and combining them with the results in the previous chapter, we will provide axiomatizations of specific forms of extended-anonymous social welfare quasi-orderings that are associated with specific sequences of finite-horizon social welfare orderings or quasi-orderings.

The next section presents a definition of a permutation matrix, which is needed for the formal analysis of the structure of a set of permutations that can be used to define a Pareto-compatible anonymity axiom. Section 4.3 provides the necessary and sufficient condition for a set of permutations to define a Pareto-compatible anonymity axiom. In Sect. 4.4, we present a general form of social welfare quasi-ordering, which is an analogue of the dominance-in-tails criterion but it satisfies an extended anonymity. Then, a characterization of this general form of social welfare quasi-ordering is established. Using the general result, we then present axiomatizations of specific forms of social welfare quasi-orderings associated with a specific sequence of finite-horizon social welfare orderings or quasi-orderings. Analogous analysis will be conducted for a general overtaking criterion using fixed-step anonymity in Sect. 4.5. In contrast to a finitely anonymous general catching-up criterion, it is impossible to formulate a fixed-step anonymous catching-up criterion. This impossibility will be analyzed in detail using a generalized formulation of the Pareto axiom in Sect. 4.6. Section 4.7 provides concluding remarks.

## 4.2 Preliminaries

### 4.2.1 Social Welfare Relation

We will work within the same framework as that used in Chap. 3. The only additional notions required in this chapter are coherence properties of a binary relation $\succsim$ on the set $\mathbb{R}^{\mathbb{N}}$ of infinite utility streams and representations of several kinds of permutations of generations.

We consider three coherence properties of a binary relation in addition to transitivity. A binary relation $\succsim$ on $\mathbb{R}^{\mathbb{N}}$ is (i) *Suzumura-consistent* if and only if, for all $K \in \mathbb{N}\setminus\{1\}$ and all $\boldsymbol{u}^0, \ldots, \boldsymbol{u}^K \in \mathbb{R}^{\mathbb{N}}$, if $\boldsymbol{u}^{k-1} \succsim \boldsymbol{u}^k$ for all $k \in \{1, \ldots K\}$, then not $\boldsymbol{u}^K \succ \boldsymbol{u}^0$; (ii) *quasi-transitive* if and only if, for all $\boldsymbol{u}, \boldsymbol{v}, \boldsymbol{w} \in \mathbb{R}^{\mathbb{N}}$, $\boldsymbol{u} \succ \boldsymbol{w}$ if $\boldsymbol{u} \succ \boldsymbol{v}$ and $\boldsymbol{v} \succ \boldsymbol{w}$; (iii) *acyclic* if and only if, for all $K \in \mathbb{N}\setminus\{1\}$ and all $\boldsymbol{u}^0, \ldots, \boldsymbol{u}^K \in \mathbb{R}^{\mathbb{N}}$, if $\boldsymbol{u}^{k-1} \succ \boldsymbol{u}^k$ for all $k \in \{1, \ldots K\}$, then not $\boldsymbol{u}^K \succ \boldsymbol{u}^0$. Suzumura consistency was introduced by Suzumura (1976), who showed that it is necessary and sufficient for the existence of an ordering extension. (See Chap. 2 for the definition of ordering extension.) Transitivity implies Suzumura consistency and quasi-transitivity, each of which in turn implies acyclicity. There is no logical relationship between Suzumura consistency and quasi-transitivity.

A *social welfare relation* is a reflexive binary relation on $\mathbb{R}^{\mathbb{N}}$. Thus, a social welfare quasi-ordering is a transitive social welfare relation on $\mathbb{R}^{\mathbb{N}}$. We consider social welfare relations that satisfies the strong Pareto principle requiring that $\boldsymbol{u} \succ \boldsymbol{v}$ if $\boldsymbol{u}, \boldsymbol{v} \in \mathbb{R}^{\mathbb{N}}$ and $\boldsymbol{u} > \boldsymbol{v}$; see Chap. 3. Throughout this chapter, a social welfare relation satisfying the strong Pareto principle is referred to as a *Paretian* social welfare relation.

### 4.2.2 Permutation Matrix

Following Mitra and Basu (2007), we represent any permutation on $\mathbb{N}$ by a permutation matrix. A permutation matrix is an infinite matrix $\boldsymbol{P} = (p_{ij})_{i,j\in\mathbb{N}}$ such that (i) for all $i \in \mathbb{N}$, there exists $j(i) \in \mathbb{N}$ such that $p_{ij(i)} = 1$ and $p_{ij} = 0$ for all $j \neq j(i)$; and (ii) for all $j \in \mathbb{N}$, there exists $i(j) \in \mathbb{N}$ such that $p_{i(j)j} = 1$ and $p_{ij} = 0$ for all $i \neq i(j)$. Let $\mathcal{P}$ be the set of all permutation matrices. Since, for any $\boldsymbol{P} \in \mathcal{P}$, the corresponding permutation on $\mathbb{N}$ is associated and the converse is also true, we will use the terms "permutation" and "permutation matrix" interchangeably. For all $\boldsymbol{u} \in \mathbb{R}^{\mathbb{N}}$ and all $\boldsymbol{P} \in \mathcal{P}$, the product $\boldsymbol{P}\boldsymbol{u}$ is the stream $\boldsymbol{v} \in \mathbb{R}^{\mathbb{N}}$ defined by $v_i = \sum_{k\in\mathbb{N}} p_{ik}u_k$ for all $i \in \mathbb{N}$. For all $\boldsymbol{P} = (p_{ij})_{i,j\in\mathbb{N}} \in \mathcal{P}$ and all $n \in \mathbb{N}$, $\boldsymbol{P}(n)$ denotes the $n \times n$ matrix $(p_{ij})_{i,j\in\{1,\ldots,n\}}$. Let $\boldsymbol{I}$ denote the infinite identity matrix. For any $\boldsymbol{P} \in \mathcal{P}$, let $\boldsymbol{P}'$ be the inverse of $\boldsymbol{P}$ satisfying $\boldsymbol{P}'\boldsymbol{P} = \boldsymbol{P}\boldsymbol{P}' = \boldsymbol{I}$.[1] A permutation $\boldsymbol{P} = (p_{ij})_{i,j\in\mathbb{N}} \in \mathcal{P}$ is said to be a *finite permutation* if there exists $n \in \mathbb{N}$ such that $p_{ii} = 1$ for all $i > n$. The set of all finite permutations is denoted by $\mathcal{F}$.

A permutation $\boldsymbol{P} = (p_{ij})_{i,j\in\mathbb{N}} \in \mathcal{P}$ is said to be *cyclic* if, for any $i \in \mathbb{N}$, there exist $k(i) \in \mathbb{N}$ and $\{i_1, \ldots, i_{k(i)}\} \subset \mathbb{N}$ such that

$$i_1 = i \text{ and } p_{i_2 i_1} = \cdots = p_{i_{k(i)} i_{k(i)-1}} = p_{i_1 i_{k(i)}} = 1. \tag{4.1}$$

Figure 4.1 illustrates the case where $k(1) = 4$ and $(i_1, \ldots, i_4) = (1, 7, 3, 5)$. This definition is used by Kamaga and Kojima (2009), which is equivalent to the original one used in Mitra and Basu (2007). The set of all cyclic permutations is denoted by $\mathcal{C}$. For any $\boldsymbol{P} = (p_{ij})_{i,j\in\mathbb{N}} \in \mathcal{C}$ and any $i \in \mathbb{N}$, $C(\boldsymbol{P}, i)$ denotes the set $\{i_1, \ldots, i_{k(i)}\}$

[1]For any $\boldsymbol{P}, \boldsymbol{Q} \in \mathcal{P}$, the product $\boldsymbol{P}\boldsymbol{Q}$ is defined by $(r_{ij})_{i,j\in\mathbb{N}}$ with $r_{ij} = \sum_{k\in\mathbb{N}} p_{ik}q_{kj}$.

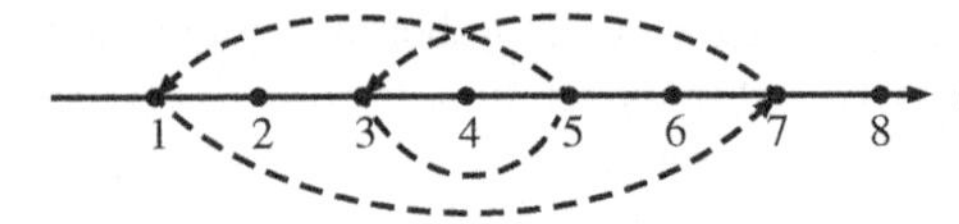


**Fig. 4.1** Cycle of a cyclic permutation

satisfying (4.1). Note that for any $i, j \in \mathbb{N}$ with $j \notin C(\boldsymbol{P}, i)$, $C(\boldsymbol{P}, i) \cap C(\boldsymbol{P}, j) = \emptyset$, since otherwise there exist $i' \in C(\boldsymbol{P}, i)$ and $j' \in C(\boldsymbol{P}, j)$ with $j \notin C(\boldsymbol{P}, i)$ and $i^* \in C(\boldsymbol{P}, i) \cap C(\boldsymbol{P}, j)$ such that $p_{i^*i'} = p_{i^*j'} = 1$; hence, $\boldsymbol{P}$ is not a permutation matrix.

It is well-known that $\mathcal{C} \subset \mathcal{P}$, i.e., the set of all permutations is not a set of cyclic permutations. For instance, consider $\boldsymbol{P} \in \mathcal{P}$ defined by $p_{21} = 1$ and $p_{ij} = 1$ if (i) $i = j - 2$ and $j > 1$ is odd or (ii) $i = j + 2$ and $j$ is even. Then, $\boldsymbol{P} \notin \mathcal{C}$. Moreover, let $\boldsymbol{u} \in \mathbb{R}^{\mathbb{N}}$ be $\boldsymbol{u} = (1, 0, 1, 0, 1, 0, \ldots)$. Then, $\boldsymbol{Pu} = (1, 1, 1, 0, 1, 0, \ldots)$ follows, so that the anonymity axiom defined by all possible permutations is incompatible with the strong Pareto principle (Lauwers 1997a; van Liedekerke 1995).

The following characterization of a cyclic permutation is presented by Lauwers (2012) and Mitra and Basu (2007).[2] It shows that the cyclicity of a permutation is necessary and sufficient for the set of permutation to yield the anonymity axiom that is compatible with the strong Pareto principle.

**Lemma 4.1** (Lauwers 2012; Mitra and Basu 2007) *A permutation $\boldsymbol{P} \in \mathcal{P}$ is cyclic if and only if there is no $\boldsymbol{u} \in \mathbb{R}^{\mathbb{N}}$ satisfying $\boldsymbol{Pu} > \boldsymbol{u}$.*

A set $\mathcal{Q}$ of permutations is a *group* of permutations (with respect to matrix multiplication) if and only if it satisfies Property 4.1(matrix multiplication is a closed binary operation on $\mathcal{Q}$), Property 4.2 (existence of the unit element), and Property 4.3 (existence of the inverse element).[3]

**Property 4.1** *For all $\boldsymbol{P}, \boldsymbol{Q} \in \mathcal{Q}$, $\boldsymbol{PQ} \in \mathcal{Q}$.*

**Property 4.2** *For all $\boldsymbol{P} \in \mathcal{Q}$, there exists $\boldsymbol{Q} \in \mathcal{Q}$ such that $\boldsymbol{PQ} = \boldsymbol{QP} = \boldsymbol{P}$.*

**Property 4.3** *For all $\boldsymbol{P} \in \mathcal{Q}$, there exists $\boldsymbol{Q} \in \mathcal{Q}$ such that $\boldsymbol{PQ} = \boldsymbol{QP} = \boldsymbol{I}$.*

Since $\mathcal{Q}$ is a set of permutations, the permutation $\boldsymbol{Q}$ in Property 4.2 must be $\boldsymbol{I}$ and the permutation $\boldsymbol{Q}$ in Property 4.3 must be $\boldsymbol{P}'$.

We also consider Property 4.1*, which requires that any product of the finite number of elements in a given set $\mathcal{Q}$ of permutations must be cyclic.

**Property 4.1*** *For any finite sequence $\{\boldsymbol{P}^k\}_{k=1}^K$ in $\mathcal{Q}$ with $K > 1$, the product $\boldsymbol{P}^1 \cdots \boldsymbol{P}^K$ belongs to $\mathcal{C}$.*

Note that, for any set $\mathcal{Q}$ of cyclic permutations, Property 4.1 implies Property 4.1*.

---

[2]In Mitra and Basu (2007), the result is established for domain $X = [0, 1]^{\mathbb{N}}$. Lauwers (2012) strengthens their result by showing that it holds for any domain $X$ satisfying $\{0, 1\}^{\mathbb{N}} \subseteq X$.

[3]In algebra, a set of objects is said to be a group if it satisfies *associativity* in addition to Properties 4.1, 4.2, and 4.3. Given a set $\mathcal{O}$ of objects, $\mathcal{O}$ together with an operation $\circ$ satisfy associativity if, for all $A, B, C \in \mathcal{O}$, $A \circ (B \circ C) = (A \circ B) \circ C$. Since any set of permutations is associative with respect to matrix multiplication, we omit associativity in the definition of a group of permutations.

## 4.3 Pareto-Compatible Extended Anonymity

### 4.3.1 Characterizations

The concept of *permissible permutations* was introduced by Mitra and Basu (2007). Given a binary relation $\succsim$ on $\mathbb{R}^{\mathbb{N}}$, the set of permissible permutations of $\succsim$ is the set of all permutations with respect to which every utility stream $\boldsymbol{u}$ is declared to be indifferent to the permuted stream $\boldsymbol{Pu}$ by $\succsim$. Formally, for any binary relation $\succsim$ on $\mathbb{R}^{\mathbb{N}}$, the set $\Pi(\succsim)$ of permissible permutations of $\succsim$ is defined by

$$\Pi(\succsim) = \{\boldsymbol{P} \in \mathcal{P} : \boldsymbol{Pu} \sim \boldsymbol{u} \text{ for all } \boldsymbol{u} \in \mathbb{R}^{\mathbb{N}}\}. \tag{4.2}$$

For any set $\mathcal{Q}$ of permutations, the anonymity axiom associated with $\mathcal{Q}$ is defined as follows.

**$\mathcal{Q}$-Anonymity**: For all $\boldsymbol{u} \in \mathbb{R}^{\mathbb{N}}$ and all $\boldsymbol{P} \in \mathcal{Q}$, $\boldsymbol{Pu} \sim \boldsymbol{u}$.

If $\mathcal{Q} = \mathcal{F}$, we obtain $\mathcal{F}$-anonymity, which is also called finite anonymity (see Chap. 3). If $\mathcal{F} \subset \mathcal{Q}$, we say that $\mathcal{Q}$-anonymity is an extended anonymity. Examples of extended anonymity axioms will be presented in the next section. Note that a social welfare relation $\succsim$ satisfies $\mathcal{Q}$-anonymity if and only if $\mathcal{Q} \subseteq \Pi(\succsim)$. Hence, $\Pi(\succsim)$-anonymity is the strongest anonymity that can be satisfied by a given social welfare relation $\succsim$.

Mitra and Basu (2007) characterized the set of permissible permutations of a Paretian social welfare quasi-ordering using the cyclicity of a permutation and the group notion in algebra. For a proof, see Mitra and Basu (2007).

**Theorem 4.1** (Mitra and Basu 2007) *$\mathcal{Q}$ is a group of cyclic permutations if and only if there exists a Paretian social welfare quasi-ordering $\succsim$ on $\mathbb{R}^{\mathbb{N}}$ that satisfies $\Pi(\succsim) = \mathcal{Q}$.*

Adachi et al. (2014) characterized the set of permissible permutations of a Paretian social welfare relation, assuming coherence properties weaker than transitivity. As the following theorem shows, the set of permissible permutations of a Paretian Suzumura-consistent social welfare relation is more restrictive than that of a Paretian quasi-transitive or acyclic social welfare relation. For a proof, see Adachi et al. (2014).

**Theorem 4.2** (Adachi et al. 2014) *Let $\mathcal{Q}$ be a set of permutations.*

*(i) $\mathcal{Q}$ is a set of cyclic permutations that satisfies Properties 4.2 and 4.3 if and only if there exists a Paretian acyclic social welfare relation $\succsim$ on $\mathbb{R}^{\mathbb{N}}$ that satisfies $\Pi(\succsim) = \mathcal{Q}$.*

*(ii) $\mathcal{Q}$ is a set of cyclic permutations that satisfies Properties 4.2 and 4.3 if and only if there exists a Paretian quasi-transitive social welfare relation $\succsim$ on $\mathbb{R}^{\mathbb{N}}$ that satisfies $\Pi(\succsim) = \mathcal{Q}$.*

*(iii)* $\mathcal{Q}$ *is a set of cyclic permutations that satisfies Properties 4.1*, 4.2, and 4.3 if and only if there exists a Paretian Suzumura-consistent social welfare relation* $\succsim$ *on* $\mathbb{R}^{\mathbb{N}}$ *that satisfies* $\Pi(\succsim) = \mathcal{Q}$.

The set of permissible permutation of a Paretian Suzumura-consistent social welfare relation can be related to that of a Paretian social welfare quasi-ordering. We define the closure of a set of permutations with respect to matrix multiplication. For any set $\mathcal{Q}$ of permutations, the closure $\overline{\mathcal{Q}}$ of $\mathcal{Q}$ is defined as follows:

$$\overline{\mathcal{Q}} = \left\{ \boldsymbol{P} \in \mathcal{P} : \begin{array}{l} \text{there exists a finite sequence } \{\boldsymbol{P}^k\}_{k=1}^K \text{ in } \mathcal{Q} \text{ satisfying} \\ \boldsymbol{P} = \boldsymbol{P}^1 \cdots \boldsymbol{P}^K \end{array} \right\}. \tag{4.3}$$

Note that $\mathcal{Q} \subseteq \overline{\mathcal{Q}}$ for all $\mathcal{Q} \subseteq \mathcal{P}$.

The following theorem shows that, for any set $\mathcal{Q}$ of cyclic permutations satisfying Properties 4.1*, 4.2, and 4.3, the closure $\overline{\mathcal{Q}}$ is the smallest group of cyclic permutations that includes $\mathcal{Q}$. Again, see Adachi et al. (2014) for its proof.

**Theorem 4.3** (Adachi et al. 2014) *Let* $\mathcal{Q}$ *be a set of cyclic permutations satisfying Properties 4.1*, 4.2, and 4.3.*

*(i)* $\overline{\mathcal{Q}}$ *is a group of cyclic permutations.*
*(ii)* $\overline{\mathcal{Q}} \subseteq \tilde{\mathcal{Q}}$ *for any group of cyclic permutations with* $\mathcal{Q} \subseteq \tilde{\mathcal{Q}}$.

Lauwers (2012) showed that a maximal group of cyclic permutations is non-constructible object. Thus, from Theorem 4.3, we cannot explicitly formulate a maximal anonymity axiom for a Paretian Suzumura-consistent social welfare relation and a Paretian social welfare quasi-ordering. However, Theorem 4.3 offers us a useful technique for finding a non-maximal anonymity axiom for these Paretian relations. To explain this, let $\mathcal{Q}_1$ and $\mathcal{Q}_2$ be constructible groups of cyclic permutations. Note that the union $\mathcal{Q}_1 \cup \mathcal{Q}_2$ is a set of cyclic permutations satisfying Properties 4.2 and 4.3. From Theorem 4.3, if $\mathcal{Q}_1 \cup \mathcal{Q}_2$ satisfies Property 4.1*, the closure $\overline{\mathcal{Q}_1 \cup \mathcal{Q}_2}$ is a group of cyclic permutations and it includes both $\mathcal{Q}_1$ and $\mathcal{Q}_2$ as a subset.

### 4.3.2 Examples of a Set of Cyclic Permutations

Each of the sets of permutations we present below is a strict superset of the set $\mathcal{F}$ of all finite permutations.[4] Thus, each of the corresponding anonymity axioms is an extended anonymity. We begin with two particular sets of cyclic permutations that satisfy Properties 4.2 and 4.3 but violate Properties 4.1 and 4.1*.

**Example 4.1** First, the set $\mathcal{C}$ of all cyclic permutations is a set of cyclic permutations and it satisfies Properties 4.2 and 4.3. Second, the set $\mathcal{V}$ of all *variable-step permutations* defined by

[4] Other examples are presented by Fleurbaey and Michel (2003), Lauwers (1998), and Sakai (2010b).

$$\mathcal{V} = \left\{ \boldsymbol{P} \in \mathcal{P} : \begin{array}{l} \text{for all } n \in \mathbb{N}, \text{ there exists } n' \in \mathbb{N} \text{ with } n' \geq n \text{ such that} \\ \boldsymbol{P}(n') \text{ is a finite-dimensional permutation matrix} \end{array} \right\}$$

is a set of cyclic permutations that satisfies Properties 4.2 and 4.3. This was first introduced by Lauwers (1997b) and was further discussed by Fleurbaey and Michel (2003). By definition, $\mathcal{V} \subset \mathcal{C}$. Neither $\mathcal{C}$ nor $\mathcal{V}$ satisfy Property 4.1* (thus, and Property 4.1). ■

By Theorem 4.2, $\mathcal{C}$-anonymity and $\mathcal{V}$-anonymity (or variable-step anonymity) are compatible with the existence of a Paretian acyclic and a Paretian quasi-transitive social welfare relations but are not compatible with the existence of a Paretian Suzumura-consistent social welfare relation.[5] Since $\mathcal{C}$ is the unique maximal of the class of all sets of cyclic permutations that satisfy Properties 4.2 and 4.3, $\mathcal{C}$-anonymity is the unique maximal anonymity axiom that is compatible with the existence of a Paretian acyclic and a Paretian quasi-transitive social welfare relations.

Next, we present sets of cyclic permutations that satisfy Properties 4.1, 4.2, and 4.3 (i.e., groups of cyclic permutations). One well-known example of a group of cyclic permutations is the set $\mathcal{F}$ of all finite permutations. We present two groups of cyclic permutations, which include $\mathcal{F}$ as a strict subset.

**Example 4.2** Let $\mathcal{S}$ and $\mathcal{V}_p$ be the sets of permutations defined as follows:

$$\mathcal{S} = \left\{ \boldsymbol{P} \in \mathcal{P} : \begin{array}{l} \text{there exists } s \in \mathbb{N} \text{ such that, for all } n \in \mathbb{N}, \\ \boldsymbol{P}(ns) \text{ is a finite-dimensional permutation matrix} \end{array} \right\},$$

$$\mathcal{V}_p = \left\{ \boldsymbol{P} \in \mathcal{P} : \begin{array}{l} \text{there exists } m \in \mathbb{N} \text{ such that, for all } n \in \mathbb{N}\setminus\{1\}, \\ \boldsymbol{P}(n^m) \text{ is a finite-dimensional permutation matrix} \end{array} \right\}.$$

$\mathcal{S}$ is the set of all *fixed-step permutations* introduced by Lauwers (1997b). $\mathcal{V}_p$ was introduced by Adachi et al. (2014). It consists of the variable-step permutations that reshuffle generations within each block of contiguous generations taken by a power function. By definition, $\mathcal{S} \subset \mathcal{V}$ and $\mathcal{V}_p \subset \mathcal{V}$. The set inclusion does not hold between $\mathcal{S}$ and $\mathcal{V}_p$. This can be verified as follows. Since any permutation in $\mathcal{V}_p$ uses a power function to take blocks of generations, the size of a block of generations becomes larger as we consider succeeding generations. Thus, $\mathcal{V}_p \not\subseteq \mathcal{S}$. On the other hand, since $3^m$ is odd for all $m \in \mathbb{N}$, $\mathcal{V}_p$ does not contain the fixed-step permutation that reshuffles two contiguous generations. Thus, $\mathcal{S} \not\subseteq \mathcal{V}_p$. ■

From Theorem 4.1, $\mathcal{S}$-anonymity (or fixed-step anonymity) and $\mathcal{V}_p$-anonymity are compatible with the existence of a Paretian social welfare quasi-ordering.

Finally, we present an example of a set of cyclic permutations that satisfies Properties 4.1*, 4.2, and 4.3 but violates Property 4.1. The example is given by the union of $\mathcal{S}$ and $\mathcal{V}_p$ in Example 4.2.

[5] Fleurbaey and Michel (2003) and Sakai (2010a) present Paretian quasi-transitive SWRs that satisfy $\mathcal{V}$-anonymity.

**Example 4.3** Let $\mathcal{Q} = \mathcal{S} \cup \mathcal{V}_p$. By Example 4.2, $\mathcal{Q}$ is a set of cyclic permutations and it satisfies Properties 4.2 and 4.3. It can be verified that $\mathcal{Q}$ satisfies Property 4.1* but violates Property 4.1; see Adachi et al. (2014) for its proof. ■

Since $\mathcal{S} \subset \mathcal{S} \cup \mathcal{V}_p$ and $\mathcal{V}_p \subset \mathcal{S} \cup \mathcal{V}_p$, $\mathcal{Q}$-anonymity defined by $\mathcal{Q} = \mathcal{S} \cup \mathcal{V}_p$ is stronger than $\mathcal{S}$-anonymity and $\mathcal{V}_p$-anonymity. However, since $\mathcal{S} \cup \mathcal{V}_p \subset \mathcal{V}$, it is weaker than $\mathcal{V}$-anonymity. By Theorem 4.2, $\mathcal{Q}$-anonymity defined by $\mathcal{Q} = \mathcal{S} \cup \mathcal{V}_p$ is compatible with the existence of a Paretian Suzumura-consistent social welfare relation as well as the existence of a Paretian quasi-transitive social welfare relation.

## 4.4 Dominance-in-Tails Criteria and Extended Anonymity

### *4.4.1 Generalized Definition and Characterizations*

We consider a general extension of the dominance-in-tails criterion that satisfies an extended anonymity defined by a group of cyclic permutations. Given a group $\mathcal{Q}$ of cyclic permutations with $\mathcal{F} \subseteq \mathcal{Q}$ and an independent sequence $(\succsim^n)$ of finite-horizon Paretian and anonymous quasi-orderings, the *$\mathcal{Q}$-anonymous extension of the dominance-in-tails criterion* $\succsim^D$ associated with $(\succsim^n)_{n\in\mathbb{N}}$ is defined as the following binary relation $\succsim^{\mathcal{Q}D}$ on $\mathbb{R}^{\mathbb{N}}$. For all $\boldsymbol{u}, \boldsymbol{v} \in \mathbb{R}^{\mathbb{N}}$,

$$\boldsymbol{u} \succsim^{\mathcal{Q}D} \boldsymbol{v} \Leftrightarrow \text{there exists } \boldsymbol{P} \in \mathcal{Q} \text{ such that } \boldsymbol{P}\boldsymbol{u} \succsim^{D} \boldsymbol{v}. \tag{4.4}$$

This extension method was analyzed by Banerjee (2006) and Kamaga and Kojima (2009).

The following lemma shows that the $\mathcal{Q}$-anonymous extension $\succsim^{\mathcal{Q}D}$ of the dominance-in-tails criterion is well-defined as a social welfare quasi-ordering. Furthermore, it characterizes its asymmetric and symmetric parts. This result was established by Kamaga and Kojima (2009).

**Lemma 4.2** (Kamaga and Kojima 2009) *Let $(\succsim^n)_{n\in\mathbb{N}}$ be an independent sequence of finite-horizon Paretian and anonymous quasi-orderings and $\mathcal{Q}$ be a group of cyclic permutations.*

*(i) $\succsim^{\mathcal{Q}D}$ is a quasi-ordering on $\mathbb{R}^{\mathbb{N}}$.*
*(ii) For any $\boldsymbol{u}, \boldsymbol{v} \in \mathbb{R}^{\mathbb{N}}$,*

$$\boldsymbol{u} \succ^{\mathcal{Q}D} \boldsymbol{v} \Leftrightarrow \textit{there exists } \boldsymbol{P} \in \mathcal{Q} \textit{ such that } \boldsymbol{P}\boldsymbol{u} \succ^{D} \boldsymbol{v}, \tag{4.5a}$$

$$\boldsymbol{u} \sim^{\mathcal{Q}D} \boldsymbol{v} \Leftrightarrow \textit{there exists } \boldsymbol{P} \in \mathcal{Q} \textit{ such that } \boldsymbol{P}\boldsymbol{u} \sim^{D} \boldsymbol{v}. \tag{4.5b}$$

***Proof*** (i) Let $\boldsymbol{u}, \boldsymbol{v} \in \mathbb{R}^{\mathbb{N}}$ and $\boldsymbol{P} = (p_{ij})_{i,j\in\mathbb{N}} \in \mathcal{Q}$. We begin by showing that

$$\boldsymbol{u} \succsim^{D} \boldsymbol{v} \Leftrightarrow \boldsymbol{P}\boldsymbol{u} \succsim^{D} \boldsymbol{P}\boldsymbol{v}. \tag{4.6}$$

First, suppose $\boldsymbol{u} \succsim^D \boldsymbol{v}$. We show that $\boldsymbol{Pu} \succsim^D \boldsymbol{Pv}$. By (3.3), there exists $n \in \mathbb{N}$ such that $\boldsymbol{u}^{-n} \succsim^n \boldsymbol{v}^{-n}$ and $\boldsymbol{u}^{+n} \geq \boldsymbol{v}^{+n}$. Let $\bar{n} = \max\{i \in \mathbb{N} : p_{ij} = 1,\ j \in \{1, \dots, n\}\}$. Note that $\bar{n} \geq n$. Furthermore, $\boldsymbol{Pu}^{+\bar{n}} \geq \boldsymbol{Pv}^{+\bar{n}}$ follows since $\boldsymbol{x}^{+n} \geq \boldsymbol{y}^{+n}$. If $\bar{n} = n$, then we obtain $\boldsymbol{Pu}^{-n} \succsim^n \boldsymbol{Pv}^{-n}$ since $\succsim^n$ is anonymous and transitive. Thus, by (3.3), $\boldsymbol{Pu} \succsim^D \boldsymbol{Pv}$ follows. Now assume that $\bar{n} > n$. We define $M \subset \{1, \dots, \bar{n}\}$ by $M = \{i : p_{ij} = 1 \text{ for } j \in \{n+1, n+2, \dots\}\}$. Note that $|M| = \bar{n} - n$. Let $\tilde{i}$ denote the $i$th smallest number in $M$. Define $\boldsymbol{w}^{-\bar{n}}, \boldsymbol{z}^{-\bar{n}} \in \mathbb{R}^{\bar{n}}$ by $\boldsymbol{w}^{-n} = \boldsymbol{u}^{-n}$, $\boldsymbol{z}^{-n} = \boldsymbol{v}^{-n}$ and for all $i \in \{1, \dots, \bar{n} - n\}$, $w_{n+i} = Pu_{\tilde{i}}$ and $z_{n+i} = Pv_{\tilde{i}}$. Since $\boldsymbol{u}^{+n} \geq \boldsymbol{v}^{+n}$, $w_{n+i} \geq z_{n+i}$ for all $i \in \{1, \dots, \bar{n} - n\}$. Since $(\succsim^n)_{n \in \mathbb{N}}$ is an independent sequence of finite-horizon Paretian and anonymous quasi-orderings, we obtain $\boldsymbol{w}^{-\bar{n}} \succsim^{\bar{n}} \boldsymbol{z}^{-\bar{n}}$, $\boldsymbol{w}^{-\bar{n}} \sim^{\bar{n}} \boldsymbol{Pu}^{-\bar{n}}$ and $\boldsymbol{z}^{-\bar{n}} \sim^{\bar{n}} \boldsymbol{Pv}^{-\bar{n}}$. By the transitivity of $\succsim^{\bar{n}}$, $\boldsymbol{Px}^{-\bar{n}} \succsim^{\bar{n}} \boldsymbol{Py}^{-\bar{n}}$ follows. Thus, by (3.3), we obtain $\boldsymbol{Px} \succsim^D \boldsymbol{Py}$. Since $\boldsymbol{u}$, $\boldsymbol{v}$ and $\boldsymbol{P}$ were chosen arbitrarily and $\boldsymbol{P}' \in \mathcal{Q}$, $\boldsymbol{Pu} \succsim^D \boldsymbol{Pv}$ implies $\boldsymbol{P}'\boldsymbol{Pu} \succsim^D \boldsymbol{P}'\boldsymbol{Pv}$, that is, $\boldsymbol{u} \succsim^D \boldsymbol{v}$.

We now show that $\succsim^{\mathcal{Q}D}$ is a quasi-ordering. From Lemma 3.4, $\succsim^D$ is a quasi-ordering. Since $\boldsymbol{I} \in \mathcal{Q}$ and $\succsim^D$ is reflexive, $\succsim^{\mathcal{Q}D}$ is reflexive. To show that $\succsim^{\mathcal{Q}D}$ is transitive, let $\boldsymbol{u}, \boldsymbol{v}, \boldsymbol{w} \in \mathbb{R}^{\mathbb{N}}$ and suppose that $\boldsymbol{u} \succsim^{\mathcal{Q}D} \boldsymbol{v}$ and $\boldsymbol{v} \succsim^{\mathcal{Q}D} \boldsymbol{w}$. From (4.4), there exist $\boldsymbol{P}, \boldsymbol{Q} \in \mathcal{Q}$ such that $\boldsymbol{Pu} \succsim^D \boldsymbol{v}$ and $\boldsymbol{Qv} \succsim^D \boldsymbol{w}$. By (4.6), we obtain $\boldsymbol{QPu} \succsim^D \boldsymbol{Qv}$. Since $\succsim^D$ is transitive, $\boldsymbol{QPu} \succsim^D \boldsymbol{w}$ follows. Since $\boldsymbol{QP} \in \mathcal{Q}$, we obtain $\boldsymbol{u} \succsim^{\mathcal{Q}D} \boldsymbol{v}$ by (4.4).

(ii) We begin with the proof of (4.5a). 'If.' Let $\boldsymbol{u}, \boldsymbol{v} \in \mathbb{R}^{\mathbb{N}}$ and $\boldsymbol{P} \in \mathcal{Q}$. Suppose $\boldsymbol{Pu} \succ^D \boldsymbol{v}$. From (4.4), $\boldsymbol{u} \succsim^{\mathcal{Q}D} \boldsymbol{v}$ follows. By way of contradiction, suppose $\boldsymbol{v} \succsim^{\mathcal{Q}D} \boldsymbol{u}$. From (4.4), there exists $\boldsymbol{Q} \in \mathcal{Q}$ such that $\boldsymbol{Qv} \succsim^D \boldsymbol{u}$. Let $\boldsymbol{R} = (r_{ij})_{i,j \in \mathbb{N}} = \boldsymbol{QP} \in \mathcal{Q}$. By (4.6), $\boldsymbol{Pu} \succ^D \boldsymbol{v}$ implies $\boldsymbol{Ru} \succ^D \boldsymbol{Qv}$. Since $\succsim^D$ is transitive, we obtain $\boldsymbol{Ru} \succ^D \boldsymbol{u}$. From (3.4a), there exists $n \in \mathbb{N}$ such that $\boldsymbol{Ru}^{-n} \succ^n \boldsymbol{u}^{-n}$ and $\boldsymbol{Ru}^{+n} \geq \boldsymbol{u}^{+n}$. Let $M = \{i \in \mathbb{N} : i > n \text{ and } Ru_i > u_i\}$. We distinguish two cases.

*Case 1.* $|M| < \infty$. Since $(\succsim^n)_{n \in \mathbb{N}}$ is an independent sequence of Paretian quasi-orderings, there exists $m > n$ such that $\boldsymbol{Ru}^{-m} \succ^m \boldsymbol{u}^{-m}$ and $\boldsymbol{Ru}^{-m} = \boldsymbol{u}^{-m}$. Let $i \in \{1, \dots, m\}$. Since $\boldsymbol{R} = (r_{ij})_{i,j \in \mathbb{N}}$ is a cyclic permutation, there exists $k(i) \in \mathbb{N}$ such that $C(\boldsymbol{R}, i) = \{i_1, \dots, i_{k(i)}\}$. It follows from (4.1) that

$$i_1 = i \text{ and } r_{i_2 i_1} = \cdots = r_{i_{k(i)} i_{k(i)-1}} = r_{i_1 i_{k(i)}} = 1.$$

Define $k^*(i) \leq k(i)$ by

$$k^*(i) = \begin{cases} \min\{t \in \{2, \dots, k(i)\} : i_t \in \{1, \dots, m\}\} & \text{if } \{i_2, \dots, i_{k(i)}\} \cap \{1, \dots, m\} \neq \emptyset, \\ 1 & \text{otherwise.} \end{cases}$$

Since $Ru_j = u_j$ for all $j > m$ and $Ru_{i_t} = u_{i_{t-1}}$ for all $t \in \{2, \dots, k(i)\}$, it follows that

$$u_i = u_{i_1} = Ru_{i_2} = u_{i_2} = \cdots = u_{i_{k^*(i)-1}} = Ru_{i_{k^*(i)}}.$$

Note that for any $i \in \{1, \ldots, m\}$, for any $i' \in C(\boldsymbol{R}, i)$ with $i' \neq i$ and for any $j \notin C(\boldsymbol{R}, i)$, $j_{k^*(j)} \neq i_{k^*(i)}, i'_{k^*(i')}$ since $C(\boldsymbol{R}, i) \cap C(\boldsymbol{R}, j) = \varnothing$. Further, $i_{k^*(i)} \neq i'_{k^*(i')}$. Thus, $\boldsymbol{R}\boldsymbol{u}^{-m}$ is a permutation of $\boldsymbol{u}^{-m}$. Since $\succsim^m$ is anonymous, we obtain $\boldsymbol{R}\boldsymbol{u}^{-m} \sim^m \boldsymbol{u}^{-m}$. However, this is a contradiction because $\boldsymbol{R}\boldsymbol{u}^{-m} \succ^m \boldsymbol{u}^{-m}$.

*Case 2.* $|M| = \infty$. Let $i \in M$. Since $Ru_i > u_i$, there exists $i^* \in C(\boldsymbol{R}, i) = \{i_1, \ldots, i_{k(i)}\}$ such that $Ru_{i^*} < u_{i^*}$, since otherwise it follows from (4.1) that

$$u_i = u_{i_1} = Ru_{i_2} \geq u_{i_2} = \cdots = Ru_{i(k)} \geq u_{i(k)} = Ru_{i_1} > u_{i_1},$$

which is a contradiction. Since $|C(\boldsymbol{R}, i)| < \infty$, it follows that $|\{i \in \mathbb{N} : Ru_i < u_i\}| = \infty$. However, this is a contradiction since $|\{i \in \mathbb{N} : Ru_i < u_i\}| < \infty$.

'Only if.' Let $\boldsymbol{u}, \boldsymbol{v} \in \mathbb{R}^{\mathbb{N}}$ and suppose $\boldsymbol{u} \succ^{\mathcal{Q}D} \boldsymbol{v}$. From (4.4), there exists $\boldsymbol{P} \in \mathcal{Q}$ such that $\boldsymbol{P}\boldsymbol{u} \succsim^D \boldsymbol{v}$. By way of contradiction, suppose $\boldsymbol{P}\boldsymbol{u} \sim^D \boldsymbol{v}$. Since $\boldsymbol{P}'\boldsymbol{P}\boldsymbol{u} = \boldsymbol{u}$, by (4.6), we obtain $\boldsymbol{u} \sim^D \boldsymbol{P}'\boldsymbol{v}$. Since $\boldsymbol{P}' \in \mathcal{Q}$, it follows from (4.4) that $\boldsymbol{v} \succsim^{\mathcal{Q}D} \boldsymbol{u}$. However, this is a contradiction because $\boldsymbol{u} \succ^{\mathcal{Q}D} \boldsymbol{v}$. Thus, $\boldsymbol{P}\boldsymbol{u} \succ^D \boldsymbol{v}$ holds.

Next, we prove (4.5b). 'If.' Let $\boldsymbol{u}, \boldsymbol{v} \in \mathbb{R}^{\mathbb{N}}$ and $\boldsymbol{P} \in \mathcal{Q}$. Suppose $\boldsymbol{P}\boldsymbol{u} \sim^D \boldsymbol{v}$. From (4.4), $\boldsymbol{u} \succsim^{\mathcal{Q}D} \boldsymbol{v}$ follows. By way of contradiction, suppose $\boldsymbol{u} \sim^{\mathcal{Q}D} \boldsymbol{v}$ does not hold. Then, by (4.4), there is no $\boldsymbol{Q} \in \mathcal{Q}$ such that $\boldsymbol{Q}\boldsymbol{v} \succsim^D \boldsymbol{u}$. However, this is a contradiction because $\boldsymbol{P}' \in \mathcal{Q}$ and $\boldsymbol{P}'\boldsymbol{v} \succsim^D \boldsymbol{u}$ follows from (4.6). Thus, $\boldsymbol{u} \sim^{\mathcal{Q}D} \boldsymbol{v}$ holds.

'Only if.' Let $\boldsymbol{u}, \boldsymbol{v} \in \mathbb{R}^{\mathbb{N}}$ and suppose $\boldsymbol{u} \sim^{\mathcal{Q}D} \boldsymbol{v}$. Then, there exists $\boldsymbol{P} \in \mathcal{Q}$ such that $\boldsymbol{P}\boldsymbol{u} \succsim^D \boldsymbol{v}$. If $\boldsymbol{P}\boldsymbol{u} \succ^D \boldsymbol{v}$, then $\boldsymbol{u} \succ^{\mathcal{Q}D} \boldsymbol{v}$ follows from (4.5a), which is a contradiction since $\boldsymbol{u} \sim^{\mathcal{Q}D} \boldsymbol{v}$. Thus, $\boldsymbol{P}\boldsymbol{u} \sim^D \boldsymbol{v}$. ■

Since $\boldsymbol{I} \in \mathcal{Q}$, the dominance-in-tails criterion $\succsim^D$ associated with an independent sequence $(\succsim^n)_{n \in \mathbb{N}}$ of finite-horizon Paretina and anonymous quasi-orderings is a subrelation of its $\mathcal{Q}$-anonymous extension $\succsim^{\mathcal{Q}D}$.

The following theorem characterizes the $\mathcal{Q}$-anonymous extension $\succsim^{\mathcal{Q}D}$ of the dominance-in-tails criterion $\succsim^D$ associated with an independent sequence $(\succsim^n)_{n \in \mathbb{N}}$ of finite-horizon Paretian and anonymous quasi-orderings. It shows that the characterization is obtained by replacing finite anonymity with $\mathcal{Q}$-anonymity in Theorem 3.1.

**Theorem 4.4** *Let $(\succsim^n)_{n \in \mathbb{N}}$ be an independent sequence of finite-horizon Paretian and anonymous quasi-orderings and $\mathcal{Q}$ be a group of cyclic permutations with $\mathcal{F} \subseteq \mathcal{Q}$. A social welfare quasi-ordering $\succsim$ on $\mathbb{R}^{\mathbb{N}}$ is an extension of $(\succsim^n)_{n \in \mathbb{N}}$ and satisfies strong Pareto and $\mathcal{Q}$-anonymity if and only if $\succsim^{\mathcal{Q}D}$ associated with $(\succsim^n)_{n \in \mathbb{N}}$ is a subrelation of $\succsim$.*

***Proof*** 'If.' Since $\succsim^D$ associated with $(\succsim^n)_{n \in \mathbb{N}}$ is a subrelation of $\succsim^{\mathcal{Q}D}$ associated with $(\succsim^n)_{n \in \mathbb{N}}$, $\succsim^D$ is a subrelation of $\succsim$. From Theorem 3.1, $\succsim$ is an extension of $(\succsim^n)_{n \in \mathbb{N}}$ and satisfies strong Pareto. To show that $\succsim$ satisfies $\mathcal{Q}$-anonymity, let $\boldsymbol{u} \in \mathbb{R}^{\mathbb{N}}$ and $\boldsymbol{P} \in \mathcal{Q}$. Since $\succsim^D$ is reflexive, we obtain $\boldsymbol{P}\boldsymbol{u} \sim^D \boldsymbol{P}\boldsymbol{u}$. From (4.5b), $\boldsymbol{u} \sim^{\mathcal{Q}D} \boldsymbol{P}\boldsymbol{u}$ follows. Since $\succsim^{\mathcal{Q}D}$ is a subrelation of $\succsim$, we obtain $\boldsymbol{u} \sim \boldsymbol{P}\boldsymbol{u}$.

'Only if.' Let $\boldsymbol{u}, \boldsymbol{v} \in \mathbb{R}^{\mathbb{N}}$ and suppose $\boldsymbol{u} \succ^{\mathcal{Q}D} \boldsymbol{v}$. By (4.5a), there exists $\boldsymbol{P} \in \mathcal{Q}$ such that $\boldsymbol{P}\boldsymbol{u} \succ^D \boldsymbol{v}$. From Theorem 3.1, $\succsim^D$ associated with $(\succsim^n)_{n \in \mathbb{N}}$ is a subrelation of $\succsim$. Thus, $\boldsymbol{P}\boldsymbol{u} \succ \boldsymbol{v}$. From $\mathcal{Q}$-anonymity, $\boldsymbol{u} \sim \boldsymbol{P}\boldsymbol{u}$ follows. Since $\succsim$ is transitive, we obtain $\boldsymbol{u} \succ \boldsymbol{v}$. Using (4.5b) instead of (4.5a), the proof that $\boldsymbol{u} \sim^{QD} \boldsymbol{v}$ implies $\boldsymbol{u} \sim \boldsymbol{v}$ is analogous. ■

In the following theorem, we assqume the finite completeness of a social welfare quasi-ordering and present an axiomatization of the $\mathcal{Q}$-anonymous extension $\succsim^{QD}$ of the dominance-in-tails criterion $\succsim^{D}$ associated with an independent sequence $(\succsim^{n})_{n\in\mathbb{N}}$ of finite-horizon Paretian and anonymous orderings. The characterization is established by replacing finite anonymity with $\mathcal{Q}$-anonymity in Theorem 3.2.

**Theorem 4.5** *Let $\mathcal{Q}$ be a group of cyclic permutations with $\mathcal{F} \subseteq \mathcal{Q}$. A finitely complete social welfare quasi-ordering $\succsim$ on $\mathbb{R}^{\mathbb{N}}$ satisfies strong Pareto, $\mathcal{Q}$-anonymity, and separable present if and only if there exists an independent sequence $(\succsim^{n})_{n\in\mathbb{N}}$ of finite-horizon Paretian and anonymous orderings such that $\succsim^{QD}$ associated with $(\succsim^{n})_{n\in\mathbb{N}}$ is a subrelation of $\succsim$.*

***Proof*** 'If.' Since $\succsim^{D}$ associated with $(\succsim^{n})_{n\in\mathbb{N}}$ is a subrelation of $\succsim^{QD}$, it follows from Theorem 3.2 that $\succsim$ satisfies strong Pareto and separable present. By Theorem 4.4, $\succsim$ satisfies $\mathcal{Q}$-anonymity.

'Only if.' Since $\mathcal{F} \subseteq \mathcal{Q}$, $\succsim$ satisfies finite anonymity. Thus, from Theorem 3.2, there exists an independent sequence $(\succsim^{n})_{n\in\mathbb{N}}$ of finite-horizon Paretian and anonymous orderings such that $\succsim^{D}$ associated with $(\succsim^{n})_{n\in\mathbb{N}}$ is a subrelation of $\succsim$. By Theorem 3.1, $\succsim$ is an extension of $(\succsim^{n})_{n\in\mathbb{N}}$. From Theorem 4.4, $\succsim^{QD}$ associated with $(\succsim^{n})_{n\in\mathbb{N}}$ is a subrelation of $\succsim$. ■

### *4.4.2 Dominance in Tails Criteria Associated with Specific Sequences and Extended Anonymity*

Let $\mathcal{Q}$ be a group of cyclic permutations with $\mathcal{F} \subseteq \mathcal{Q}$. Using the general results—Theorems 4.4 and 4.5—together with Theorem 3.1, we provide axiomatizations of the $\mathcal{Q}$-anonymous extensions of the specific forms of the dominance-in-tails criterion provided in Chap. 3. All theorems we present below show that those extensions are axiomatized by replacing finite anonymity with $\mathcal{Q}$-anonymity in the corresponding results in Chap. 3. Since the proofs are straightforward from the general results, we omit their proofs.

From Theorems 3.3 and 3.4, the *$\mathcal{Q}$-anonymous extension* $\succsim_U^{QD}$ of the *utilitarian* social welfare quasi-ordering $\succsim_U^{D}$ is characterized as follows. Banerjee (2006) presents a related result to the equivalence between part (i) and (iii).

**Theorem 4.6** (Kamaga and Kojima 2009) *Let $\succsim$ be a social welfare quasi-ordering on $\mathbb{R}^{\mathbb{N}}$ and $\mathcal{Q}$ be a group of cyclic permutations with $\mathcal{F} \subseteq \mathcal{Q}$. The following three statements are equivalent:*

*(i) $\succsim_U^{QD}$ is a subrelation of $\succsim$,*
*(ii) $\succsim$ satisfies strong Pareto, $\mathcal{Q}$-anonymity, and incremental equity,*

*(iii)* $\succsim$ *satisfies strong Pareto, $\mathcal{Q}$-anonymity, and translation-scale invariance.*

Another axiomatization of $\succsim_U^{QD}$ follows from Theorem 3.5.

**Theorem 4.7** *Let $\mathcal{Q}$ be a group of cyclic permutations with $\mathcal{F} \subseteq \mathcal{Q}$. A finitely complete social welfare quasi-ordering $\succsim$ on $\mathbb{R}^{\mathbb{N}}$ satisfies strong Pareto, $\mathcal{Q}$-anonymity, separable present, cardinal full comparability, and restricted continuity if and only if $\succsim_U^{QD}$ is a subrelation of $\succsim$.*

Let $G$ be the set of continuous and increasing functions $g : \mathbb{R} \to \mathbb{R}$ with $g(0) = 0$. Using Theorem 3.6, the *$\mathcal{Q}$-anonymous extension* $\succsim_{U,g}^{QD}$ of the *generalized utilitarian* social welfare quasi-ordering $\succsim_{U,g}^{D}$ associated with $g \in G$ is characterized as follows.

**Theorem 4.8** *Let $\mathcal{Q}$ be a group of cyclic permutations with $\mathcal{F} \subseteq \mathcal{Q}$. A finitely complete social welfare quasi-ordering $\succsim$ on $\mathbb{R}^{\mathbb{N}}$ satisfies strong Pareto, $\mathcal{Q}$-anonymity, separable present, and restricted continuity if and only if there exists $g \in G$ such that $\succsim_{U,g}^{QD}$ is a subrelation of $\succsim$.*

The following axiomatization of the *$\mathcal{Q}$-anonymous extension* $\succsim_L^{QD}$ of the *leximin* social welfare quasi-ordering $\succsim_L^{D}$ is obtained by using Theorem 3.7. This result was presented by Kamaga and Kojima (2009).

**Theorem 4.9** (Kamaga and Kojima 2009) *Let $\mathcal{Q}$ be a group of cyclic permutations with $\mathcal{F} \subseteq \mathcal{Q}$. A social welfare quasi-ordering $\succsim$ on $\mathbb{R}^{\mathbb{N}}$ satisfies strong Pareto, $\mathcal{Q}$-anonymity, and Hammond equity if and only if $\succsim_L^{QD}$ is a subrelation of $\succsim$.*

Using Theorem 3.8, we can axiomatize the *$\mathcal{Q}$-anonymous extension* $\succsim_\cap^{QD}$ of the *intersection* $\succsim_\cap^{D}$ of the utilitarian and leximin social welfare quasi-orderings as follows.

**Theorem 4.10** *Let $\mathcal{Q}$ be a group of cyclic permutations with $\mathcal{F} \subseteq \mathcal{Q}$. A social welfare quasi-ordering $\succsim$ on $\mathbb{R}^{\mathbb{N}}$ satisfies strong Pareto, $\mathcal{Q}$-anonymity, the strong Pigou–Dalton principle, and the composite transfer principle if and only if $\succsim_\cap^{QD}$ is a subrelation of $\succsim$.*

From Theorems 3.9 and 3.10, we obtain the following joint characterizations involving the *$\mathcal{Q}$-anonymous extension* $\succsim_{UL}^{QD}$ of the *utilitarianism-first and leximin-second* social welfare quasi-ordering $\succsim_{UL}^{D}$.

**Theorem 4.11** *Let $\mathcal{Q}$ be a group of cyclic permutations with $\mathcal{F} \subseteq \mathcal{Q}$.*

*(i) A finitely complete social welfare quasi-ordering $\succsim$ on $\mathbb{R}^{\mathbb{N}}$ satisfies strong Pareto, $\mathcal{Q}$-anonymity, the weak Pigou–Dalton principle, the composite transfer principle, separable present, and cardinal full comparability if and only if any one of $\succsim_U^{QD}$, $\succsim_{UL}^{QD}$, and $\succsim_L^{QD}$ is a subrelation of $\succsim$.*

*(ii) A finitely complete social welfare quasi-ordering $\succsim$ on $\mathbb{R}^{\mathbb{N}}$ satisfies strong Pareto, $\mathcal{Q}$-anonymity, the strong Pigou–Dalton principle, the composite transfer principle, separable present, and cardinal full comparability if and only if either $\succsim_{UL}^{QD}$ or $\succsim_L^{QD}$ is a subrelation of $\succsim$.*

## 4.5 Fixed-Step Anonymous Overtaking Criteria

### *4.5.1 Generalized Definitions and Characterizations*

In this section, we consider $\mathcal{S}$-anonymity (or fixed-step anonymity). We provide and characterize two types of $\mathcal{S}$-anonymous extensions of the genralized overtaking criterion. One is the extension that applies the overtaking criterion to the permuted streams constructed by using fixed-step permutations, which is analogous to the $\mathcal{Q}$-anonymous extension of the dominance-in-tails criterion. The other extension uses a periodic modification of the overtaking criterion, which we call the *fixed-step overtaking criterion.*

Given an independent sequence $(\succsim^n)_{n \in \mathbb{N}}$ of finite-horizon Paretian and anonymous orderings, the $\mathcal{S}$*-anonymous overtaking criterion* associated with $(\succsim^n)_{n \in \mathbb{N}}$ is defined as the following binary relation $\succsim^{\mathcal{S}O}$ on $\mathbb{R}^{\mathbb{N}}$. For any $\boldsymbol{u}, \boldsymbol{v} \in \mathbb{R}^{\mathbb{N}}$,

$$\boldsymbol{u} \succsim^{\mathcal{S}O} \boldsymbol{v} \;\Leftrightarrow\; \text{there exist } \boldsymbol{P}, \boldsymbol{Q} \in \mathcal{S} \text{ such that } \boldsymbol{Pu} \succsim^{O} \boldsymbol{Qv}, \tag{4.7}$$

where $\succsim^O$ is the overtaking criterion associated with $(\succsim^n)_{n \in \mathbb{N}}$; see Chap. 3.

Characterizations of the asymmetric and symmetric parts of $\succsim^{\mathcal{S}O}$ are given by the following lemma.

**Lemma 4.3** (Kamaga and Kojima 2010) *Let $(\succsim^n)_{n \in \mathbb{N}}$ be an independent sequence of finite-horizon Paretian and anonymous orderings. For any $\boldsymbol{u}, \boldsymbol{v} \in \mathbb{R}^{\mathbb{N}}$,*

$$\boldsymbol{u} \succ^{\mathcal{S}O} \boldsymbol{v} \;\Leftrightarrow\; \textit{there exist } \boldsymbol{P}, \boldsymbol{Q} \in \mathcal{S} \textit{ such that } \boldsymbol{Pu} \succ^{O} \boldsymbol{Qv}, \tag{4.8a}$$

$$\boldsymbol{u} \sim^{\mathcal{S}O} \boldsymbol{v} \;\Leftrightarrow\; \textit{there exists } \boldsymbol{P} \in \mathcal{S} \textit{ such that } \boldsymbol{Pu} \sim^{O} \boldsymbol{v}. \tag{4.8b}$$

***Proof*** We first prove (4.8a). 'If.' Let $\boldsymbol{u}, \boldsymbol{v} \in \mathbb{R}^{\mathbb{N}}$ and suppose that there exist $\boldsymbol{P}, \boldsymbol{Q} \in \mathcal{S}$ such that $\boldsymbol{Pu} \succ^{O} \boldsymbol{Qv}$. From (4.7), $\boldsymbol{u} \succsim^{\mathcal{S}O} \boldsymbol{v}$ follows. Since $\boldsymbol{P}, \boldsymbol{Q} \in \mathcal{S}$, there exist $p, q \in \mathbb{N}$ such that $\boldsymbol{P}(np)$ and $\boldsymbol{Q}(nq)$ are finite-dimensional permutation matrices for all $n \in \mathbb{N}$. Let $s = p \cdot q$. Since $\succsim^n$ is anonymous and transitive for all $n \in \mathbb{N}$, from (3.6a), $\boldsymbol{Pu} \succ^{O} \boldsymbol{Qv}$ implies that there exists $\bar{n} \in \mathbb{N}$ such that for all $n \geq \bar{n}$, $\boldsymbol{Pu}^{-sn} \succ^{sn} \boldsymbol{Qv}^{-sn}$. Thus, none of $\boldsymbol{R}, \boldsymbol{S} \in \mathcal{S}$ satisfies $\boldsymbol{Rv} \succsim^{O} \boldsymbol{Su}$ because, for all $n \in \mathbb{N}$, there exists $n^* \in \mathbb{N}$ such that $\boldsymbol{R}(sn^*)$ and $\boldsymbol{S}(sn^*)$ are finite-dimensional permutation matrices, so that $\boldsymbol{Pu}^{-sn^*} \succ^{sn^*} \boldsymbol{Qv}^{-sn^*}$. Thus, by (4.7), $\boldsymbol{v} \succsim^{\mathcal{S}O} \boldsymbol{u}$ does not hold. Hence, $\boldsymbol{u} \succ^{\mathcal{S}O} \boldsymbol{v}$.

'Only if.' Let $\boldsymbol{u}, \boldsymbol{v} \in \mathbb{R}^{\mathbb{N}}$ and suppose $\boldsymbol{u} \succ^{\mathcal{S}O} \boldsymbol{v}$. From (4.7), there exist $\boldsymbol{P}, \boldsymbol{Q} \in \mathcal{S}$ such that $\boldsymbol{Pu} \succsim^{O} \boldsymbol{Qv}$. If $\boldsymbol{Qv} \succsim^{O} \boldsymbol{Pu}$ holds, then by (4.7), we obtain $\boldsymbol{v} \succsim^{\mathcal{S}O} \boldsymbol{u}$, a contradiction. Thus, $\boldsymbol{Pu} \succ^{O} \boldsymbol{Qv}$ must hold.

Next, we prove (4.8b). 'If.' Let $\boldsymbol{u}, \boldsymbol{v} \in \mathbb{R}^{\mathbb{N}}$ and suppose that there exists $\boldsymbol{P} \in \mathcal{S}$ such that $\boldsymbol{Pu} \sim^{O} \boldsymbol{v}$. Since $\boldsymbol{I} \in \mathcal{S}$, it follows from (4.7) that $\boldsymbol{u} \succsim^{\mathcal{S}O} \boldsymbol{v}$ and $\boldsymbol{v} \succsim^{\mathcal{S}O} \boldsymbol{u}$, that is, $\boldsymbol{u} \sim^{\mathcal{S}O} \boldsymbol{v}$.

'Only if.' Let $\boldsymbol{u}, \boldsymbol{v} \in \mathbb{R}^{\mathbb{N}}$ and suppose $\boldsymbol{u} \sim^{\mathcal{S}O} \boldsymbol{v}$. From (4.7), there exist $\boldsymbol{P}, \boldsymbol{Q} \in \mathcal{S}$ such that $\boldsymbol{Pu} \succsim^{O} \boldsymbol{Qv}$. If $\boldsymbol{Pu} \succ^{O} \boldsymbol{Qv}$, then from (4.8a), we obtain $\boldsymbol{u} \succ^{\mathcal{S}O} \boldsymbol{v}$, a contradiction. Thus, $\boldsymbol{Pu} \sim^O \boldsymbol{Qv}$ must hold. From Lemma 3.8 (ii) and (4.6) in the proof of Lemma 4.2, $\boldsymbol{Pu} \sim^O \boldsymbol{Qv}$ implies $\boldsymbol{Q'Pu} \sim^O \boldsymbol{Q'Qv}$. Letting $\boldsymbol{R} = \boldsymbol{Q'P}$, we obtain $\boldsymbol{Ru} \sim^O \boldsymbol{v}$ and $\boldsymbol{R} \in \mathcal{S}$. ■

Since $\boldsymbol{I} \in \mathcal{S}$, the overtaking criterion $\succsim^O$ associated with an independent sequence $(\succsim^n)_{n\in\mathbb{N}}$ of finite-horizon Paretian and anonymous orderings is a subrelation of the $\mathcal{S}$-anonymous overtaking criterion associated with $(\succsim^n)_{n\in\mathbb{N}}$.

Now we move on to another extension method. Given an independent sequence $(\succsim^n)_{n\in\mathbb{N}}$ of finite-horizon Paretian and anonymous orderings, the *fixed-step overtaking criterion* associated with $(\succsim^n)_{n\in\mathbb{N}}$ is defined as the following binary relation $\succsim^{FO}$ on $\mathbb{R}^{\mathbb{N}}$. For any $\boldsymbol{u}, \boldsymbol{v} \in \mathbb{R}^{\mathbb{N}}$,

$$\boldsymbol{u} \succ^{FO} \boldsymbol{v} \Leftrightarrow \text{there exists } k \in \mathbb{N} \text{ such that } \boldsymbol{u}^{-nk} \succ^{nk} \boldsymbol{v}^{-nk} \text{ for all } n \in \mathbb{N}, \tag{4.9a}$$

$$\boldsymbol{u} \sim^{FO} \boldsymbol{v} \Leftrightarrow \text{there exists } k \in \mathbb{N} \text{ such that } \boldsymbol{u}^{-nk} \sim^{nk} \boldsymbol{v}^{-nk} \text{ for all } n \in \mathbb{N}. \tag{4.9b}$$

Note that $\succsim^{FO}$ is a finitely complete social welfare quasi-ordering.

The next lemma shows that $\succsim^{SO}$ associated with an independent sequence $(\succsim^n)_{n\in\mathbb{N}}$ of finite-horizon Paretian and anonymous orderings is a subrelation of $\succsim^{FO}$ associated with $(\succsim^n)_{n\in\mathbb{N}}$. Further, their asymmetric parts coincide with each other. This result is based on Lemma 3 of Kamaga and Kojima (2010).

**Lemma 4.4** *Let $(\succsim^n)_{n\in\mathbb{N}}$ be an independent sequence of finite-horizon Paretian and anonymous orderings. Then, $\succ^{SO} = \succ^{FO}$ and $\sim^{SO} \subseteq \sim^{FO}$.*

***Proof*** We begin by showing $\succ^{FO} \subseteq \succ^{SO}$. Let $\boldsymbol{u}, \boldsymbol{v} \in \mathbb{R}^{\mathbb{N}}$ and suppose $\boldsymbol{u} \succ^{FO} \boldsymbol{v}$. From (4.9a), there exists $s \in \mathbb{N}$ such that $\boldsymbol{u}^{-ns} \succ^{ns} \boldsymbol{v}^{-ns}$ for all $n \in \mathbb{N}$. Let $\boldsymbol{P}, \boldsymbol{Q} \in \mathcal{S}$ such that, for all $n \in \mathbb{N}$, $\boldsymbol{P}(ns)$ and $\boldsymbol{Q}(ns)$ are finite-dimensional permutation matrices,

$$(Pu)_{(n-1)s+1} \geq (Pu)_{(n-1)s+2} \geq \cdots \geq (Pu)_{ns}$$

and

$$(Qv)_{(n-1)s+1} \leq (Qv)_{(n-1)s+2} \leq \cdots \leq (Qv)_{ns}$$

Note that for all $n \in \mathbb{N}$,

$$(Pu)_{(n-1)s+1} - (Qv)_{(n-1)s+1} \geq (Pu)_{(n-1)s+2} - (Qv)_{(n-1)s+2} \geq \cdots \geq (Pu)_{ns} - (Qv)_{ns}.$$

Since $\succsim^n$ is anonymous and transitive for all $n \in \mathbb{N}$, $(\boldsymbol{Px})^{-nk} \succ^{nk} (\boldsymbol{Py})^{-nk}$ for all $n \in \mathbb{N}$. Thus, applying the same argument as the proof of Theorem 3.11, we obtain that $(\boldsymbol{Pu})^{-n} \succ^n (\boldsymbol{Qv})^{-n}$ for all $n \in \mathbb{N}$. From (3.6a), $\boldsymbol{Pu} \succ^O \boldsymbol{Qv}$ follows. By (4.8a), we obtain $\boldsymbol{u} \succ^{SO} \boldsymbol{v}$.

Next, we show $\succ^{SO} \subseteq \succ^{FO}$. Let $\boldsymbol{u}, \boldsymbol{v} \in \mathbb{R}^{\mathbb{N}}$ and suppose $\boldsymbol{u} \succ^{SO} \boldsymbol{v}$. By (4.8a), there exist $\boldsymbol{P}, \boldsymbol{Q} \in \mathcal{S}$ such that $\boldsymbol{Pu} \succ^O \boldsymbol{Qv}$. Since $\boldsymbol{P}, \boldsymbol{Q} \in \mathcal{S}$, there exists $p, q \in \mathbb{N}$ such that $\boldsymbol{P}(np)$ and $\boldsymbol{Q}(nq)$ are permutation matrices for each $n \in \mathbb{N}$. Further, since

$\boldsymbol{Pu} \succ^{O} \boldsymbol{Qv}$, there exists $\bar{n} \in \mathbb{N}$ such that $\boldsymbol{Pu}^{-n} \succ^{n} \boldsymbol{Qv}^{-n}$ for all $n \geq \bar{n}$. Define $k \in \mathbb{N}$ by $k = p \cdot q \cdot \bar{n}$. Since $\succsim^{n}$ is anonymous for each $n \in \mathbb{N}$, we obtain $\boldsymbol{Pu}^{-nk} \sim^{nk} \boldsymbol{u}^{-nk}$ and $\boldsymbol{Qv}^{-nk} \sim^{nk} \boldsymbol{v}^{-nk}$ for all $n \in \mathbb{N}$. Since $\succsim^{n}$ is transitive for each $n \in \mathbb{N}$, it follows that $\boldsymbol{u}^{-nk} \succ^{nk} \boldsymbol{v}^{-nk}$ for all $n \in \mathbb{N}$. By (4.9a), we obtain $\boldsymbol{u} \succ^{FO} \boldsymbol{v}$. Using the identity matrix $\boldsymbol{I}$ instead of $\boldsymbol{Q}$, the proof that $\sim^{\mathcal{S}O} \subseteq \sim^{FO}$ is analogous. ■

As we will see in the next subsection, the set inclusion between the symmetric parts, $\sim^{\mathcal{S}O}$ and $\sim^{FO}$, may become equality depending on the choice of a specific sequence $(\succsim^{n})_{n\in\mathbb{N}}$ of finite-horizon Paretian and anonymous orderings. Thus, for some specific sequences of finite-horizon Paretian and anonymous orderings, the associated criteria $\succsim^{\mathcal{S}O}$ and $\succsim^{FO}$ coincide with each other.

Using Lemma 4.4, it can be shown that the $\mathcal{S}$-anonymous overtaking criterion is a finitely complete social welfare quasi-ordering. We state the following lemma.

**Lemma 4.5** *Let $(\succsim^{n})_{n\in\mathbb{N}}$ be an independent sequence of finite-horizon Paretian and anonymous orderings, and suppose that $\succsim^{\mathcal{S}O}$ is associated with $(\succsim^{n})_{n\in\mathbb{N}}$. Then, $\succsim^{\mathcal{S}O}$ is a finitely complete social welfare quasi-ordering.*

***Proof*** Since $\boldsymbol{I} \in \mathcal{S}$ and $\mathcal{F} \subset \mathcal{S}$, it follows from Lemma 3.8 (i) that $\succsim^{\mathcal{S}O}$ is reflexive and finitely complete. To show that $\succsim^{\mathcal{S}O}$ is transitive, let $\boldsymbol{u}, \boldsymbol{v}, \boldsymbol{w} \in \mathbb{R}^{\mathbb{N}}$ and suppose that $\boldsymbol{u} \succsim^{\mathcal{S}O} \boldsymbol{v}$ and $\boldsymbol{v} \succsim^{\mathcal{S}O} \boldsymbol{w}$. From Lemma 4.4, if $\boldsymbol{u} \succ^{\mathcal{S}O} \boldsymbol{v}$ and $\boldsymbol{v} \succ^{\mathcal{S}O} \boldsymbol{w}$, then $\boldsymbol{u} \succ^{\mathcal{S}O} \boldsymbol{w}$ since $\succsim^{FO}$ is transitive. We suppose $\boldsymbol{u} \succ^{\mathcal{S}O} \boldsymbol{v}$ and $\boldsymbol{v} \sim^{\mathcal{S}O} \boldsymbol{w}$. From Lemma 4.3, there exist $\boldsymbol{P}, \boldsymbol{Q}, \boldsymbol{R} \in \mathcal{S}$ such that $\boldsymbol{Pu} \succ^{O} \boldsymbol{Qv}$ and $\boldsymbol{Rv} \sim^{O} \boldsymbol{w}$. Let $\boldsymbol{S} = \boldsymbol{QR}' \in \mathcal{S}$. Then, from Lemma 3.8 (ii) and (4.6) in the proof of Lemma 4.2, $\boldsymbol{Rv} \sim^{O} \boldsymbol{w}$ implies $\boldsymbol{Qv} \sim^{O} \boldsymbol{Sw}$. By Lemma 3.8, $\succsim^{O}$ is transitive. Thus, we obtain $\boldsymbol{Pu} \succ^{O} \boldsymbol{Sw}$. Hence, from (4.8a), $\boldsymbol{u} \succ^{\mathcal{S}O} \boldsymbol{w}$ follows. Analogously, it can be shown that $\boldsymbol{u} \sim^{\mathcal{S}O} \boldsymbol{v}$ and $\boldsymbol{v} \succ^{\mathcal{S}O} \boldsymbol{w}$ imply $\boldsymbol{u} \succ^{\mathcal{S}O} \boldsymbol{w}$ and that $\boldsymbol{u} \sim^{\mathcal{S}O} \boldsymbol{v}$ and $\boldsymbol{v} \sim^{\mathcal{S}O} \boldsymbol{w}$ imply $\boldsymbol{u} \sim^{\mathcal{S}O} \boldsymbol{w}$; we omit its proof. ■

We now present characterizations of the $\mathcal{S}$-anonymous overtaking criterion $\succsim^{\mathcal{S}O}$ associated with an independent sequence $(\succsim^{n})_{n\in\mathbb{N}}$ of finite-horizon Paretian and anonymous orderings. The following theorem is a restatement of the result of Asheim and Banerjee (2010) that was established using a proliferating sequence $(\succsim^{n})_{n\in\mathbb{N}}$ of Paretian and anonymous orderings and a slightly stronger consistency axiom. The theorem shows that adding $\mathcal{S}$-anonymity to the set of axioms in Theorem 3.11 gives us a characterization of $\succsim^{\mathcal{S}O}$.

**Theorem 4.12** *Let $(\succsim^{n})_{n\in\mathbb{N}}$ be an independent sequence of finite-horizon Paretian and anonymous orderings. A social welfare quasi-ordering $\succsim$ on $\mathbb{R}^{\mathbb{N}}$ is an extension of $(\succsim^{n})_{n\in\mathbb{N}}$ and satisfies $\mathcal{S}$-anonymity and weak preference consistency if and only if $\succsim^{\mathcal{S}O}$ associated with $(\succsim^{n})_{n\in\mathbb{N}}$ is a subrelation of $\succsim$.*

***Proof*** 'If.' Since $\succsim^{O}$ assciated with $(\succsim^{n})_{n\in\mathbb{N}}$ is a subrelation of $\succsim^{\mathcal{S}O}$, it follows from Theorem 3.11 that $\succsim$ is an extension of $(\succsim^{n})_{n\in\mathbb{N}}$ and satisfies weak preference consistency. From (4.8b), $\succsim^{\mathcal{S}O}$ satisfies $\mathcal{S}$-anonymity.

'Only if.' Since $\mathcal{F} \subset \mathcal{S}$, $\mathcal{S}$-anonymity implies finite anonymity. Thus, from Theorem 3.11, $\succsim^{O}$ associated with $(\succsim^{n})_{n\in\mathbb{N}}$ is a subrelation of $\succsim$. To show that $\succsim^{\mathcal{S}O}$

associated with $(\succsim^n)_{n\in\mathbb{N}}$ is a subrelation of $\succsim$, let $\boldsymbol{u}, \boldsymbol{v} \in \mathbb{R}^{\mathbb{N}}$ and suppose $\boldsymbol{u} \succ^{SO} \boldsymbol{v}$. From (4.8a), there exist $\boldsymbol{P}, \boldsymbol{Q} \in \mathcal{S}$ such that $\boldsymbol{Pu} \succ^{O} \boldsymbol{Qv}$. Since $\succsim^O$ is a subrelation of $\succsim$, $\boldsymbol{Pu} \succ \boldsymbol{Qv}$ follows. Since $\succsim$ satisfies $\mathcal{S}$-anonymity, we obtain $\boldsymbol{Pu} \sim \boldsymbol{u}$ and $\boldsymbol{Qv} \sim \boldsymbol{v}$. By the transitivity of $\succsim$, $\boldsymbol{u} \succ \boldsymbol{v}$ follows. The proof that $\boldsymbol{u} \sim^{SO} \boldsymbol{v}$ implies $\boldsymbol{u} \sim \boldsymbol{v}$ is analogous. ■

Next, assuming the finite completeness of a social welfare quasi-ordering, we present an axiomatization of an $\mathcal{S}$-anonymous overtaking criterion using $\mathcal{S}$-anonymity. The theorem shows the consequence of strengthening finite anonymity to $\mathcal{S}$-anonymity in Theorem 3.12.

**Theorem 4.13** *A finitely complete social welfare quasi-ordering $\succsim$ on $\mathbb{R}^{\mathbb{N}}$ satisfies strong Pareto, $\mathcal{S}$-anonymity, separable present, and weak preference consistency if and only if there exists an independent sequence $(\succsim^n)_{n\in\mathbb{N}}$ of finite-horizon Paretian and anonymous orderings such that $\succsim^{SO}$ associated with $(\succsim^n)_{n\in\mathbb{N}}$ is a subrelation of $\succsim$.*

***Proof*** 'If.' Since $\succsim^O$ assciated with $(\succsim^n)_{n\in\mathbb{N}}$ is a subrelation of $\succsim^{SO}$, it follows from Theorem 3.12 that $\succsim$ satisfies strong Pareto, separable present and weak preference consistency. From Theorem 4.12, $\succsim$ satisfies $\mathcal{S}$-anonymity.

'Only if.' Since $\mathcal{S}$-anonymity implies finite anonymity, it follows from Theorem 3.12 that there exists an independent sequence $(\succsim^n)_{n\in\mathbb{N}}$ of finite-horizon Paretian and anonymous orderings such that $\succsim^O$ associated with $(\succsim^n)_{n\in\mathbb{N}}$ is a subrelation of $\succsim$. From Theorem 3.11, $\succsim$ is an extension of $(\succsim^n)_{n\in\mathbb{N}}$. From Theorem 4.12, $\succsim^{SO}$ associated with $(\succsim^n)_{n\in\mathbb{N}}$ is a subrelation of $\succsim$. ■

We present a characterization of a fixed-step overtaking criterion using the following consistency axiom. It is a fixed-step periodic analogue of weak preference consistency defined for indifference relations. It asserts that the evaluation of two streams must be consistent with indifference relations that are periodically obtained when their tails are replaced with a common one. This axiom was used by Kamaga and Kojima (2010). See also Asheim and Banerjee (2010) for a similar axiom.

**Fixed-step Indifference Consistency**: For all $\boldsymbol{u}, \boldsymbol{v} \in \mathbb{R}^{\mathbb{N}}$, if there exists $k \in \mathbb{N}$ such that $(\boldsymbol{u}^{-kn}, \boldsymbol{w}^{-kn}) \sim (\boldsymbol{v}^{-kn}, \boldsymbol{w}^{-kn})$ for all $n \in \mathbb{N}$ and for all $\boldsymbol{w} \in \mathbb{R}^{\mathbb{N}}$, then $\boldsymbol{u} \sim \boldsymbol{v}$.

In the next theorem, we present a characterization of the fixed-step overtaking criterion associated with an independent sequence of finite-horizon Paretian and anonymous orderings. It is based on the result of Kamaga and Kojima (2010) and is also a restatement of the result of Asheim and Banerjee (2010) that was established in terms of a proliferating sequence of finite-horizon Paretian and anonymous orderings using slightly stronger consistency axioms.

**Theorem 4.14** *Let $(\succsim^n)_{n\in\mathbb{N}}$ be an independent sequence of finite-horizon Paretian and anonymous orderings. A social welfare quasi-ordering $\succsim$ on $\mathbb{R}^{\mathbb{N}}$ is an extension of $(\succsim^n)_{n\in\mathbb{N}}$ and satisfies weak preference consistency and fixed-step indifference consistency if and only if $\succsim^{FO}$ associated with $(\succsim^n)_{n\in\mathbb{N}}$ is a subrelation of $\succsim$.*

***Proof*** 'If.' From Lemma 4.4, $\succsim^{SO}$ associated with $(\succsim^n)_{n\in\mathbb{N}}$ is a subrelation of $\succsim^{FO}$. Thus, by Theorem 4.12, $\succsim$ is an extension of $(\succsim^n)_{n\in\mathbb{N}}$ and satisfies weak preference consistency. To show that $\succsim$ satisfies fixed-step indifference consistency, let $\boldsymbol{u}, \boldsymbol{v} \in \mathbb{R}^{\mathbb{N}}$ and $k \in \mathbb{N}$. Suppose that $(\boldsymbol{u}^{-kn}, \boldsymbol{w}^{-kn}) \sim (\boldsymbol{v}^{-kn}, \boldsymbol{w}^{-kn})$ for all $n \in \mathbb{N}$ and for all $\boldsymbol{w} \in \mathbb{R}^{\mathbb{N}}$. Since $\succsim$ is an extension of $(\succsim^n)_{n\in\mathbb{N}}$, it follows that $\boldsymbol{u}^{-kn} \sim^{kn} \boldsymbol{v}^{-kn}$ for all $n \in \mathbb{N}$. From (4.9b), $\boldsymbol{u} \sim^{FO} \boldsymbol{v}$ follows. Since $\succsim^{FO}$ is a subrelation of $\succsim$, we obtain $\boldsymbol{u} \sim \boldsymbol{v}$.

'Only if.' Let $\boldsymbol{u}, \boldsymbol{v} \in \mathbb{R}^{\mathbb{N}}$. Note that $\succsim$ satisfies $\mathcal{S}$-anonymity because $\succsim$ is an extension of $(\succsim^n)_{n\in\mathbb{N}}$ and satisfies fixed-step indifference consistency and $\succsim^n$ is anonymous for all $n \in \mathbb{N}$. Thus, from Lemma 4.4, it suffices to show that $\boldsymbol{u} \sim^{FO} \boldsymbol{v}$ implies $\boldsymbol{u} \sim \boldsymbol{v}$. Suppose $\boldsymbol{u} \sim^{FO} \boldsymbol{v}$. From (4.9b), there exists $k \in \mathbb{N}$ such that $\boldsymbol{u}^{-kn} \sim^{kn} \boldsymbol{v}^{-kn}$ for all $n \in \mathbb{N}$. Since $\succsim$ is an extension of $(\succsim^n)_{n\in\mathbb{N}}$, it follows that $(\boldsymbol{u}^{-kn}, \boldsymbol{w}^{-kn}) \sim (\boldsymbol{v}^{-kn}, \boldsymbol{w}^{-kn})$ for all $n \in \mathbb{N}$ and for all $\boldsymbol{w} \in \mathbb{R}^{\mathbb{N}}$. By fixed-step indifference consistency, we obtain $\boldsymbol{u} \sim \boldsymbol{v}$. ■

Assuming that a social welfare quasi-ordering is finitely complete, an axiomatization of the fixed-step overtaking criterion is given by adding fixed-step indifference consistency to the set of axioms in Theorem 3.12 that characterizes the overtaking criterion.

**Theorem 4.15** *A finitely complete social welfare quasi-ordering $\succsim$ on $\mathbb{R}^{\mathbb{N}}$ satisfies strong Pareto, finite anonymity, separable present, weak preference consistency, and fixed-step indifference consistency if and only if there exists an independent sequence $(\succsim^n)_{n\in\mathbb{N}}$ of finite-horizon Paretian and anonymous orderings such that $\succsim^{FO}$ associated with $(\succsim^n)_{n\in\mathbb{N}}$ is a subrelation of $\succsim$.*

***Proof*** 'If.' Since $\succsim^{O}$ associated with $(\succsim^n)_{n\in\mathbb{N}}$ is a subrelation of $\succsim^{FO}$, it follows from Theorem 3.12 that $\succsim$ satisfies strong Pareto, finite anonymity, separable present and weak preference consistency. From Theorem 4.14, $\succsim$ satisfies fixed-step indifference consistency.

'Only if.' From Theorem 3.12, there exists an independent sequence $(\succsim^n)_{n\in\mathbb{N}}$ of finite-horizon Paretian and anonymous orderings such that $\succsim^{O}$ associated with $(\succsim^n)_{n\in\mathbb{N}}$ is a subrelation of $\succsim$. From Theorem 3.11, $\succsim$ is an extension of $(\succsim^n)_{n\in\mathbb{N}}$. From Theorem 4.14, $\succsim^{FO}$ associated with $(\succsim^n)_{n\in\mathbb{N}}$ is a subrelation of $\succsim$. ■

### *4.5.2 Fixed-Step Anonymous Overtaking Criteria Associated with Specific Sequences*

Combining the axiomatizations of the specific forms of overtaking criteria in Chap. 3 with the general characterization results in the previous subsection, we provide axiomatizations of the $\mathcal{S}$-anonymous overtaking criteria and the fixed-step overtaking criteria associated with specific sequences of finite-horizon orderings. We omit the proofs of the axiomatization results because they are straightforward from the general results.

We begin with the following lemma, which shows that the symmetric parts of $\succsim^{SO}$ and $\succsim^{FO}$ coincide with each other if $(\succsim^n)_{n\in\mathbb{N}}$ is a sequence of finite-horizon leximin orderings or utilitarianism-first and leximin-second orderings.

**Lemma 4.6** *If* $(\succsim^n)_{n\in\mathbb{N}} = (\succsim^n_L)$ *or* $(\succsim^n)_{n\in\mathbb{N}} = (\succsim^n_{UL})_{n\in\mathbb{N}}$, *then* $\sim^{FO} \subseteq \sim^{SO}$.

***Proof*** Let $\boldsymbol{u}, \boldsymbol{v} \in \mathbb{R}^{\mathbb{N}}$ with $\boldsymbol{u} \sim^{FO} \boldsymbol{v}$ and suppose $\succsim^{FO}$ is associated with $(\succsim^n)_{n\in\mathbb{N}} = (\succsim^n_L)$ or $(\succsim^n)_{n\in\mathbb{N}} = (\succsim^n_{UL})_{n\in\mathbb{N}}$. From (4.9b), in either case, there exists $k \in \mathbb{N}$ such that $\boldsymbol{u}^{-nk} \sim^{nk} \boldsymbol{v}^{-nk}$ for all $n \in \mathbb{N}$ since $\sim^n_L = \sim^n_{UL}$ for all $n \in \mathbb{N}$. Thus, there exists $\boldsymbol{P} \in \mathcal{S}$ such that $\boldsymbol{P}\boldsymbol{u} = \boldsymbol{v}$. From (4.8b), $\boldsymbol{u} \sim^{SO} \boldsymbol{v}$ follows. ■

From Lemmas 4.4 and 4.6, axiomatizing the $\mathcal{S}$-anonymous overtaking criteria $\succsim^{SO}_L$ and $\succsim^{SO}_{UL}$ that are associated with the sequences $(\succsim^n_L)_{n\in\mathbb{N}}$ and $(\succsim^n_{UL})_{n\in\mathbb{N}}$ of finite-horizon leximin orderings and utilitarianism-first and leximin-second orderings, respectively, means that we establish axiomatizations of the fixed-step overtaking criteria $\succsim^{FO}_L$ and $\succsim^{FO}_{UL}$ associated with $(\succsim^n_L)_{n\in\mathbb{N}}$ and $(\succsim^n_{UL})_{n\in\mathbb{N}}$, and vice versa.

Contrary to these coincidences, if $(\succsim^n)_{n\in\mathbb{N}}$ is the sequence $(\succsim^n_{U,g})_{n\in\mathbb{N}}$ of finite-horizon generalized utilitarian orderings associated with $g \in G$ (including the special case of $(\succsim^n_U)_{n\in\mathbb{N}}$), the associated $\succsim^{SO}$ and $\succsim^{FO}$ do not coincide. For instance, let $g \in G$ and consider

$$\boldsymbol{u} = \left(g^{-1}(1), g^{-1}(\tfrac{1}{2}), g^{-1}(1), g^{-1}(\tfrac{1}{2}), \ldots\right) \text{ and } \boldsymbol{v} = \left(g^{-1}(\tfrac{3}{4}), g^{-1}(\tfrac{3}{4}), g^{-1}(\tfrac{3}{4}), \ldots\right).$$

From (4.9b), $\boldsymbol{u} \sim^{FO} \boldsymbol{v}$ follows, while these streams are non-comparable according to $\succsim^{SO}$. Thus, $\sim^{SO} \subset \sim^{FO}$.

In the following theorems, we present axiomatizations of the *$\mathcal{S}$-anonymous overtaking criterion* $\succsim^{SO}_U$ associated with the sequence $(\succsim^n_U)_{n\in\mathbb{N}}$ of finite-horizon *utilitarian* orderings. These follow from Theorems 3.13 and 3.14. The equivalence between part (i) and (iii) in the first theorem was presented by Kamaga and Kojima (2010).

**Theorem 4.16** *Let $\succsim$ be a social welfare quasi-ordering on $\mathbb{R}^{\mathbb{N}}$. The following three statements are equivalent:*

*(i)* $\succsim^{SO}_U$ *is a subrelation of* $\succsim$,
*(ii)* $\succsim$ *satisfies strong Pareto, $\mathcal{S}$-anonymity, incremental equity, and weak preference consistency,*
*(iii)* $\succsim$ *satisfies strong Pareto, $\mathcal{S}$-anonymity, translation-scale invariance, and weak preference consistency.*

**Theorem 4.17** *A finitely complete social welfare quasi-ordering $\succsim$ on $\mathbb{R}^{\mathbb{N}}$ satisfies strong Pareto, $\mathcal{S}$-anonymity, separable present, cardinal full comparability, restricted continuity, and weak preference consistency if and only if $\succsim^{SO}_U$ is a subrelation of $\succsim$.*

Using Theorem 3.15, we obtain the following axiomatization of the *$\mathcal{S}$-anonymous overtaking criterion* $\succsim^{SO}_{U,g}$ associated with the sequence $(\succsim^n_{U,g})_{n\in\mathbb{N}}$ of finite-horizon *generalized utilitarian* orderings associated with $g \in G$.

**Theorem 4.18** *A finitely complete social welfare quasi-ordering $\succsim$ on $\mathbb{R}^{\mathbb{N}}$ satisfies strong Pareto, $\mathcal{S}$-anonymity, separable present, restricted continuity, and weak preference consistency if and only if there exists $g \in G$ such that $\succsim_{U,g}^{SO}$ is a subrelation of $\succsim$.*

The *$\mathcal{S}$-anonymous overtaking criterion* $\succsim_L^{SO}$ associated with the sequence $(\succsim_L^n)_{n\in\mathbb{N}}$ of finite-horizon *leximin* orderings is obtained as follows. This result was provided by Kamaga and Kojima (2010).

**Theorem 4.19** (Kamaga and Kojima 2010) *A social welfare quasi-ordering $\succsim$ on $\mathbb{R}^{\mathbb{N}}$ satisfies strong Pareto, $\mathcal{S}$-anonymity, Hammond equity, and weak preference consistency if and only if $\succsim_L^{SO}$ is a subrelation of $\succsim$.*

From Theorems 3.17 and 3.18, we obtain the following joint axiomatizations involving the *$\mathcal{S}$-anonymous overtaking criterion* $\succsim_{UL}^{SO}$ associated with the sequence $(\succsim_{UL}^n)_{n\in\mathbb{N}}$ of finite-horizon *utilitarianism-first and leximin-second* orderings.

**Theorem 4.20** *(i) A finitely complete social welfare quasi-ordering $\succsim$ on $\mathbb{R}^{\mathbb{N}}$ satisfies strong Pareto, $\mathcal{S}$-anonymity, the weak Pigou–Dalton principle, the composite transfer principle, separable present, cardinal full comparability, and weak preference consistency if and only if any one of $\succsim_U^{SO}$, $\succsim_{UL}^{SO}$, and $\succsim_L^{SO}$ is a subrelation of $\succsim$.*

*(ii) A finitely complete social welfare quasi-ordering $\succsim$ on $\mathbb{R}^{\mathbb{N}}$ satisfies strong Pareto, $\mathcal{S}$-anonymity, the strong Pigou–Dalton principle, the composite transfer principle, separable present, cardinal full comparability, and weak preference consistency if and only if either $\succsim_{UL}^{SO}$ or $\succsim_L^{SO}$ is a subrelation of $\succsim$.*

Next, we provide axiomatizations of specific forms of the fixed-step overtaking criteria. The following theorems present axiomatizations of the *fixed-step overtaking criterion* $\succsim_U^{FO}$ associated with the sequence $(\succsim_U^n)_{n\in\mathbb{N}}$ of finite-horizon *utilitarian* orderings. The equivalence between part (i) and (iii) in the first theorem was presented by Kamaga and Kojima (2010).

**Theorem 4.21** *Let $\succsim$ be a social welfare quasi-ordering on $\mathbb{R}^{\mathbb{N}}$. The following three statements are equivalent:*

*(i) $\succsim_U^{FO}$ is a subrelation of $\succsim$,*

*(ii) $\succsim$ satisfies strong Pareto, incremental equity, weak preference consistency, and fixed-step indifference consistency,*

*(iii) $\succsim$ satisfies strong Pareto, finite anonymity, translation-scale invariance, weak preference consistency, and fixed-step indifference consistency.*

**Theorem 4.22** *A finitely complete social welfare quasi-ordering $\succsim$ on $\mathbb{R}^{\mathbb{N}}$ satisfies strong Pareto, finite anonymity, separable present, cardinal full comparability, restricted continuity, weak preference consistency, and fixed-step indifference consistency if and only if $\succsim_U^{FO}$ is a subrelation of $\succsim$.*

The following theorem axiomatizes the *fixed-step overtaking criterion* $\succsim_{U,g}^{FO}$ that is associated with the sequence $(\succsim_{U,g}^{n})_{n\in\mathbb{N}}$ of finite-horizon *generalized utilitarian* orderings associated with $g \in G$.

**Theorem 4.23** *A finitely complete social welfare quasi-ordering* $\succsim$ *on* $\mathbb{R}^{\mathbb{N}}$ *satisfies strong Pareto, finite anonymity, separable present, restricted continuity, weak preference consistency, and fixed-step indifference consistency if and only if there exists* $g \in G$ *such that* $\succsim_{U,g}^{FO}$ *is a subrelation of* $\succsim$.

The *fixed-step overtaking criterion* $\succsim_{L}^{FO}$ associated with the sequence $(\succsim_{L}^{n})_{n\in\mathbb{N}}$ of finite-horizon *leximin* orderings is axiomatized as follows. This result was presented by Kamaga and Kojima (2010).

**Theorem 4.24** (Kamaga and Kojima 2010) *A social welfare quasi-ordering* $\succsim$ *on* $\mathbb{R}^{\mathbb{N}}$ *satisfies strong Pareto, finite anonymity, Hammond equity, weak preference consistency, and fixed-step indifference consistency if and only if* $\succsim_{L}^{FO}$ *is a subrelation of* $\succsim$.

Finally, the following theorem presents joint characterizations involving the *fixed-step overtaking criterion* $\succsim_{UL}^{FO}$ associated with the sequence $(\succsim_{UL}^{n})_{n\in\mathbb{N}}$ of finite-horizon *utilitarianism-first and leximin-second* orderings.

**Theorem 4.25** *(i) A finitely complete social welfare quasi-ordering* $\succsim$ *on* $\mathbb{R}^{\mathbb{N}}$ *satisfies strong Pareto, finite anonymity, the weak Pigou–Dalton principle, the composite transfer principle, separable present, cardinal full comparability, weak preference consistency, and fixed-step indifference consistency if and only if any one of* $\succsim_{U}^{FO}$, $\succsim_{UL}^{FO}$, *and* $\succsim_{L}^{FO}$ *is a subrelation of* $\succsim$.

*(ii) A finitely complete social welfare quasi-ordering* $\succsim$ *on* $\mathbb{R}^{\mathbb{N}}$ *satisfies strong Pareto, finite anonymity, the strong Pigou–Dalton principle, the composite transfer principle, separable present, cardinal full comparability, weak preference consistency, and fixed-step indifference consistency if and only if either* $\succsim_{UL}^{FO}$ *or* $\succsim_{L}^{FO}$ *is a subrelation of* $\succsim$.

## 4.6 Impossibility of a Fixed-Step Anonymous Extension of the Catching-Up Criterion

In this section, we examine the impossibility of a fixed-step anonymous extensions of the catching-up criterion with a focus on Pareto axioms. Banerjee (2006) was the first to point out that any extension of the utilitarian catching-up social welfare quasi-ordering $\succsim_{U}^{C}$ violates $\mathcal{S}$-anonymity. Kamaga and Kojima (2010) generalize this impossibility by showing that there is no social welfare quasi-ordering on $D \subseteq \mathbb{R}^{\mathbb{N}}$ that satisfies weak dominance, $\mathcal{S}$-anonymity, and strong preference consistency as long as $D$ includes a binary domain (e.g., $\{0, 1\}^{\mathbb{N}}$); see Chap. 3 for the definition of strong preference consistency. Weak dominance is a Pareto axiom that was introduced by Basu and Mitra (2003) that is weaker than the strong Pareto principle.

**Weak Dominance**: For all $\boldsymbol{u}, \boldsymbol{v} \in \mathbb{R}^{\mathbb{N}}$, if there exists $i \in \mathbb{N}$ such that $u_i > v_i$ and $u_j = v_j$ for all $j \in \mathbb{N} \setminus \{i\}$, then $\boldsymbol{u} \succ \boldsymbol{v}$.

The above mentioned impossibility result is stated as follows. For a proof, see Kamaga and Kojima (2010, Proposition 3).

**Theorem 4.26** (Kamaga and Kojima 2010) *Let $D \supseteq \{a, b\}^{\mathbb{N}}$ with $a, b \in \mathbb{R}$ and $a > b$. There is no social welfare quasi-ordering on $D$ that satisfies weak dominance, $\mathcal{S}$-anonymity, and strong preference consistency.*

Recall that the catching-up criterion $\succsim^C$ associated with an independent sequence $(\succsim^n)_{n\in\mathbb{N}}$ of finite-horizon Paretian and anonymous orderings satisfies strong Pareto and strong preference consistency; see Theorem 3.20 in Chap. 3. Since strong Pareto implies weak dominance, it follows from Theorem 4.26 that there is no $\mathcal{S}$-anonymous extension of $\succsim^C$ associated with $(\succsim^n)_{n\in\mathbb{N}}$. Specifically, any social welfare quasi-ordering that includes $\succsim^C$ associated with $(\succsim^n)_{n\in\mathbb{N}}$ as a subrelation violates $\mathcal{S}$-anonymity.

While strong Pareto is incompatible with $\mathcal{S}$-anonymity and strong preference consistency, as Kamaga and Kojima (2010) showed, the weak Pareto axiom is compatible with $\mathcal{S}$-anonymity and strong preference consistency.

**Weak Pareto**: For all $\boldsymbol{u}, \boldsymbol{v} \in \mathbb{R}^{\mathbb{N}}$, if $\boldsymbol{u} \gg \boldsymbol{v}$, then $\boldsymbol{u} \succ \boldsymbol{v}$.

The possibility result is stated as follows. For a proof, see Kamaga and Kojima (2010, Proposition 4)

**Theorem 4.27** (Kamaga and Kojima 2010) *There exists a social welfare quasi-ordering on $\mathbb{R}^{\mathbb{N}}$ that satisfies weak Pareto, $\mathcal{S}$-anonymity, and strong preference consistency.*

By Theorems 4.26 and 4.27, not all but some implications of strong Pareto are essential for the impossibility of a fixed-step anonymous extension of a catching-up criterion. To examine what implication of strong Pareto is essential, Kamaga (2013) introduced a generalized Pareto axiom which we call $\mathcal{N}$-Pareto. Given an arbitrary family of non-empty sets of generations $\mathcal{N} \subseteq 2^{\mathbb{N}}\backslash\{\varnothing\}$, the $\mathcal{N}$-Pareto axiom associated with $\mathcal{N}$ asserts that the evaluation must be positively sensitive to utilities of generations in any $N \in \mathcal{N}$.

**$\mathcal{N}$-Pareto**: For all $\boldsymbol{u}, \boldsymbol{v} \in \mathbb{R}^{\mathbb{N}}$ with $\boldsymbol{u} \geq \boldsymbol{v}$, if $\{i \in \mathbb{N} : u_i > v_i\} \in \mathcal{N}$, then $\boldsymbol{u} \succ \boldsymbol{v}$.

By definition, for any subsets $\mathcal{N}, \mathcal{N}' \subseteq 2^{\mathbb{N}}\backslash\{\varnothing\}$, if $\mathcal{N} \subseteq \mathcal{N}'$ then $\mathcal{N}'$-Pareto implies $\mathcal{N}$-Pareto. According to the choice of $\mathcal{N}$, $\mathcal{N}$-Pareto represents various Pareto axioms. First, if $\mathcal{N} = 2^{\mathbb{N}}\backslash\{\varnothing\}$, $\mathcal{N}$-Pareto represents strong Pareto. Second, weak Pareto corresponds to $\mathcal{N}$-Pareto defined by $\mathcal{N} = \{\mathbb{N}\}$. Third, weak dominance is obtained by setting $\mathcal{N} = \{N \in 2^{\mathbb{N}} : |N| = 1\}$. Finally, if $\mathcal{N} = \{N \in 2^{\mathbb{N}} : |N| = \infty\}$, $\mathcal{N}$-Pareto represents *strong monotonicity for infinite generations* proposed by Sakai (2006).[6]

The following theorem, established by Kamaga (2013), presents a characterization of an $\mathcal{N}$-Pareto axiom that is compatible with $\mathcal{S}$-anonymity and strong preference consistency. It shows that $\mathcal{N}$-Pareto defined by a family of sets of more than one generations is compatible with $\mathcal{S}$-anonymity and strong preference consistency.

**Theorem 4.28** (Kamaga 2013) *Let $\mathcal{N} \subseteq 2^{\mathbb{N}} \setminus \{\varnothing\}$. There exists a social welfare quasi-ordering on $\mathbb{R}^{\mathbb{N}}$ that satisfies $\mathcal{N}$-Pareto, $\mathcal{S}$-anonymity, and strong preference consistency if and only if $|N| > 1$ for all $N \in \mathcal{N}$.*

***Proof*** 'If.' Suppose that $|N| > 1$ for all $N \in \mathcal{N}$. Define the binary relation $\succsim$ on $\mathbb{R}^{\mathbb{N}}$ as follows. For all $\boldsymbol{u}, \boldsymbol{v} \in \mathbb{R}^{\mathbb{N}}$,

$$\boldsymbol{u} \succsim \boldsymbol{v} \Leftrightarrow \text{there exists } \boldsymbol{P} \in \mathcal{S} \text{ such that} \begin{cases} \text{(i) } \boldsymbol{Pu} \geq \boldsymbol{v} \text{ and } |\{i \in \mathbb{N} : (\boldsymbol{Pu})_i > v_i\}| > 1 \\ \text{or (ii) } \boldsymbol{Pu} = \boldsymbol{v}. \end{cases} \tag{4.10}$$

It can be verified that $\succsim$ is a social welfare quasi-ordering and that the asymmetric and symmetric parts of $\succsim$ are given as follows. For all $\boldsymbol{u}, \boldsymbol{v} \in \mathbb{R}^{\mathbb{N}}$,

$$\boldsymbol{u} \succ \boldsymbol{v} \Leftrightarrow \text{there exists } \boldsymbol{P} \in \mathcal{S} \text{ such that } \boldsymbol{Pu} \geq \boldsymbol{v} \text{ and } |\{i \in \mathbb{N} : (\boldsymbol{Pu})_i > v_i\}| > 1, \tag{4.11}$$

$$\boldsymbol{u} \sim \boldsymbol{v} \Leftrightarrow \text{there exists } \boldsymbol{P} \in \mathcal{S} \text{ such that } \boldsymbol{Pu} = \boldsymbol{v}. \tag{4.12}$$

For the detailed proof, see Kamaga (2013). We show that $\succsim$ satisfies $\mathcal{N}$-Pareto, $\mathcal{S}$-anonymity and strong preference consistency. Since $\boldsymbol{I} \in \mathcal{S}$, it follows from (4.11) that $\succsim$ satisfies $\mathcal{N}$-Pareto. Further, from (4.12), $\succsim$ satisfies $\mathcal{S}$-anonymity. Finally, we show that $\succsim$ satisfies strong preference consistency. We show by mathematical induction that the premise of strong preference consistency is never satisfied by $\succsim$. From (4.11) and (4.12), $(\boldsymbol{u}^{-1}, \boldsymbol{w}^{+1}) \succsim (\boldsymbol{v}^{-1}, \boldsymbol{w}^{+1})$ implies $u_1 = v_1$. Further, for all $n \in \mathbb{N}$, if $\boldsymbol{u}^{-n} = \boldsymbol{v}^{-n}$ and $(\boldsymbol{u}^{-(n+1)}, \boldsymbol{w}^{+(n+1)}) \succsim (\boldsymbol{v}^{-(n+1)}, \boldsymbol{w}^{+(n+1)})$, then $u_{n+1} = v_{n+1}$. Therefore, if $(\boldsymbol{u}^{-n}, \boldsymbol{w}^{+n}) \succsim (\boldsymbol{v}^{-n}, \boldsymbol{w}^{+n})$ for all $n \in \mathbb{N}$, then $\boldsymbol{u} = \boldsymbol{v}$, and thus, from (4.12), it follows that for all $n \in \mathbb{N}$, $(\boldsymbol{u}^{-n}, \boldsymbol{w}^{+n}) \sim (\boldsymbol{v}^{-n}, \boldsymbol{w}^{+n})$. Thus, the premise of strong preference consistency is never satisfied by $\succsim$. Therefore, $\succsim$ satisfies strong preference consistency.

'Only if.' Suppose that there exists a social welfare quasi-ordering $\succsim$ on $\mathbb{R}^{\mathbb{N}}$ that satisfies $\mathcal{N}$-Pareto, $\mathcal{S}$-anonymity and strong preference consistency. By way of contradiction, assume that there exists $n \in \mathbb{N}$ such that $\{n\} \in \mathcal{N}$. We begin by showing that $\succsim$ satisfies weak dominance. Let $\boldsymbol{u}, \boldsymbol{v} \in X$ and suppose that there exists

[6] Strong monotonicity for infinite generations is called the infinite Pareto principle in Crespo et al. (2009).

$n' \in \mathbb{N}$ such that $u_{n'} > v_{n'}$ and $u_i = v_i$ for all $i \in \mathbb{N} \setminus \{n'\}$. Consider $\boldsymbol{w}, \boldsymbol{z} \in X$ such that

$$\begin{cases} w_n = u_{n'}, \; w_{n'} = u_n, \text{ and } w_i = u_i \text{ for all } i \in \mathbb{N} \setminus \{n, n'\}, \\ z_n = v_{n'}, \; z_{n'} = v_n, \text{ and } z_i = v_i \text{ for all } i \in \mathbb{N} \setminus \{n, n'\}. \end{cases}$$

By $\mathcal{N}$-Pareto, we obtain $\boldsymbol{w} \succ \boldsymbol{z}$. From $\mathcal{S}$-anonymity, it follows that $\boldsymbol{u} \sim \boldsymbol{w}$ and $\boldsymbol{z} \sim \boldsymbol{v}$. Since $\succsim$ is transitive, $\boldsymbol{u} \succ \boldsymbol{v}$. Thus, $\succsim$ satisfies weak dominance. However, from Theorem 4.26, this is a contradiction since $\succsim$ satisfies $\mathcal{S}$-anonymity and strong preference consistency. Thus, there is no $n \in \mathbb{N}$ such that $\{n\} \in \mathcal{N}$. This implies that $|N| > 1$ for all $N \in \mathcal{N}$. ∎

From Theorem 4.28, the impossibility of a fixed-step anonymous extension of a catching-up criterion is ascribed to the incompatibility between the three axioms, namely, weak dominance, $\mathcal{S}$-anonymity and strong preference consistency. The strongest Paretian axiom that is compatible with $\mathcal{S}$-anonymity and strong preference consistency is given by $\mathcal{N}$-Pareto defined by $\mathcal{N} = \{N \in 2^{\mathbb{N}} : |N| \geq 2\}$.

## 4.7 Concluding Remarks

An extended anonymity axiom such as fixed-step anonymity is a more plausible representation of the equal treatment of generations than finite anonymity is because it can realize the equal treatment of infinitely many generations. Taking the closure of a set of cyclic permutations that is compatible with a Paretian Suzumura-consistent social welfare relation is shown to be a useful for exploring a constructible group of cyclic permutations.

Although fixed-step anonymity is compatible with a general overtaking criterion, it is incompatible with a general catching-up criterion. Consequently, exploring fixed-step anonymous overtaking criteria associated with sequences of finite-horizon social welfare orderings or quasi-orderings seems to a reasonable way to obtain more comparable social welfare quasi-orderings for infinite utility streams.

The framework we used in this chapter is restrictive because it cannot deal with the infinite-horizon social evaluation of social alternatives that entail the demographic changes across generations. The extension of this framework to the social evaluation problem involving variable population sizes will be addressed in the next chapter.

## References

Adachi, T., Cato, S., & Kamaga, K. (2014). Extended anonymity and Paretian relations on infinite utility streams. *Mathematical Social Sciences*, *72*, 24–32.

Asheim, G. B., & Banerjee, K. (2010). Fixed-step anonymous overtaking and catching-up. *International Journal of Economic Theory*, *6*, 149–165.

Banerjee, K. (2006). On the extension of the utilitarian and Suppes-Sen social welfare relations to infinite utility streams. *Social Choice and Welfare*, *27*, 327–339.
Basu, K., & Mitra, T. (2003). Aggregating infinite utility streams with intergenerational equity: The impossibility of being Paretian. *Econometrica*, *71*, 1557–1563.
Crespo, J. A., Nuñez, C., & Rincón-Zapatero, J. P. (2009). On the impossibility of representing infinite utility streams. *Economic Theory*, *40*, 47–56.
Fleurbaey, M., & Michel, P. (2003). Intertemporal equity and the extension of the Ramsey criterion. *Journal of Mathematical Economics*, *39*, 777–802.
Kamaga, K. (2013). The impossibility of a fixed-step anonymous extension of the catching-up criterion: A re-examination. *Sophia Economic Review*, *58*, 73–85.
Kamaga, K., & Kojima, T. (2009). $\mathcal{Q}$-anonymous social welfare relations on infinite utility streams. *Social Choice and Welfare*, *33*, 405–413.
Kamaga, K., & Kojima, T. (2010). On the leximin and utilitarian overtaking criteria with extended anonymity. *Social Choice and Welfare*, *35*, 377–392.
Lauwers, L. (1997a). Rawlsian equity and generalized utilitarianism with and infinite population. *Economic Theory*, *9*, 143–150.
Lauwers, L. (1997b). Infinite utility: Insisting on strong monotonicity. *Australasian Journal of Philosophy*, *75*, 222–233.
Lauwers, L. (1998). Intertemporal objective functions: Strong Pareto versus anonymity. *Mathematical Social Sciences*, *35*, 37–55.
Lauwers, L. (2012). Intergenerational equity, efficiency, and constructibility. *Economic Theory*, *49*, 227–242.
Mitra, T., & Basu, K. (2007). On the extension of Paretian social welfare quasi-orderings for infinite utility streams with extended anonymity. In J. E. Roemer & K. Suzumura (Eds.), *Intergenerational equity and sustainability*. Palgrave-Macmillan: Basingstoke.
Sakai, T. (2006). Equitable intergenerational preferences on restricted domains. *Social Choice and Welfare*, *27*, 41–54.
Sakai, T. (2010a). Intertemporal equity and an explicit construction of welfare criteria. *Social Choice and Welfare*, *35*, 393–414.
Sakai, T. (2010b). A characterization and an impossibility of finite length anonymity for infinite generations. *Journal of Mathematical Economics*, *46*, 877–883.
Suzumura, K. (1976). Remarks on the theory of collective choice. *Economica*, *43*, 381–390.
van Liedekerke, L. (1995). Should utilitarians be cautious about an infinite future? *Australasian Journal of Philosophy*, *73*, 405–407.

# Chapter 5
# Intergenerational Social Welfare Evaluation with Variable Population Size

**Abstract** This chapter presents an extended framework for social evaluation with variable population size. We establish the welfarism theorem in the extended framework. Then, using the welfarist framework, we will present and axiomatize infinite-horizon extensions of critical-level generalized utilitarianism. The population ethics property of infinite-horizon extensions of critical-level generalized utilitarianism will be discussed.

**Keywords** Variable-population social choice · Welfarism · Critical-level utilitarianism · Population ethics

## 5.1 Introduction

The framework for ranking infinite utility streams has two restrictive aspects when used to deal with complicated intergenerational problems. While some intergenerational problems, such as the prevention of global warming, require a consideration of the conflict of interest within a generation as well as between generations, it cannot take into account the diverse well-being levels among individuals within a generation, nor can it deal with demographic changes across generations. For intergenerational problems where demographic changes across generations matter, such as for the design of a population policy for reversing a declining birthrate, the population size of each generation needs to be considered.

This chapter provides an extended framework that can deal with intergenerational social evaluation with variable population size, which was proposed by Kamaga (2016). It is an infinite-horizon extension of the framework for variable-population social choice initiated by Blackorby and Donaldson (1984). Social alternatives are paths of temporal social states. Although we begin by presenting the welfarist framework established by Kamaga (2016), we present the analysis of a social welfare functional that transforms a profile of utility functions of potential individuals into an ordering or a quasi-ordering on the set of paths of temporal social states. Then, we present the welfarism theorem, which is analogous to those established in finite- and infinite-horizon fixed population settings. The welfarism theorem present the



K. Kamaga, *Social Welfare Evaluation and Intergenerational Equity*,
Development Bank of Japan Research Series,
https://doi.org/10.1007/978-981-15-4254-1_5

axiomatic foundation for the analysis of a social welfare quasi-ordering for infinite streams of utility vectors.

Using the welfarist framework, we examine and axiomatize infinite-horizon extensions of critical-level generalized utilitarianism that includes infinite-horizon extensions of critical-level utilitarianism as special cases. Parfit's (1976, 1982, 1984) repugnant conclusion is reformulated in the infinite-horizon framework, and the population ethics property of those infinite-horizon critical-level utilitarianism is examined. An infinite-horizon reformulation of the very sadistic conclusion discussed by Arrhenius (2000, 2011) is also examined.

The next section presents of a basic framework, and the welfarism theorems are established in Sect. 5.3. In Sect. 5.4, we present the definitions of infinite-horizon extensions of critical-level generalized utilitarianism and provide their axiomatizations. Their population ethics property is examined using an infinite-horizon reformulation of the axiom that postulates avoidance of the repugnant conclusion in Sect. 5.5. Section 5.6 provides concluding remarks.

## 5.2 Framework

We consider the welfarist framework of infinite-horizon variable population social choice presented in Kamaga (2016). A justification of the welfarist framework will be presented in the next section.

Let $\mathbb{R}$ (resp. $\mathbb{R}_{++}$ and $\mathbb{R}_{--}$) be the set of all (resp. all positive and all negative) real numbers and $\mathbb{N}$ be the set of all positive integers. For all $n \in \mathbb{N}$, $\mathbf{1}_n$ is the vector consisting of $n$ ones. Let $\Omega = \cup_{n\in\mathbb{N}}\mathbb{R}^n$, and let $\Omega^{\mathbb{N}}$ be the set of all streams of generational utility vectors $\boldsymbol{u} = (\boldsymbol{u}^1, \boldsymbol{u}^2, \ldots)$. For all $\boldsymbol{u} \in \Omega$ and all $t \in \mathbb{N}$, $\mathbf{n}(\boldsymbol{u}^t)$ is the number of components in $\boldsymbol{u}^t$, i.e., the population size at the $t$-th generation. Thus, $\boldsymbol{u}^t = \left(u_1^t, \ldots, u_{\mathbf{n}(\boldsymbol{u}^t)}^t\right)$. For all $\boldsymbol{u} \in \Omega^{\mathbb{N}}$ and all $t \in \mathbb{N}$, we interpret $\boldsymbol{u}^t$ as the utility distribution among $\mathbf{n}(\boldsymbol{u}^t)$ individuals in the $t$-th generation, while we ignore the identities of individuals in each generation. This simplification does not affect the analysis since the evaluation relations we consider do not depend on the identities of individuals. Any individual's life is neutral if it is as good as a life without any experience, and thus, an individual's life is worth living if her/his utility level is above neutrality. We employ the population ethics convention that a utility level of zero represents neutrality and a utility level above zero represents that life is worth living. See Broome (1993) for a discussion of neutrality and its normalization to zero.

For any $\boldsymbol{u} \in \Omega^{\mathbb{N}}$ and any $t \in \mathbb{N}$, let $\boldsymbol{u}^{-t}$ denote $(\boldsymbol{u}^1, \ldots, \boldsymbol{u}^t) \in \Omega^t$ and $\boldsymbol{u}^{+t}$ denote $(\boldsymbol{u}^{t+1}, \boldsymbol{u}^{t+2}, \ldots) \in \Omega^{\mathbb{N}}$. Thus, $\boldsymbol{u} = (\boldsymbol{u}^{-t}, \boldsymbol{u}^{+t}) = (\boldsymbol{u}^{-(t-1)}, \boldsymbol{u}^t, \boldsymbol{u}^{+t})$. We refer to $\boldsymbol{u}^{-t}$ as $t$-head of a stream of utility vectors and $\boldsymbol{u}^{+t}$ as $t$-tail of a stream of utility vectors. For any $\boldsymbol{u}, \boldsymbol{v} \in \Omega^{\mathbb{N}}$ and any $t \in \mathbb{N}$, we write $[\boldsymbol{u}^t, \boldsymbol{v}^t]$ as $[\boldsymbol{u}^t, \boldsymbol{v}^t] = \left(u_1^t, \ldots, u_{\mathbf{n}(\boldsymbol{u}^t)}^t, v_1^t, \ldots, v_{\mathbf{n}(\boldsymbol{v}^t)}^t\right) \in \Omega$.

A binary relation on $\Omega^{\mathbb{N}}$ is generically denoted by $\succsim^*$. We write $\boldsymbol{u} \succsim^* \boldsymbol{v}$ for $(\boldsymbol{u}, \boldsymbol{v}) \in \succsim^*$. The asymmetric and symmetric parts of $\succsim^*$ is denoted by $\succ^*$ and $\sim^*$, respectively. A binary relation $\succsim^*$ on $\Omega^{\mathbb{N}}$ is a quasi-ordering if it is reflexive and transitive. A binary relation $\succsim^*$ on $\Omega^{\mathbb{N}}$ is *intratemporally anonymous* if and only if, for all $\boldsymbol{u}, \boldsymbol{v} \in \Omega^{\mathbb{N}}$, $\boldsymbol{u} \sim^* \boldsymbol{v}$ if, for all $t \in \mathbb{N}$, there exists a bijection $\pi^t : \{1, \ldots, \mathbf{n}(\boldsymbol{u}^t)\} \to \{1, \ldots, \mathbf{n}(\boldsymbol{v}^t)\}$ such that $\boldsymbol{u}^t = \left(v^t_{\pi^t(1)}, \ldots, v^t_{\pi^t(\mathbf{n}(\boldsymbol{u}^t))}\right)$. A binary relation $\succsim^*$ on $\Omega^{\mathbb{N}}$ is *finitely complete* if and only if $\boldsymbol{u} \succsim^* \boldsymbol{v}$ or $\boldsymbol{v} \succsim^* \boldsymbol{u}$ for all $\boldsymbol{u}, \boldsymbol{v} \in \Omega^{\mathbb{N}}$ with $\boldsymbol{u}^{+t} = \boldsymbol{v}^{+t}$ for some $t \in \mathbb{N}$. In this chapter, we say that a binary relation on $\Omega^{\mathbb{N}}$ is a social welfare relation if it is an intratemporally anonymous quasi-ordering. Given binary relations $\succsim^*_A$ and $\succsim^*_B$ on $\Omega^{\mathbb{N}}$, we say that $\succsim^*_A$ is a *subrelation* of $\succsim^*_B$ if $\boldsymbol{u} \sim^*_A \boldsymbol{v}$ implies $\boldsymbol{u} \sim^*_B \boldsymbol{v}$ and $\boldsymbol{u} \succ^*_A \boldsymbol{v}$ implies $\boldsymbol{u} \succ^*_B \boldsymbol{v}$.

## 5.3 Welfarism

### *5.3.1 Social Welfare Functional*

In this section, we present a theoretical justification for the analysis of a social welfare relation for streams of variable-dimensional utility vectors. Specifically, we establish the welfarism theorem, which shows that the analysis of the evaluation of paths of temporal social states is equivalently represented by the analysis of a social welfare relation for streams of variable-dimensional utility vectors.

We consider the framework used in Kamaga (2016), which is an infinite-horizon extension of the finite-horizon framework of variable-population social choice in Blackorby et al. (2005), where social alternatives are infinite-horizon paths of temporal social states and the original finite-horizon framework is used to describe a temporal social state. We begin with the description of a temporal social state. We generically use $t \in \mathbb{N}$ to denote the time period of the society. For all $t \in \mathbb{N}$, $X^t$ is a set of temporal social states $x^t$ at $t$ and $x^t$ is a complete description of all aspects of the society at $t$ including the identities of the individuals alive, their population size, and their actions such as their consumption and fertility choices.

Different individuals may be alive in different states $x^t, y^t \in X^t$. For each time period $t \in \mathbb{N}$, we assume that there are infinitely many individuals who will potentially be alive in some $x^t \in X^t$ at $t$ and that each of the potential individuals lives one period, so that there is no overlap between generations. For all $t \in \mathbb{N}$, we denote an individual potentially alive at $t$ by the ordered pair $(i, t) \in \mathbb{N} \times \{t\}$. This means that any individual who is potentially alive at $t$ is never alive at different time periods $t' \neq t$. For each period $t \in \mathbb{N}$, the set of all individuals potentially alive at $t$ is $\mathbb{N} \times \{t\}$ and the set of all non-empty and finite subsets of $\mathbb{N} \times \{t\}$ is denoted by $\mathcal{N}^t$. For all $t \in \mathbb{N}$ and all $x^t \in X^t$, the set of all individuals alive in $x^t$ is denoted by $\mathbf{N}(x^t)$, and $\mathbf{n}(x^t) = |\mathbf{N}(x^t)|$ is the population size. We assume that, for all $t \in \mathbb{N}$ and all $x^t \in X^t$, $0 < \mathbf{n}(x^t) < \infty$, and thus, $\mathbf{N}(x^t) \in \mathcal{N}^t$. For all $t \in \mathbb{N}$ and all $\mathbf{N} \in \mathcal{N}^t$, let

$X^t_{\mathbf{N}} \subseteq X^t$ be the set of all temporal social states $x^t$ that satisfy $\mathbf{N}(x^t) = \mathbf{N}$. We assume that $|X^t_{\mathbf{N}}| \geq 3$ for all $t \in \mathbb{N}$ and all $\mathbf{N} \in \mathcal{N}^t$. This assumption is needed to establish the two versions of the welfarism theorem in the next section. Since $|\mathcal{N}^t| = |\mathbb{N}|$, $|X^t| \geq |\mathbb{N}|$ for all $t \in \mathbb{N}$.

$X^\infty = \Pi_{t\in\mathbb{N}} X^t$ is the set of all infinite-horizon paths of temporal social states $\boldsymbol{x} = \{x^t\}_{t\in\mathbb{N}}$. Thus, $X^\infty$ is the set of social alternatives to be ranked. For all $\boldsymbol{x} \in X^\infty$ and all $t \in \mathbb{N}$, we refer to $\mathbf{N}(x^t)$ as the $t$-th *generation* in $\boldsymbol{x}$. For all $\boldsymbol{x} \in X^\infty$, $\mathbf{N}(\boldsymbol{x}) = (\mathbf{N}(x^t))_{t\in\mathbb{N}}$ is the profile of generations in $\boldsymbol{x}$, and $\mathbf{n}(\boldsymbol{x}) = (\mathbf{n}(x^t))_{t\in\mathbb{N}}$ is the stream of their population sizes. Since $X^t_{\mathbf{N}} \neq \varnothing$ for all $t \in \mathbb{N}$ and all $\mathbf{N} \in \mathcal{N}^t$, the set of all possible generation profiles is $\Pi_{t\in\mathbb{N}} \mathcal{N}^t$.

For all $t \in \mathbb{N}$ and all $(i, t) \in \mathbb{N} \times \{t\}$, $U^t_i : X^t_i \to \mathbb{R}$ is a utility function of individual $(i, t)$, where $X^t_i = \{x^t \in X^t : (i, t) \in \mathbf{N}(x^t)\}$ is the set of all temporal social states at $t$ in which individual $(i, t)$ is alive. For all $t \in \mathbb{N}$, a profile of utility functions of all potential individuals at $t$ is denoted by $U^t = (U^t_i)_{i\in\mathbb{N}} = (U^t_1, \ldots, U^t_i, \ldots)$. A profile of the utility functions of all individuals who are potentially alive at some $t \in \mathbb{N}$ is a list of infinitely many components, one for each profile $U^t$ of utility functions at $t$, and is denoted by $U = (U^t)_{t\in\mathbb{N}} = (U^1, \ldots, U^t, \ldots)$. We refer to $U$ as the profile of utility functions. The set of all logically possible profiles of utility functions is denoted by $\mathcal{U}$.

A binary relation $B$ on $X^\infty$ is finitely complete if, for all $\boldsymbol{x}, \boldsymbol{y} \in X^\infty$, $\boldsymbol{x} B \boldsymbol{y}$ or $\boldsymbol{y} B \boldsymbol{x}$ whenever there exists $t \in \mathbb{N}$ such that $x^{t'} = y^{t'}$ for all $t' \geq t$. Let $\mathcal{Q}$ be the set of all logically possible quasi-orderings on $X^\infty$. Moreover, let $\mathcal{Q}^f \subset \mathcal{Q}$ be the set of all logically possible finitely complete quasi-orderings on $X^\infty$. Letting $\mathcal{Q}^* \in \{\mathcal{Q}, \mathcal{Q}^f\}$, a *social welfare functional* is a mapping $F : \mathcal{D} \to \mathcal{Q}^*$ that associates a (finitely complete) quasi-ordering on $X^\infty$ with each profile of utility functions in $\mathcal{D}$, where $\mathcal{D}$ is the domain of $F$ that satisfies $\varnothing \neq \mathcal{D} \subseteq \mathcal{U}$. Thus, a social welfare functional is an aggregation rule that transforms each profile of utility functions to a social ranking of social alternatives. For all $U \in \mathcal{D}$, we write $F(U) = R_U$, and $P_U$ and $I_U$ denote, respectively, the asymmetric and symmetric parts of $R_U$.

### 5.3.2 *Welfarism Theorem*

To outline the welfarism theorem, we present three axioms defined for a social welfare functional. The axioms we use for the two versions of the welfarism theorem are all reformulations of those used in the finite-horizon framework of variable-population social choice (e.g., Blackorby, Bossert and Donaldson 1999, 2005). The assumption of the unlimited domain of $F$ is stated as the following axiom.

**Unlimited Domain**: $\mathcal{D} = \mathcal{U}$.

Binary independence of irrelevant alternatives requires that the ranking of any two paths of temporal social states depends only on the utilities of the individuals alive.

**Binary Independence of Irrelevant Alternatives**: For all $\boldsymbol{x}, \boldsymbol{y} \in X^\infty$ and all $U, V \in \mathcal{D}$, if $\mathbf{U}(\boldsymbol{x}) = \mathbf{V}(\boldsymbol{x})$ and $\mathbf{U}(\boldsymbol{y}) = \mathbf{V}(\boldsymbol{y})$, then $\boldsymbol{x} R_U \boldsymbol{y} \Leftrightarrow \boldsymbol{x} R_V \boldsymbol{y}$.

Intratemporal anonymity asserts that any two paths of temporal social states are equally good if the corresponding streams of the utility vectors of generations coincide using a permutation in each generation. This means that, even if the individuals alive are *different* in two paths of temporal social states, these paths are declared equally good if the corresponding streams of the utility vectors coincide using a permutation in each generation. In this sense, this requirement is stronger than the standard requirement of anonymity.

**Intratemporal Anonymity**: For all $\boldsymbol{x}, \boldsymbol{y} \in X^\infty$ and all $U \in \mathcal{D}$, if, for all $t \in \mathbb{N}$, there exists a bijection $\mu^t : \mathbf{N}(x^t) \longrightarrow \mathbf{N}(y^t)$ such that $U_i^t(x^t) = U_j^t(y^t)$ for all $(i, t) \in \mathbf{N}(x^t)$ and all $(j, t) = \mu^t((i, t))$, then $\boldsymbol{x} I_U \boldsymbol{y}$.

Note that intratemporal anonymity implies the following property: for all $\boldsymbol{x}, \boldsymbol{y} \in X^\infty$ and all $U \in \mathcal{D}$, $\boldsymbol{x} I_U \boldsymbol{y}$ if $\mathbf{U}(\boldsymbol{x}) = \mathbf{U}(\boldsymbol{y})$. This property implies the so-called Pareto indifference axiom.

We now present the welfarism theorem. It is an infinite-horizon variant of those obtained by Blackorby et al. (1999, 2005) in the finite-horizon framework of variable-population social choice; see also d'Aspremont (1985, 2007), d'Aspremont and Gevers (1977), and Hammond (1979) for similar results in the finite- and infinite-horizon fixed-population frameworks.

The theorem shows that, assuming a social welfare functional $F$ has an unlimited domain, $F$ satisfies the axioms of binary independence of irrelevant alternatives and intratemporal anonymity if and only if the ranking $F(U) = R_U$ of the paths of temporal social states is determined by a single (finitely complete) social welfare relation defined for streams $\mathbf{U}(\boldsymbol{x})$ of utility vectors irrespective of the profile of the utility functions $U$ considered. In the following theorem, part (ii) was presented in Kamaga (2016).

**Theorem 5.1** *Suppose that a social welfare functional $F$ satisfies unlimited domain.*

*(i) Let $\mathcal{Q}^* = \mathcal{Q}$. $F$ satisfies binary independence of irrelevant alternatives and intratemporal anonymity if and only if there exists a social welfare relation $\succsim^*$ on $\Omega^{\mathbb{N}}$ such that for all $\boldsymbol{x}, \boldsymbol{y} \in X^\infty$ and all $U \in \mathcal{D}$,*

$$\boldsymbol{x} R_U \boldsymbol{y} \;\Leftrightarrow\; \mathbf{U}(\boldsymbol{x}) \succsim^* \mathbf{U}(\boldsymbol{y}). \tag{5.1}$$

*(ii) Let $\mathcal{Q}^* = \mathcal{Q}^f$. $F$ satisfies binary independence of irrelevant alternatives and intratemporal anonymity if and only if there exists a finitely complete social welfare relation $\succsim^*$ on $\Omega^{\mathbb{N}}$ such that for all $\boldsymbol{x}, \boldsymbol{y} \in X^\infty$ and all $U \in \mathcal{D}$,*

$$\boldsymbol{x} R_U \boldsymbol{y} \;\Leftrightarrow\; \mathbf{U}(\boldsymbol{x}) \succsim^* \mathbf{U}(\boldsymbol{y}). \tag{5.2}$$

To prove Theorem 5.1, we begin by showing that binary independence of irrelevant alternatives and intratemporal anonymity together imply strong neutrality. Strong neutrality asserts that the ranking of the paths of social states $\boldsymbol{x}$ and $\boldsymbol{y}$ must be the same as that obtained for $\boldsymbol{x}'$ and $\boldsymbol{y}'$ as long as utility profiles coincide between these pairs of paths of social states. Note that it does not require that the individuals alive be the same between the paths of social states. This axiom is seen as an variant of the strong neutrality property appeared in finite-horizon variable population framework (Blackorby et al. 2005) and finite- or infinite-horizon fixed-population frameworks (d'Aspremont and Gevers 1977; d'Aspremont 2007).

**Strong Neutrality**: For all $\boldsymbol{x}, \boldsymbol{y}, \boldsymbol{x}', \boldsymbol{y}' \in X^{\infty}$ and all $U, V \in \mathcal{D}$, if $\mathbf{U}(\boldsymbol{x}) = \mathbf{V}(\boldsymbol{x}')$ and $\mathbf{U}(\boldsymbol{y}) = \mathbf{V}(\boldsymbol{y}')$, then

$$\boldsymbol{x} R_U \boldsymbol{y} \;\Leftrightarrow\; \boldsymbol{x}' R_V \boldsymbol{y}'.$$

**Lemma 5.1** *If a social welfare functional $F$ satisfies unlimited domain, binary independence of irrelevant alternatives and intratemporal anonymity, then it satisfies strong neutrality.*

***Proof*** The proof is performed by applying an argument analogous to that used in d'Aspremont (1985). Let $\boldsymbol{x}, \boldsymbol{y}, \boldsymbol{x}', \boldsymbol{y}' \in X^{\infty}$ and all $U, V \in \mathcal{D}$. Suppose that $\mathbf{U}(\boldsymbol{x}) = \mathbf{V}(\boldsymbol{x}')$ and $\mathbf{U}(\boldsymbol{y}) = \mathbf{V}(\boldsymbol{y}')$. Let $\boldsymbol{u}, \boldsymbol{v} \in \Omega^{\mathbb{N}}$ satisfy $\boldsymbol{u} = \mathbf{U}(\boldsymbol{x})$ and $\boldsymbol{v} = \mathbf{U}(\boldsymbol{y})$. Since $F$ satisfies unlimited domain and $X^t_{\mathbf{N}} \neq \varnothing$ for all $\mathbf{N} \in \mathcal{N}^t$ and for all $t \in \mathbb{N}$, there exist $\bar{U}, \tilde{U}, \hat{U} \in \mathcal{D}$ and $\boldsymbol{z} \in X^{\infty} \setminus \{\boldsymbol{x}, \boldsymbol{x}'\}$ such that

$$\bar{\mathbf{U}}(\boldsymbol{x}) = \boldsymbol{u} \text{ and } \bar{\mathbf{U}}(\boldsymbol{y}) = \bar{\mathbf{U}}(\boldsymbol{z}) = \boldsymbol{v},$$
$$\tilde{\mathbf{U}}(\boldsymbol{x}) = \tilde{\mathbf{U}}(\boldsymbol{x}') = \boldsymbol{u} \text{ and } \tilde{\mathbf{U}}(\boldsymbol{z}) = \boldsymbol{v},$$
$$\hat{\mathbf{U}}(\boldsymbol{x}') = \boldsymbol{u} \text{ and } \hat{\mathbf{U}}(\boldsymbol{y}') = \bar{\mathbf{U}}(\boldsymbol{z}) = \boldsymbol{v}.$$

Since $F$ satisfies binary independence of irrelevant alternatives, we obtain

$$\boldsymbol{x} R_U \boldsymbol{y} \;\Leftrightarrow\; \boldsymbol{x} R_{\bar{U}} \boldsymbol{y}.$$

Since $F$ satisfies intratemporal anonymity, $\boldsymbol{y} I_{\bar{U}} \boldsymbol{z}$ follows. Thus, from the transitivity of $R_{\bar{U}}$, we obtain

$$\boldsymbol{x} R_{\bar{U}} \boldsymbol{y} \;\Leftrightarrow\; \boldsymbol{x} R_{\bar{U}} \boldsymbol{z}.$$

From binary independence of irrelevant alternatives, it follows that

$$\boldsymbol{x} R_{\bar{U}} \boldsymbol{z} \;\Leftrightarrow\; \boldsymbol{x} R_{\tilde{U}} \boldsymbol{z}.$$

By intratemporal anonymity and the transitivity of $R_{\tilde{U}}$, we obtain

$$\boldsymbol{x} R_{\tilde{U}} \boldsymbol{z} \;\Leftrightarrow\; \boldsymbol{x}' R_{\tilde{U}} \boldsymbol{z}.$$

Again, from binary independence of irrelevant alternatives, it follows that

$$\boldsymbol{x}' R_{\tilde{U}} \boldsymbol{z} \;\Leftrightarrow\; \boldsymbol{x}' R_{\hat{U}} \boldsymbol{z}.$$

Further, by intratemporal anonymity and the transitivity of $R_{\hat{U}}$, we obtain

$$x' R_{\hat{U}} z \Leftrightarrow x' R_{\hat{U}} y'.$$

Finally, by binary independence of irrelevant alternatives, we obtain

$$x' R_{\hat{U}} y' \Leftrightarrow x' R_V y'.$$

Thus, combining the equivalence assertions we obtained above, it follows that

$$\boldsymbol{x} R_U \boldsymbol{y} \Leftrightarrow x' R_V y'.$$

Thus, $F$ satisfies strong neutrality. ■

*Proof of Theorem* 5.1

(i) 'If.' From (5.1), it is straightforward that $F$ satisfies binary independence of irrelevant alternatives. We show that $F$ satisfies intratemporal anonymity. Let $\boldsymbol{x}, \boldsymbol{v} \in X^\infty$ and $U \in \mathcal{D}$. We suppose that for all $t \in \mathbb{N}$, there exists $\mu^t : \mathbf{N}(x^t) \to \mathbf{N}(y^t)$ such that $U_i^t(x^t) = U_j^t(y^t)$ for all $(i, t) \in \mathbf{N}(x^t)$ and for all $(j, t) = \mu^t((i, t))$. Since $\succsim^*$ is intratemporally anonymous, $\mathbf{U}(\boldsymbol{x}) \sim^* \mathbf{U}(\boldsymbol{y})$ follows. From (5.1), we obtain $\boldsymbol{x} I_U \boldsymbol{y}$.
'Only if.' We define the binary relation $\succsim^*$ on $\Omega^{\mathbb{N}}$ as follows. For all $\boldsymbol{u}, \boldsymbol{v} \in \Omega^{\mathbb{N}}$, $\boldsymbol{u} \succsim^* \boldsymbol{v}$ if and only if there exist $\boldsymbol{x}, \boldsymbol{y} \in X^\infty$ and $U \in \mathcal{D}$ such that $\boldsymbol{u} = \mathbf{U}(\boldsymbol{x})$, $\boldsymbol{v} = \mathbf{U}(\boldsymbol{y})$ and $\boldsymbol{x} R_U \boldsymbol{y}$. From Lemma 5.1, $F$ satisfies strong neutrality. Thus, $\succsim^*$ satisfies that for all $\boldsymbol{x}, \boldsymbol{y} \in X^\infty$ and for all $U \in \mathcal{D}$, $\boldsymbol{x} R_U \boldsymbol{y}$ if and only if $\mathbf{U}(\boldsymbol{x}) \succsim^* \mathbf{U}(\boldsymbol{y})$. Hence, $\succsim^*$ satisfies (5.1).
We show that $\succsim^*$ is a social welfare relation. We begin by showing that $\succsim^*$ is reflexive. Let $\boldsymbol{u} \in \Omega^{\mathbb{N}}$. Since $F$ satisfies unlimited domain and $X_{\mathbf{N}}^t \neq \varnothing$ for all $\mathbf{N} \in \mathcal{N}^t$ and for all $t \in \mathbb{N}$, there exists $\boldsymbol{x} \in X^\infty$ and $U \in \mathcal{D}$ such that $\boldsymbol{u} = \mathbf{U}(\boldsymbol{x})$. Since $R_U$ is reflexive, we obtain $\boldsymbol{x} R_U \boldsymbol{x}$. From (5.1), $\boldsymbol{u} \succsim^* \boldsymbol{u}$ follows.
Next, we show that $\succsim^*$ is transitive. Let $\boldsymbol{u}, \boldsymbol{v}, \boldsymbol{w} \in \Omega^{\mathbb{N}}$ and suppose that $\boldsymbol{u} \succsim^* \boldsymbol{v}$ and $\boldsymbol{v} \succsim^* \boldsymbol{w}$. Since $F$ satisfies unlimited domain and $X_{\mathbf{N}}^t \neq \varnothing$ for all $\mathbf{N} \in \mathcal{N}^t$ and for all $t \in \mathbb{N}$, there exist $\boldsymbol{x}, \boldsymbol{y}, \boldsymbol{z} \in X^\infty$ and $U \in \mathcal{U}$ such that $\boldsymbol{u} = \mathbf{U}(\boldsymbol{x})$, $\boldsymbol{v} = \mathbf{U}(\boldsymbol{y})$ and $\boldsymbol{w} = \mathbf{U}(\boldsymbol{z})$. By (5.1), we obtain $\boldsymbol{x} R_U \boldsymbol{y}$ and $\boldsymbol{y} R_U \boldsymbol{z}$. From the transitivity of $R_U$, $\boldsymbol{x} R_U \boldsymbol{z}$ follows. From (5.1), we obtain $\boldsymbol{u} \succsim^* \boldsymbol{w}$.
Finally, we show that $\succsim^*$ is intratemporally anonymous. Let $\boldsymbol{u}, \boldsymbol{v} \in \Omega^{\mathbb{N}}$ and suppose that for all $t \in \mathbb{N}$, there exists a bijection $\mu^t : \{1, \ldots, \mathbf{n}(\boldsymbol{u}^t)\} \to \{1, \ldots, \mathbf{n}(\boldsymbol{v}^t)\}$ such that $\boldsymbol{u}^t = (\boldsymbol{v}^t_{\mu^t(1)}, \ldots, \boldsymbol{v}^t_{\mu^t(\mathbf{n}(\boldsymbol{u}^t))})$. Since $F$ satisfies unlimited domain and $X_{\mathbf{N}}^t \neq \varnothing$ for all $\mathbf{N} \in \mathcal{N}^t$ and for all $t \in \mathbb{N}$, there exist $\boldsymbol{x}, \boldsymbol{y} \in X^\infty$ and $U \in \mathcal{U}$ such that $\boldsymbol{u} = \mathbf{U}(\boldsymbol{x})$ and $\boldsymbol{v} = \mathbf{U}(\boldsymbol{y})$. Since $F$ satisfies intratemporal anonymity, we obtain $\boldsymbol{x} I_U \boldsymbol{y}$. From (5.1), $\boldsymbol{u} \sim^* \boldsymbol{v}$ follows.

(ii) 'If.' From Theorem 5.1 (i), $F$ satisfies binary independence of irrelevant alternatives and intratemporal anonymity.
'Only if.' From Theorem 5.1 (i), there exists a social welfare relation $\succsim^*$ on $\Omega^{\mathbb{N}}$ that satisfies (5.2). We show that $\succsim^*$ is finitely complete. Let $\boldsymbol{u}, \boldsymbol{v} \in \Omega^{\mathbb{N}}$ and suppose that there exists $T \in \mathbb{N}$ such that $\boldsymbol{u}^t = \boldsymbol{v}^t$ for all $t \geq T$. Since F satisfies unlimited domain and $X_{\mathbf{N}}^t \neq \varnothing$ for all $\mathbf{N} \in \mathcal{N}^t$ and for all $t \in \mathbb{N}$, there

exist $\boldsymbol{x}, \boldsymbol{y} \in X^{\infty}$ and $U \in \mathcal{D}$ such that $\boldsymbol{u} = \mathbf{U}(\boldsymbol{x})$, $\boldsymbol{v} = \mathbf{U}(\boldsymbol{y})$ and $x^t = y^t$ for all $t \geq T$. Since $R_U$ is finitely complete, we obtain $\boldsymbol{x} R_U \boldsymbol{y}$ or $\boldsymbol{y} R_U \boldsymbol{x}$. From (5.2), it follows that $\boldsymbol{u} \succsim^* \boldsymbol{v}$ or $\boldsymbol{v} \succsim^* \boldsymbol{u}$. ■

## 5.4 Critical-Level Utilitarianism

### *5.4.1 Definitions*

We present three types of an infinite-horizon extension of critical-level (generalized) utilitarianism, which were presented by Kamaga (2016). We begin with the infinite-horizon extension that we call the critical-level (generalized) utilitarian social welfare relation, which corresponds to the dominance-in-tails criterion. Since we need a dominance relation for tails of streams of utility vectors, defining the critical-level utilitarian and critical-level generalized utilitarian social welfare relations requires that we first define the quasi-ordering on $\Omega$ from Suppes (1966) and Sen (1970), which we call the *intratemporal Suppes–Sen grading principle*. It is defined as the following binary relation $\succsim_S$ on $\Omega$: for all $(u_1, \ldots, u_m), (v_1, \ldots, v_n) \in \Omega$, $(u_1, \ldots, u_m) \succsim_S (v_1, \ldots, v_n)$ if and only if $m = n$ and there exists a permutation $\mu$ on $\{1, \ldots, n\}$ such that $(u_1, \ldots, u_n) \geq (v_{\mu(1)}, \ldots, v_{\mu(n)})$. We denote the asymmetric and symmetric parts of $\succsim_S$ by $\succ_S$ and $\sim_S$, respectively. It is easy to verify that $\succsim$ is a quasi-ordering. Further, for all $(u_1, \ldots, u_n), (v_1, \ldots, v_n) \in \Omega$, (i) $(u_1, \ldots, u_n) \succ_S (v_1, \ldots, v_n)$ if and only if there exists a permutation $\mu$ on $\{1, \ldots, n\}$ such that $(u_1, \ldots, u_n) > (v_{\mu(1)}, \ldots, v_{\mu(n)})$, and (ii) $(u_1, \ldots, u_n) \sim_S (v_1, \ldots, v_n)$ if and only if there exists a permutation $\mu$ on $\{1, \ldots, n\}$ such that $(u_1, \ldots, u_n) = (v_{\mu(1)}, \ldots, v_{\mu(n)})$.

Let $G$ be the set of all possible continuous and increasing functions $g : \mathbb{R} \to \mathbb{R}$ with $g(0) = 0$. Given $g \in G$ and $\alpha \in \mathbb{R}$, the *critical-level generalized utilitarian* social welfare relation associated with $g$ and $\alpha$ ranks the streams of utility vectors by (i) comparing the total sum of the gains of individuals' transformed utilities over $g(\alpha)$ in $T$-heads of streams and (ii) applying the intratemporal Suppes–Sen grading principle to each generation in $T$-tails of streams. Formally, the critical-level generalized utilitarian social welfare relation associated with $g$ and $\alpha$ is defined as the following binary relation $\succsim^*_{U,g,\alpha}$ on $\Omega^{\mathbb{N}}$: for all $\boldsymbol{u}, \boldsymbol{v} \in \Omega^{\mathbb{N}}$,

$$\boldsymbol{u} \succsim^*_{U,g,\alpha} \boldsymbol{v} \Leftrightarrow \text{ there exists } T \in \mathbb{N} \text{ such that } \boldsymbol{u}^t \succsim_S \boldsymbol{v}^t \text{ for all } t > T \text{ and}$$
$$\sum_{t=1}^{T} \sum_{i=1}^{\mathbf{n}(\boldsymbol{u}^t)} [g(u_i^t) - g(\alpha)] \geq \sum_{t=1}^{T} \sum_{i=1}^{\mathbf{n}(\boldsymbol{v}^t)} [g(v_i^t) - g(\alpha)]. \tag{5.3}$$

The evaluation of $T$-heads of streams in (5.3) is a direct application of the critical-level generalized utilitarian ordering. It is easy to verify that, for any choice of $g \in G$ and $\alpha \in \mathbb{R}$, $\succsim^*_{U,g\alpha}$ is a social welfare relation. Further, by (5.3), $\alpha$ is the unique critical level for *all* $\boldsymbol{u} \in \Omega^{\mathbb{N}}$ at *any* $t$-th generation. That is, the addition of individuals with the utility level of $\alpha$ at any generation does not change social goodness.

According to the choice of $g \in G$ and $\alpha \in \mathbb{R}$, the critical-level generalized utilitarian social welfare relation represents different evaluation relations. If a critical-level generalized utilitarian social welfare relation is associated with a (strictly) concave function $g \in G$, the application of the critical-level generalized utilitarian ordering to the heads of streams with the same total population represents (strict) inequality aversion. If it is associated with the identity mapping $g \in G$, it is the *critical-level utilitarian* social welfare relation, which we denote by $\succsim^*_{U,\alpha}$.

It is easy to verify that the asymmetric and symmetric parts of $\succsim^*_{U,g,\alpha}$ are characterized respectively as follows. For all $\boldsymbol{u}, \boldsymbol{v} \in \Omega^{\mathbb{N}}$,

$$\boldsymbol{u} \succ^*_{U,g,\alpha} \boldsymbol{v} \Leftrightarrow \text{there exists } T \in \mathbb{N} \text{ such that } \boldsymbol{u}^t \succsim \boldsymbol{v}^t \text{ for all } t > T \text{ and}$$
$$\sum_{t=1}^{T}\sum_{i=1}^{\mathbf{n}(\boldsymbol{u}^t)}[g(u_i^t) - g(\alpha)] > \sum_{t=1}^{T}\sum_{i=1}^{\mathbf{n}(\boldsymbol{v}^t)}[g(v_i^t) - g(\alpha)]; \tag{5.4a}$$

$$\boldsymbol{u} \sim^*_{U,g,\alpha} \boldsymbol{v} \Leftrightarrow \text{there exists } T \in \mathbb{N} \text{ such that } \boldsymbol{u}^t \sim \boldsymbol{v}^t \text{ for all } t > T \text{ and}$$
$$\sum_{t=1}^{T}\sum_{i=1}^{\mathbf{n}(\boldsymbol{u}^t)}[g(u_i^t) - g(\alpha)] = \sum_{t=1}^{T}\sum_{i=1}^{\mathbf{n}(\boldsymbol{v}^t)}[g(v_i^t) - g(\alpha)]. \tag{5.4b}$$

Next, we present the infinite-horizon extension of critical-level (generalized) utilitarianism corresponding to the overtaking criterion of von Weizsäcker (1965). The *critical-level generalized utilitarian overtaking* social welfare relation consecutively applies critical-level generalized utilitarianism to the heads of streams of utility vectors. Given $g \in G$ and $\alpha \in \mathbb{R}$, the critical-level generalized utilitarian overtaking social welfare relation associated with $g$ and $\alpha$ is defined as the following binary relation $\succsim^*_{O,g,\alpha}$ on $\Omega^{\mathbb{N}}$. For all $\boldsymbol{u}, \boldsymbol{v} \in \Omega^{\mathbb{N}}$,

$$\boldsymbol{u} \succsim^*_{O,g,\alpha} \boldsymbol{v} \Leftrightarrow \text{there exists } T^* \in \mathbb{N} \text{ such that for all } T \geq T^*,$$
$$\sum_{t=1}^{T}\sum_{i=1}^{\mathbf{n}(\boldsymbol{u}^t)}[g(u_i^t) - g(\alpha)] > \sum_{t=1}^{T}\sum_{i=1}^{\mathbf{n}(\boldsymbol{v}^t)}[g(v_i^t) - g(\alpha)]; \tag{5.5a}$$

$$\boldsymbol{u} \sim^*_{O,g,\alpha} \boldsymbol{v} \Leftrightarrow \text{there exists } T^* \in \mathbb{N} \text{ such that for all } T \geq T^*,$$
$$\sum_{t=1}^{T}\sum_{i=1}^{\mathbf{n}(\boldsymbol{u}^t)}[g(u_i^t) - g(\alpha)] = \sum_{t=1}^{T}\sum_{i=1}^{\mathbf{n}(\boldsymbol{v}^t)}[g(v_i^t) - g(\alpha)]. \tag{5.5b}$$

It is easy to verify that, for any $g \in G$ and any $\alpha \in \mathbb{R}$, the associated $\succsim^*_{O,g,\alpha}$ is well defined as a social welfare relation. From (5.4a), (5.4b), (5.5a), and (5.5b), it follows that, given $g \in G$ and $\alpha \in \mathbb{R}$, the associated $\succsim^*_{U,g,\alpha}$ is a subrelation of the associated $\succsim^*_{O,g,\alpha}$. For any $\alpha \in \mathbb{N}$, if $\succsim^*_{O,g,\alpha}$ is associated with the identity mapping

$g$ and $\alpha$, it is the *critical-level utilitarian overtaking* social welfare relation, which we denote by $\succsim^*_{O,\alpha}$.

Finally, we present the infinite-horizon extension of critical-level (generalized) utilitarianism corresponding to the catching-up criterion of Atsumi (1965), von Weizsäcker (1965), and Svensson (1980). The *critical-level generalized utilitarian catching-up* social welfare relation also consecutively applies critical-level generalized utilitarianism to the heads of streams of utility vectors in the manner of the catching-up criterion. Given $g \in G$ and $\alpha \in \mathbb{R}$, the critical-level generalized utilitarian catching-up social welfare relation associated with $g$ and $\alpha$ is defined as the following binary relation $\succsim^*_{C,g,\alpha}$ on $\Omega^{\mathbb{N}}$. For all $\boldsymbol{u}, \boldsymbol{v} \in \Omega^{\mathbb{N}}$,

$$\boldsymbol{u} \succsim^*_{C,g,\alpha} \boldsymbol{v} \Leftrightarrow \text{there exists } T^* \in \mathbb{N} \text{ such that for all} T \geq T^*, \quad \sum_{t=1}^{T}\sum_{i=1}^{\mathrm{n}(\boldsymbol{u}^t)}[g(u_i^t) - g(\alpha)] \geq \sum_{t=1}^{T}\sum_{i=1}^{\mathrm{n}(\boldsymbol{v}^t)}[g(v_i^t) - g(\alpha)]. \tag{5.6}$$

It is easy to verify that the asymmetric and symmetric parts of $\succsim^*_{C,g,\alpha}$ are characterized as follows. For all $\boldsymbol{u}, \boldsymbol{v} \in \Omega^{\mathbb{N}}$,

$$\left.\begin{array}{l} \boldsymbol{u} \succ^*_{C,g,\alpha} \boldsymbol{v} \Leftrightarrow \text{there exists } T^* \in \mathbb{N} \text{ such that for all } T \geq T^*, \\ \quad \sum_{t=1}^{T}\sum_{i=1}^{\mathrm{n}(\boldsymbol{u}^t)}[g(u_i^t) - g(\alpha)] \geq \sum_{t=1}^{T}\sum_{i=1}^{\mathrm{n}(\boldsymbol{v}^t)}[g(v_i^t) - g(\alpha)] \\ \quad \text{and for all } T' \in \mathbb{N}, \text{ there exists} T > T' \text{ such that} \\ \quad \sum_{t=1}^{T}\sum_{i=1}^{\mathrm{n}(\boldsymbol{u}^t)}[g(u_i^t) - g(\alpha)] > \sum_{t=1}^{T}\sum_{i=1}^{\mathrm{n}(\boldsymbol{v}^t)}[g(v_i^t) - g(\alpha)]; \end{array}\right\} \tag{5.7a}$$

$$\boldsymbol{u} \sim^*_{C,g,\alpha} \boldsymbol{v} \Leftrightarrow \text{there exists } T^* \in \mathbb{N} \text{ such that for all } T \geq T^*, \quad \sum_{t=1}^{T}\sum_{i=1}^{\mathrm{n}(\boldsymbol{u}^t)}[g(u_i^t) - g(\alpha)] = \sum_{t=1}^{T}\sum_{i=1}^{\mathrm{n}(\boldsymbol{v}^t)}[g(v_i^t) - g(\alpha)]. \tag{5.7b}$$

From (5.5a), (5.5b), (5.7a), and (5.7b), it follows that, given $g \in G$ and $\alpha \in \mathbb{R}$, the associated $\succsim^*_{O,g,\alpha}$ is a subrelation of the associated $\succsim^*_{C,g,\alpha}$. Further, $\sim^*_{O,g,\alpha} = \sim^*_{C,g,\alpha}$ holds. For any $\alpha \in \mathbb{R}$, if $\succsim^*_{C,g,\alpha}$ is associated with the identity mapping $g$ and $\alpha$, it is the *critical-level utilitarian catching-up* social welfare relation, which we denote by $\succsim^*_{C,\alpha}$.

### 5.4.2 Axiomatizations

We begin with the strong Pareto principle and the finite anonymity axiom. Both are reformulations of the corresponding axioms used in the framework of ranking infinite utility streams; see Chap. 3. Strong Pareto requires that the evaluation be positively sensitive to individuals' utilities as long as every generation has the same population size.

**Strong Pareto**: For all $\boldsymbol{u}, \boldsymbol{v} \in \Omega^{\mathbb{N}}$ such that $\mathbf{n}(\boldsymbol{u}^t) = \mathbf{n}(\boldsymbol{v}^t)$ for all $t \in \mathbb{N}$, if $\boldsymbol{u}^t \geq \boldsymbol{v}^t$ for all $t \in \mathbb{N}$ and there exists $t' \in \mathbb{N}$ such that $\boldsymbol{u}^{t'} > \boldsymbol{v}^{t'}$, then $\boldsymbol{u} \succ^* \boldsymbol{v}$.

Finite anonymity formalizes the equal treatment of finitely many generations by asserting that the relative ranking of any two streams of utility vectors must be declared equally good with respect to a transposition of generations.

**Finite Anonymity**: For all $\boldsymbol{u}, \boldsymbol{v} \in \Omega^{\mathbb{N}}$, if there exist $t_1, t_2 \in \mathbb{N}$ such that $\boldsymbol{u}^{t_1} = \boldsymbol{v}^{t_2}$, $\boldsymbol{u}^{t_2} = \boldsymbol{v}^{t_1}$, and $\boldsymbol{u}^t = \boldsymbol{v}^t$ for all $t \in \mathbb{N}\backslash\{t_1, t_2\}$, then $\boldsymbol{u} \sim^* \boldsymbol{v}$.

The next two axioms are infinite-horizon reformulations of the axioms used by Blackorby, Bossert, and Donaldson (2005) in the finite-horizon framework of variable-population social choice.[1] First, we present an axiom regarding the existence of a critical level of utility. Weak existence of critical levels requires that a critical level of utility exist for at least one stream of utility vectors in at least one generation.

**Weak Existence of Critical Levels**: There exist $t \in \mathbb{N}, \alpha \in \mathbb{R}$, and $\boldsymbol{u} \in \Omega^{\mathbb{N}}$ such that $\boldsymbol{u} \sim^* (\boldsymbol{u}^{-(t-1)}, [\boldsymbol{u}^t, \alpha], \boldsymbol{u}^{+t})$.

Existence independence requires that the evaluation be independent of any addition of individuals in all generations. However, it requires this property only for the streams of utility vectors that have a common tail. Thus, the axiom is interpreted to assert that we can focus on a conflict of interest among the present and near future generations, if only we know that each of the distant future generations has the same utility vector.

**Existence Independence**: For all $\boldsymbol{u}, \boldsymbol{v}, \boldsymbol{w} \in \Omega^{\mathbb{N}}$, if there exists $T \in \mathbb{N}$ such that $\boldsymbol{u}^t = \boldsymbol{v}^t$ for all $t > T$, then

$$\boldsymbol{u} \succsim^* \boldsymbol{v} \Leftrightarrow \left([\boldsymbol{u}^t, \boldsymbol{w}^t]\right)_{t\in\mathbb{N}} \succsim^* \left([\boldsymbol{v}^t, \boldsymbol{w}^t]\right)_{t\in\mathbb{N}}.$$

Finally, the other two axioms are reformulations of the axioms defined for intragenerational fixed-population framework considered in Chap. 2. Restricted continuity asserts that small changes in individuals' utilities of a *single* generation do not lead to large changes in the evaluation. The axiom formulates this property in a restricted form, dealing with only the same dimensional utility vectors of a generation. To state the axiom, we need additional notation and definitions. For all $n, t \in \mathbb{N}$ and

[1]Their axioms also appear in Blackorby et al. (1995, 1998, 1999, 2002).

all $\boldsymbol{w} \in \Omega^{\mathbb{N}}$, let $\Omega^{\mathbb{N}}_{t,n,\boldsymbol{w}} = \{\boldsymbol{u} \in \Omega^{\mathbb{N}} : \mathbf{n}(\boldsymbol{u}^t) = n \text{ and } \boldsymbol{u}^{t'} = \boldsymbol{w}^{t'} \text{ for all } t' \neq t\}$. For all $n, t \in \mathbb{N}$ and all $\boldsymbol{w} \in \Omega^{\mathbb{N}}$, we define the metric $d$ on $\Omega^{\mathbb{N}}_{t,n,\boldsymbol{w}}$ by $d(\boldsymbol{u}, \boldsymbol{v}) = \sum_{i=1}^{n} |u_i^t - v_i^t|$ for all $\boldsymbol{u}, \boldsymbol{v} \in \Omega^{\mathbb{N}}_{t,n,\boldsymbol{w}}$. Note that, for all $n, t \in \mathbb{N}$ and all $\boldsymbol{w} \in \Omega^{\mathbb{N}}$, the pair $(\Omega^{\mathbb{N}}_{t,n,\boldsymbol{w}}, d)$ constitutes a metric space.

**Restricted Continuity**: There exist $t \in \mathbb{N}$ and $\boldsymbol{w} \in \Omega^{\mathbb{N}}$ such that for all $n \in \mathbb{N}$ and all $\boldsymbol{u} \in \Omega^{\mathbb{N}}_{t,n,\boldsymbol{w}}$, $\{\boldsymbol{v} \in \Omega^{\mathbb{N}}_{t,n,\boldsymbol{w}} : \boldsymbol{v} \succsim^* \boldsymbol{u}\}$ and $\{\boldsymbol{v} \in \Omega^{\mathbb{N}}_{t,n,\boldsymbol{w}} : \boldsymbol{u} \succsim^* \boldsymbol{v}\}$ are closed in $(\Omega^{\mathbb{N}}_{t,n,\boldsymbol{w}}, d)$.

Intratemporal incremental equity asserts that the evaluation must be neutral to the utility transfer between individuals within a *single* generation. Clearly, it is a reformulation of incremental equity we considered in Chap. 2.

**Intratemporal Incremental Equity**: There exists $t \in \mathbb{N}$ such that for all $\boldsymbol{u}, \boldsymbol{v} \in \Omega^{\mathbb{N}}$ with $\boldsymbol{u}^{t'} = \boldsymbol{v}^{t'}$ for all $t' \neq t$, if $\mathbf{n}(\boldsymbol{u}^t) = \mathbf{n}(\boldsymbol{v}^t)$ and there exist $i, j \in \{1, \ldots, \mathbf{n}(\boldsymbol{u}^t)\}$ such that $u_i^t - v_i^t = v_j^t - u_j^t$ and $u_k^t = v_k^t$ for all $k \in \{1, \ldots, \mathbf{n}(\boldsymbol{u}^t)\} \setminus \{i, j\}$, then $\boldsymbol{u} \sim^* \boldsymbol{v}$.

Given $\alpha \in \mathbb{R}$ and $g \in G$, we say that a social welfare relation $\succsim^*$ on $\Omega^{\mathbb{N}}$ is *single-generation critical-level generalized utilitarian associated with* $\alpha$ *and* $g$ if, for all $t \in \mathbb{N}$ and for all $\boldsymbol{u}, \boldsymbol{v} \in \Omega^{\mathbb{N}}$ with $u^{t'} = v^{t'}$ for all $t' \neq t$,

$$\boldsymbol{u} \succsim^* \boldsymbol{v} \;\Leftrightarrow\; \sum_{i=1}^{\mathbf{n}(u^t)} [g(u_i^t) - g(\alpha)] \geq \sum_{i=1}^{\mathbf{n}(v^t)} [g(v_i^t) - g(\alpha)].$$

The following lemma is based on Kamaga (2016).

**Lemma 5.2** *Let* $\alpha \in \mathbb{R}$ *and* $g \in G$ *and suppose that a social welfare relation* $\succsim^*$ *on* $\Omega^{\mathbb{N}}$ *is single-generation critical-level generalized utilitarian associated with* $\alpha$ *and* $g$ *and satisfies finite anonymity and existence independence. For all* $T \in \mathbb{N}$ *and for all* $\boldsymbol{u}, \boldsymbol{v} \in \Omega^{\mathbb{N}}$ *with* $\boldsymbol{u}^{+T} = \boldsymbol{v}^{+T}$,

$$\boldsymbol{u} \succsim^* \boldsymbol{v} \;\Leftrightarrow\; \sum_{t=1}^{T} \sum_{i=1}^{\mathbf{n}(u^t)} [g(u_i^t) - g(\alpha)] \geq \sum_{t=1}^{T} \sum_{i=1}^{\mathbf{n}(v^t)} [g(v_i^t) - g(\alpha)]. \tag{5.8}$$

***Proof*** *Step* 1. We show that for all $T \in \mathbb{N}$ and for all $\boldsymbol{u}, \boldsymbol{v} \in \Omega^{\mathbb{N}}$ with $\boldsymbol{u}^{+T} = \boldsymbol{v}^{+T}$,

$$\sum_{t=1}^{T} \sum_{i=1}^{\mathbf{n}(u^t)} [g(u_i^t) - g(\alpha)] = \sum_{t=1}^{T} \sum_{i=1}^{\mathbf{n}(v^t)} [g(v_i^t) - g(\alpha)] \Rightarrow \boldsymbol{u} \sim^* \boldsymbol{v}.$$

The proof is performed by induction on $T$. Since $\succsim^*$ is single-generation critical-level generalized utilitarian associated with $\alpha$ and $g$, (5.8) holds for $T = 1$. Let $T \in \mathbb{N} \setminus \{1\}$ and suppose that (5.8) holds for $T - 1$. Let $\boldsymbol{u}, \boldsymbol{v} \in \Omega^{\mathbb{N}}$ and assume that $\boldsymbol{u}^{+T} = \boldsymbol{v}^{+T}$ and

$$\sum_{t=1}^{T}\sum_{i=1}^{\mathbf{n}(\boldsymbol{u}^t)}[g(u_i^t)-g(\alpha)]=\sum_{t=1}^{T}\sum_{i=1}^{\mathbf{n}(\boldsymbol{v}^t)}[g(v_i^t)-g(\alpha)].$$

We define $\Delta$ by

$$\Delta=\sum_{t=1}^{T-1}\sum_{i=1}^{\mathbf{n}(\boldsymbol{u}^t)}[g(u_i^t)-g(\alpha)]-\sum_{t=1}^{T-1}\sum_{i=1}^{\mathbf{n}(\boldsymbol{v}^t)}[g(v_i^t)-g(\alpha)]. \tag{5.9}$$

Then,

$$\Delta=\sum_{i=1}^{\mathbf{n}(\boldsymbol{v}^T)}[g(v_i^T)-g(\alpha)]-\sum_{i=1}^{\mathbf{n}(\boldsymbol{u}^T)}[g(u_i^T)-g(\alpha)]. \tag{5.10}$$

We now distinguish two cases. (i) $\Delta=0$. From the assumption of induction and (5.9), $\boldsymbol{u}\sim^*(\boldsymbol{v}^{-(T-1)}\boldsymbol{u}^{+(T+1)})$ follows. Furthermore, since $\succsim^*$ is single-generation critical-level generalized utilitarian associated with $\alpha$ and $g$, by (5.10), we obtain $(\boldsymbol{v}^{-(T-1)}\boldsymbol{u}^{+(T-1)})\sim^*(\boldsymbol{v}^{-T},\boldsymbol{u}^{+T})$. Note that $(\boldsymbol{v}^{-T},\boldsymbol{u}^{+T})=\boldsymbol{v}$. Thus, by the transitivity of $\succsim^*$, we obtain $\boldsymbol{u}\sim^*\boldsymbol{v}$.

(ii) $\Delta\neq 0$. Without loss of generality, we assume $\Delta>0$. Let $\beta\in\mathbb{R}$ with $\beta>\alpha$. Since $g$ is increasing, $g(\beta)>g(\alpha)$. Since $\Delta<\infty$, there exists $n\in\mathbb{N}$ such that

$$g(\beta)>g(\alpha)+\frac{\Delta}{n}>g(\alpha).$$

Since $g$ is continuous on $\mathbb{R}$, it follows from the intermediate value theorem that there exists $\gamma\in(\alpha,\beta)$ such that

$$g(\gamma)=g(\alpha)+\frac{\Delta}{n}.$$

Thus,

$$n[g(\gamma)-g(\alpha)]=\Delta. \tag{5.11}$$

Define $\bar{\boldsymbol{u}},\bar{\boldsymbol{v}}\in\Omega^{\mathbb{N}}$ by

$$\boldsymbol{u}=(\boldsymbol{v}^{-(T-2)},[\boldsymbol{v}^{T-1},\gamma\mathbf{1}_n],\boldsymbol{u}^{+(T-1)})\ \text{ and }\ \bar{\boldsymbol{v}}=(\boldsymbol{v}^{-(T-1)},[\boldsymbol{u}^T,\gamma\mathbf{1}_n],\boldsymbol{v}^{+T}).$$

From (5.9) and (5.11), it follows that

$$\begin{aligned}\sum_{t=1}^{T-1}\sum_{i=1}^{\mathbf{n}(\bar{\boldsymbol{u}}^t)}[g(\bar{u}_i^t)-g(\alpha)]&=\sum_{t=1}^{T-1}\sum_{i=1}^{\mathbf{n}(\bar{\boldsymbol{u}}^t)}[g(v_i^t)-g(\alpha)]+n[g(\gamma)-g(\alpha)]\\&=\sum_{t=1}^{T-1}\sum_{i=1}^{\mathbf{n}(\boldsymbol{u}^t)}[g(u_i^t)-g(\alpha)].\end{aligned} \tag{5.12}$$

Furthermore, by (5.10) and (5.11), we obtain

$$\sum_{i=1}^{\mathrm{n}(\bar{\boldsymbol{v}}^T)}[g(\bar{v}_i^T)-g(\alpha)] = \sum_{i=1}^{\mathrm{n}(\boldsymbol{u}^T)}[g(u_i^T)-g(\alpha)]+n[g(\gamma)-g(\alpha)] = \sum_{i=1}^{\mathrm{n}(\boldsymbol{v}^T)}[g(v_i^T)-g(\alpha)]. \tag{5.13}$$

From the assumption of induction and (5.12), $\boldsymbol{u} \sim^* \bar{\boldsymbol{u}}$ follows. Further, since $\succsim^*$ is single-generation critical-level generalized utilitarian associated with $\alpha$ and $g$, it follows from (5.13) that $\boldsymbol{v} \sim^* \bar{\boldsymbol{v}}$. By the transitivity of $\succsim^*$, we obtain

$$\boldsymbol{u} \succsim^* \boldsymbol{v} \Leftrightarrow \bar{\boldsymbol{u}} \succsim^* \bar{\boldsymbol{v}}. \tag{5.14}$$

Next, we define $\hat{\boldsymbol{u}}, \hat{\boldsymbol{v}} \in \Omega^{\mathbb{N}}$ by

$$\hat{\boldsymbol{u}} = ([\bar{\boldsymbol{u}}^t, \gamma])_{t\in\mathbb{N}} \text{ and } \hat{\boldsymbol{v}} = ([\bar{\boldsymbol{v}}^t, \gamma])_{t\in\mathbb{N}}.$$

Since $\bar{\boldsymbol{u}}^{+T} = \bar{\boldsymbol{v}}^{T} = \boldsymbol{u}^{+T}$ and $\succsim^*$ satisfies existence independence, we obtain

$$\bar{\boldsymbol{u}} \succsim^* \bar{\boldsymbol{v}} \Leftrightarrow \hat{\boldsymbol{u}} \succsim^* \hat{\boldsymbol{v}}. \tag{5.15}$$

We define $\check{\boldsymbol{u}} \in \Omega^{\mathbb{N}}$ by $\check{\boldsymbol{u}}^{T-1} = \hat{\boldsymbol{u}}^{T}$, $\check{\boldsymbol{u}}^{T} = \hat{\boldsymbol{u}}^{T-1}$ and $\check{\boldsymbol{u}}^{t} = \hat{\boldsymbol{u}}^{t}$ for all $t \neq T-1, T$. From finite anonymity, $\hat{\boldsymbol{u}} \sim^* \check{\boldsymbol{u}}$ follows. By the transitivity of $\succsim^*$, we obtain

$$\hat{\boldsymbol{u}} \succsim^* \hat{\boldsymbol{v}} \Leftrightarrow \check{\boldsymbol{u}} \succsim^* \hat{\boldsymbol{v}}. \tag{5.16}$$

Note that

$$\check{\boldsymbol{u}} = ([\boldsymbol{v}^1, \gamma], \ldots, [\boldsymbol{v}^{T-2}, \gamma], [\boldsymbol{u}^T, \gamma], [\boldsymbol{v}^{T-1}, \gamma\mathbf{1}_{n+1}], [\boldsymbol{v}^{T+1}, \gamma], [\boldsymbol{v}^{T+2}, \gamma], \ldots),$$
$$\hat{\boldsymbol{v}} = ([\boldsymbol{v}^1, \gamma], \ldots, [\boldsymbol{v}^{T-2}, \gamma], [\boldsymbol{v}^{T-1}, \gamma], [\boldsymbol{u}^T, \gamma\mathbf{1}_{n+1}], [\boldsymbol{v}^{T+1}, \gamma], [\boldsymbol{v}^{T+2}, \gamma], \ldots).$$

From existence independence, we obtain

$$\check{\boldsymbol{u}} \succsim^* \hat{\boldsymbol{v}} \Leftrightarrow (\boldsymbol{v}^{-(T-2)}, \boldsymbol{u}^T, \boldsymbol{v}^{T-1}, \boldsymbol{v}^{+T}) \succsim^* (\boldsymbol{v}^{-(T-2)}, \boldsymbol{v}^{T-1}, \boldsymbol{u}^T, \boldsymbol{v}^{+T}). \tag{5.17}$$

Since $\succsim^*$ satisfies finite anonymity, we obtain

$$(\boldsymbol{v}^{-(T-2)}, \boldsymbol{u}^T, \boldsymbol{v}^{T-1}, \boldsymbol{v}^{+T}) \sim^* (\boldsymbol{v}^{-(T-2)}, \boldsymbol{v}^{T-1}, \boldsymbol{u}^T, \boldsymbol{v}^{+T}).$$

Thus, from (5.14), (5.15), (5.16) and (5.17), we obtain $\boldsymbol{u} \sim^* \boldsymbol{v}$.

*Step 2*. We show that for all $T \in \mathbb{N}$ and for all $\boldsymbol{u}, \boldsymbol{v} \in \Omega^{\mathbb{N}}$ with $\boldsymbol{u}^{+T} = \boldsymbol{v}^{+T}$,

$$\sum_{t=1}^{T} \sum_{i=1}^{\mathbf{n}(u^t)} [g(u_i^t) - g(\alpha)] > \sum_{t=1}^{T} \sum_{i=1}^{\mathbf{n}(v^t)} [g(v_i^t) - g(\alpha)] \Rightarrow \boldsymbol{u} \succ^* \boldsymbol{v}.$$

Let $T \in \mathbb{N}$ and $\boldsymbol{u}, \boldsymbol{v} \in \Omega^{\mathbb{N}}$ with $\boldsymbol{u}^{+T} = \boldsymbol{v}^{+T}$. Suppose that

$$\sum_{t=1}^{T} \sum_{i=1}^{\mathbf{n}(u^t)} [g(u_i^t) - g(\alpha)] > \sum_{t=1}^{T} \sum_{i=1}^{\mathbf{n}(v^t)} [g(v_i^t) - g(\alpha)].$$

We define $\Delta \in \mathbb{R}_{++}$ by

$$\Delta = \sum_{t=1}^{T} \sum_{i=1}^{\mathbf{n}(u^t)} [g(u_i^t) - g(\alpha)] - \sum_{t=1}^{T} \sum_{i=1}^{\mathbf{n}(v^t)} [g(v_i^t) - g(\alpha)].$$

Let $\beta \in \mathbb{R}$ with $\beta > \alpha$. Then, by the same argument as that in Step 1, there exist $n \in \mathbb{N}$ and $\gamma \in (\alpha, \beta)$ such that

$$n[g(\gamma) - g(\alpha)] = \Delta.$$

Define $\bar{\boldsymbol{u}} \in \Omega^{\mathbb{N}}$ by

$$\bar{\boldsymbol{u}} = ([v^1, \gamma \mathbf{1}_n], \boldsymbol{v}^{+1}).$$

Note that $\bar{\boldsymbol{u}}^{+T} = \boldsymbol{v}^{+T} = \boldsymbol{u}^{+T}$ and

$$\begin{aligned}
\sum_{t=1}^{T} \sum_{i=1}^{\mathbf{n}(\bar{u}^t)} [g(\bar{u}_i^t) - g(\alpha)] &= \sum_{t=1}^{T} \sum_{i=1}^{\mathbf{n}(v^t)} [g(v_i^t) - g(\alpha)] + n[g(\gamma) - g(\alpha)] \\
&= \sum_{t=1}^{T} \sum_{i=1}^{\mathbf{n}(v^t)} [g(v_i^t) - g(\alpha)] + \Delta \\
&= \sum_{t=1}^{T} \sum_{i=1}^{\mathbf{n}(u^t)} [g(u_i^t) - g(\alpha)].
\end{aligned}$$

Thus, from Step 1, $\boldsymbol{u} \sim^* \bar{\boldsymbol{u}}$ follows. Furthermore, note that $\bar{\boldsymbol{u}}^{+1} = \boldsymbol{v}^{+1}$ and

$$\begin{aligned}
\sum_{i=1}^{\mathbf{n}(\bar{u}^1)} [g(\bar{u}_i^1) - g(\alpha)] &= \sum_{i=1}^{\mathbf{n}(v^1)} [g(v_i^1) - g(\alpha)] + n[g(\gamma) - g(\alpha)] \\
&> \sum_{i=1}^{\mathbf{n}(v^1)} [g(v_i^1) - g(\alpha)].
\end{aligned}$$

Since $\succsim^*$ is single-generation critical-level generalized utilitarian associated with $\alpha$ and $g$, we obtain $\bar{\boldsymbol{u}} \succ^* \boldsymbol{v}$. By the transitivity of $\succsim^*$, we obtain $\boldsymbol{u} \succ^* \boldsymbol{v}$.

*Step 3*. We will complete the proof. Let $T \in \mathbb{N}$ and $\boldsymbol{u}, \boldsymbol{v} \in \Omega^{\mathbb{N}}$ with $\boldsymbol{u}^{+T} = \boldsymbol{v}^{+T}$. From Steps 1 and 2,

$$\sum_{t=1}^{T} \sum_{i=1}^{\mathbf{n}(u^t)} [g(u_i^t) - g(\alpha)] \geq \sum_{t=1}^{T} \sum_{i=1}^{\mathbf{n}(v^t)} [g(v_i^t) - g(\alpha)] \Rightarrow \boldsymbol{u} \succsim^* \boldsymbol{v}.$$

To show that the converse implication also holds, we now assume $\boldsymbol{u} \succsim^* \boldsymbol{v}$. If $\sum_{t=1}^{T} \sum_{i=1}^{\mathbf{n}(u^t)} [g(u_i^t) - g(\alpha)] < \sum_{t=1}^{T} \sum_{i=1}^{\mathbf{n}(v^t)} [g(v_i^t) - g(\alpha)]$, then from Step 2, we obtain $\boldsymbol{v} \succ^* \boldsymbol{u}$. However, this is a contradiction because $\boldsymbol{u} \succsim^* \boldsymbol{v}$. Thus, $\sum_{t=1}^{T} \sum_{i=1}^{\mathbf{n}(u^t)} [g(u_i^t) - g(\alpha)] \geq \sum_{t=1}^{T} \sum_{i=1}^{\mathbf{n}(v^t)} [g(v_i^t) - g(\alpha)]$ must hold. ■

The following theorem presents an axiomatization of the critical-level utilitarian social welfare relation $\succsim^*_{U,\alpha}$ using intratemporal incremental equity combined with other axioms.

**Theorem 5.2** *A social welfare relation $\succsim^*$ on $\Omega^{\mathbb{N}}$ satisfies strong Pareto, finite anonymity, intratemporal incremental equity, weak existence of critical levels, and existence independence if and only if there exists $\alpha \in \mathbb{R}$ such that $\succsim^*_{U,\alpha}$ associated with $\alpha$ is a subrelation of $\succsim^*$.*

***Proof*** 'If.' It is easy to verify that $\succsim^*$ satisfies the axioms if there exists $\alpha \in \mathbb{R}$ such that $\succsim^*_{U,\alpha}$ associated with $\alpha$ is a subrelation of $\succsim^*$; we omit its proof.

'Only if.' *Step 1*. We show that there exist $\alpha \in \mathbb{R}$ such that $\succsim^*$ is single-generation critical-level utilitarian associated with $\alpha$ and the identity mapping $g \in G$. Let $t \in \mathbb{N}$. Since $\succsim^*$ satisfies existence independence, we can define the quasi-ordering $\succsim_t$ on $\Omega$ by, for all $\boldsymbol{u}, \boldsymbol{v} \in \Omega^{\mathbb{N}}$ with $\boldsymbol{u}^{t'} = \boldsymbol{v}^{t'}$ for all $t' \neq t$,

$$\boldsymbol{u}^t \succsim_t \boldsymbol{v}^t \ \Leftrightarrow\ \boldsymbol{u} \succsim^* \boldsymbol{v}. \tag{5.18}$$

Since $\succsim^*$ is transitive and satisfies finite anonymity, it follows from strong Pareto and intratemporal incremental equity that, for each $n \in \mathbb{N}$, the restriction of $\succsim_t$ on $\mathbb{R}^n$ satisfies strong Pareto and incremental equity defined for a quasi-ordering on $\mathbb{R}^n$; see Chap. 2. From Theorem 2.1, it follows that, for all $n \in \mathbb{N}$ and for all $\boldsymbol{u}^t, \boldsymbol{v}^t \in \mathbb{R}^n$,

$$\boldsymbol{u}^t \succsim_t \boldsymbol{v}^t \ \Leftrightarrow\ \sum_{i=1}^{n} u_i^t \geq \sum_{i=1}^{n} v_i^t. \tag{5.19}$$

Since $\succsim^*$ is transitive and satisfies finite anonymity, it follows from weak existence of critical levels and existence independence that $\succsim_t$ satisfies the corresponding properties defined as follows.

**Property 5.1**. There exist $\alpha \in \mathbb{R}$ and $\boldsymbol{u}^t \in \Omega$ such that $\boldsymbol{u}^t \sim_t [\boldsymbol{u}^t, \alpha]$.

**Property 5.2**. For all $\boldsymbol{u}^t, \boldsymbol{v}^t, \boldsymbol{w}^t \in \Omega$,

$$\boldsymbol{u}^t \succsim_t \boldsymbol{v}^t \Leftrightarrow [\boldsymbol{u}^t, \boldsymbol{w}^t] \succsim_t [\boldsymbol{v}^t, \boldsymbol{w}^t].$$

As shown by Blackorby et al. (2005, Theorem 6.9), these two properties together imply that there exists $\alpha \in \mathbb{R}$ such that for all $\boldsymbol{u}^t \in \Omega$,

$$\boldsymbol{u}^t \sim_t [\boldsymbol{u}^t, \alpha]. \tag{5.20}$$

To complete Step 1, let $\boldsymbol{u}, \boldsymbol{v} \in \Omega^{\mathbb{N}}$ with $\boldsymbol{u}^{t'} = \boldsymbol{v}^{t'}$ for all $t' \neq t$. If $\mathbf{n}(\boldsymbol{u}^t) = \mathbf{n}(\boldsymbol{v}^t) = n \in \mathbb{N}$, it follows from (5.18) and (5.19) that

$$\begin{aligned} \boldsymbol{u} \succsim^* \boldsymbol{v} &\Leftrightarrow \boldsymbol{u}^t \succsim_t \boldsymbol{v}^t \\ &\Leftrightarrow \sum_{i=1}^{n} \boldsymbol{u}_i^t \geq \sum_{i=1}^{n} v_i^t \\ &\Leftrightarrow \sum_{i=1}^{n} [\boldsymbol{u}_i^t - \alpha] \geq \sum_{i=1}^{n} [v_i^t - \alpha]. \end{aligned}$$

We now suppose $\mathbf{n}(\boldsymbol{u}^t) \neq \mathbf{n}(\boldsymbol{v}^t)$. Without loss of generality, we assume $\mathbf{n}(\boldsymbol{u}^t) > \mathbf{n}(\boldsymbol{v}^t)$. Let $\mathbf{n}(\boldsymbol{u}^t) = n$ and $\mathbf{n}(\boldsymbol{v}^t) = m$. From (5.20), we obtain

$$\boldsymbol{v}^t \sim_t [\boldsymbol{v}^t, \alpha \mathbf{1}_{n-m}].$$

Thus, since $\succsim_t$ is transitive, it follows from (5.18) and (5.19) that

$$\begin{aligned} \boldsymbol{u} \succsim^* \boldsymbol{v} &\Leftrightarrow \boldsymbol{u}^t \succsim_t \boldsymbol{v}^t \\ &\Leftrightarrow \boldsymbol{u}^t \succsim_t [\boldsymbol{v}^t, \alpha \mathbf{1}_{n-m}] \\ &\Leftrightarrow \sum_{i=1}^{n} \boldsymbol{u}_i^t \geq \sum_{i=1}^{m} v_i^t + (n-m)\alpha \\ &\Leftrightarrow \sum_{i=1}^{n} [\boldsymbol{u}_i^t - \alpha] \geq \sum_{i=1}^{m} [v_i^t - \alpha]. \end{aligned}$$

*Step 2*. We show that $\succsim^*_{U,\alpha}$ is a subrelation of $\succsim^*$. Let $\boldsymbol{u}, \boldsymbol{v} \in \Omega^{\mathbb{N}}$. We suppose $\boldsymbol{u} \succ^*_{U,\alpha} \boldsymbol{v}$. From (5.4a), there exists $T \in \mathbb{N}$ such that $\boldsymbol{u}^t \succsim_S \boldsymbol{v}^t$ for all $t > T$ and

$$\sum_{t=1}^{T} \sum_{i=1}^{\mathbf{n}(\boldsymbol{u}^t)} [u_i^t - \alpha] > \sum_{t=1}^{T} \sum_{i=1}^{\mathbf{n}(\boldsymbol{v}^t)} [v_i^t - \alpha].$$

Define $\bar{\boldsymbol{u}} \in \Omega^{\mathbb{N}}$ by $\bar{\boldsymbol{u}} = (\boldsymbol{u}^{+T}, \boldsymbol{v}^{+T})$. Since $\succsim^*$ satisfies strong Pareto and is intratemporally anonymous and transitive, we obtain $\boldsymbol{u} \succsim^* \bar{\boldsymbol{u}}$. Further, from Step 1 and

Lemma 5.2, $\bar{\boldsymbol{u}} \succ^* \boldsymbol{v}$ follows. Thus, by the transitivity of $\succsim^*$, we obtain $\boldsymbol{u} \succ^* \boldsymbol{v}$. The proof that $\boldsymbol{u} \sim^*_{U,\alpha} \boldsymbol{v}$ implies $\boldsymbol{u} \sim^* \boldsymbol{v}$ is analogous. ■

Assuming the finite completeness of a social welfare relation, we obtain an axiomatization of the critical-level generalized utilitarian social welfare relation by replacing intratemporal incremental equity with restricted continuity in the axioms of Theorem 5.2. This result was presented by Kamaga (2016).

**Theorem 5.3** (Kamaga 2016) *A finitely complete social welfare relation* $\succsim^*$ *on* $\Omega^{\mathbb{N}}$ *satisfies strong Pareto, finite anonymity, weak existence of critical levels, existence independence, and restricted continuity if and only if there exist* $g \in G$ *and* $\alpha \in \mathbb{R}$ *such that* $\succsim^*_{U,g,\alpha}$ *associated with* $g$ *and* $\alpha$ *is a subrelation of* $\succsim^*$.

***Proof*** 'If.' It is easy to verify that $\succsim^*$ satisfies the axioms if there exist $g \in G$ and $\alpha \in \mathbb{R}$ such that $\succsim^*_{U,g,\alpha}$ associated with $g$ and $\alpha$ is a subrelation of $\succsim^*$; we omit its proof.

'Only if.' We begin by showing that there exist $g \in G$ and $\alpha \in \mathbb{R}$ such that $\succsim^*$ is single-generation critical-level utilitarian associated with $g$ and $\alpha$. Let $t \in \mathbb{N}$. Since $\succsim^*$ satisfies existence independence, we can define the ordering $\succsim_t$ on $\Omega$ that satisfies (5.18). Since $\succsim^*$ is intratemporally anonymous and satisfies strong Pareto, existence independence and restricted continuity, it follows from the argument analogous to that in Step 1 of the proof of Theorem 5.2 that for all $n \in \mathbb{N}$, the restriction of $\succsim_t$ on $\mathbb{R}^n$ satisfies strong Pareto, anonymity, separability and continuity; see Chap. 2. Furthermore, weak existence of critical levels and existence independence imply that $\succsim_t$ satisfies Properties 1 and 2 in the proof of Theorem 5.2. Thus, from Theorem 18 in Blackorby, Bossert and Donaldson (2002), there exist $g \in G$ and $\alpha \in \mathbb{R}$ such that for all $\boldsymbol{u}^t, \boldsymbol{v}^t \in \Omega$,

$$\boldsymbol{u}^t \succsim_t \boldsymbol{v}^t \;\Leftrightarrow\; \sum_{i=1}^{\mathrm{n}(\boldsymbol{u}^t)} [g(u_i^t) - g(\alpha)] \geq \sum_{i=1}^{\mathrm{n}(\boldsymbol{v}^t)} [g(v_i^t) - g(\alpha)].$$

Since $\succsim_t$ satisfies (5.18), $\succsim^*$ is single-generation critical-level utilitarian associated with $g$ and $\alpha$.

Using an argument analogous to that used in Step 2 of the proof of Theorem 5.2, it can be shown that $\succsim^*_{U,g,\alpha}$ associated with $g$ and $\alpha$ is a subrelation of $\succsim^*$. ■

To present the axiomatic characterizations of the critical-level (generalized) utilitarian overtaking social welfare relation and the critical-level (generalized) utilitarian catching-up social welfare relation, we consider three consistency axioms, which were presented by Kamaga (2016). The first two axioms are reformulations of the preference consistency axioms we used in Chap. 3 to characterize the overtaking and catching-up criteria. (See also Kamaga and Kojima (2010)). Both require that the strict preference relation of the evaluation be consistent with the evaluations obtained when the tails of streams of utility vectors are replaced with any common one.

**Weak Preference Consistency**: For all $\boldsymbol{u}, \boldsymbol{v} \in \Omega^{\mathbb{N}}$, if $(\boldsymbol{u}^{-t}, \boldsymbol{w}^{+t}) \succ^* (\boldsymbol{v}^{-t}, \boldsymbol{w}^{+t})$ for all $t \in \mathbb{N}$ and all $\boldsymbol{w} \in \Omega^{\mathbb{N}}$, then $\boldsymbol{u} \succ^* \boldsymbol{v}$.

**Strong Preference Consistency**: For all $\boldsymbol{u}, \boldsymbol{v} \in \Omega^{\mathbb{N}}$, if, for all $\boldsymbol{w} \in \Omega^{\mathbb{N}}$, $(\boldsymbol{u}^{-t}, \boldsymbol{w}^{+t}) \succsim^* (\boldsymbol{v}^{-t}, \boldsymbol{w}^{+t})$ for all $t \in \mathbb{N}$ and, for all $t' \in \mathbb{N}$, there exists $t > t'$ such that $(\boldsymbol{u}^{-t}, \boldsymbol{w}^{+t}) \succ^* (\boldsymbol{v}^{-t}, \boldsymbol{w}^{+t})$, then $\boldsymbol{u} \succ^* \boldsymbol{v}$.

Indifference consistency postulates a requirement similar to that of weak preference consistency for the indifference relation of the evaluation.

**Indifference Consistency**: For all $\boldsymbol{u}, \boldsymbol{v} \in \Omega^{\mathbb{N}}$, if $(\boldsymbol{u}^{-t}, \boldsymbol{w}^{+t}) I^* (\boldsymbol{v}^{-t}, \boldsymbol{w}^{+t})$ for all $t \in \mathbb{N}$ and all $\boldsymbol{w} \in \Omega^{\mathbb{N}}$, then $\boldsymbol{u} I^* \boldsymbol{v}$.

Adding weak preference consistency and indifference consistency to the axioms of Theorem 5.2, we obtain the following axiomatization of the critical-level utilitarian overtaking social welfare relation.

**Theorem 5.4** *A social welfare relation* $\succsim^*$ *on* $\Omega^{\mathbb{N}}$ *satisfies strong Pareto, finite anonymity, intratemporal incremental equity, weak existence of critical levels, existence independence, weak preference consistency, and indifference consistency if and only if there exists* $\alpha \in \mathbb{R}$ *such that* $\succsim^*_{O,\alpha}$ *associated with* $\alpha$ *is a subrelation of* $\succsim^*$.

***Proof*** 'If.' The proof is easy and we omit it.

'Only if.' From Theorem 5.2, there exists $\alpha \in \mathbb{R}$ such that $\succsim^*_{U,\alpha}$ associated with $\alpha$ is a subrelation of $\succsim^*$. We show that $\succsim^*_{O,\alpha}$ associated with $\alpha$ is a subrelation of $\succsim^*$. Let $\boldsymbol{u}, \boldsymbol{v} \in \Omega^{\mathbb{N}}$ and suppose $\boldsymbol{u} \succ^*_{O,\alpha} \boldsymbol{v}$. From (5.5a), there exists $T^* \in \mathbb{N}$ such that for all $T \geq T^*$,

$$\sum_{t=1}^{T}\sum_{i=1}^{\mathbf{n}(\boldsymbol{u}^t)}[u_i^t - \alpha] > \sum_{t=1}^{T}\sum_{i=1}^{\mathbf{n}(\boldsymbol{v}^t)}[v_i^t - \alpha].$$

Since $\succsim^*_{U,\alpha}$ is a subrelation of $\succsim^*$, letting $g \in G$ be the identity mapping in (5.8) in Lemma 5.2, $\succsim^*$ satisfies (5.8). Define $\bar{\boldsymbol{u}}, \bar{\boldsymbol{v}} \in \Omega^{\mathbb{N}}$ as follows: $\bar{\boldsymbol{u}}^1 = [\boldsymbol{u}^1, \ldots, \boldsymbol{u}^{T^*}]$, $\bar{\boldsymbol{u}}^t = \alpha$ for all $t \in \{2, \ldots, T^*\}$, $\bar{\boldsymbol{u}}^{+T^*} = \boldsymbol{u}^{T^*}$, $\bar{\boldsymbol{v}}^1 = [\boldsymbol{v}^1, \ldots, \boldsymbol{v}^{T^*}]$, $\bar{\boldsymbol{v}}^t = \alpha$ for all $t \in \{2, \ldots, T^*\}$, and $\bar{\boldsymbol{v}}^{+T^*} = \boldsymbol{v}^{T^*}$. Since $\succsim^*$ satisfies (5.8), we obtain $\boldsymbol{u} \sim^* \bar{\boldsymbol{u}}$, and $\boldsymbol{v} \sim^* \bar{\boldsymbol{v}}$. Further, by the construction of $\bar{\boldsymbol{u}}$ and $\bar{\boldsymbol{v}}$, it follows that, for all $t \in \mathbb{N}$ and for all $\boldsymbol{w} \in \Omega^{\mathbb{N}}$, $(\bar{\boldsymbol{u}}^{-t}, \boldsymbol{w}^{+t}) \succ^* (\bar{\boldsymbol{v}}^{-t}, \boldsymbol{w}^{+t})$. From weak preference consistency, we obtain $\bar{\boldsymbol{u}} \succ^* \bar{\boldsymbol{v}}$. Since $\succsim^*$ is transitive, $\boldsymbol{u} \succ^* \boldsymbol{v}$ follows.

The proof that $\boldsymbol{u} \sim^*_{O,\alpha} \boldsymbol{v}$ implies $\boldsymbol{u} \sim^* \boldsymbol{v}$ is analogous using indifference consistency instead of weak preference consistency. ∎

Analogously, the critical-level generalized utilitarian overtaking social welfare relation is axiomatized by adding the consistency axioms in the axioms of Theorem 5.3. This result is was provided by Kamaga (2016). The proof is analogous to that of Theorem 5.4 and we omit its proof.

**Theorem 5.5** (Kamaga 2016) *A finitely complete social welfare relation* $\succsim^*$ *on* $\Omega^{\mathbb{N}}$ *satisfies strong Pareto, finite anonymity, weak existence of critical levels, existence independence, restricted continuity, weak preference consistency, and indifference consistency if and only if there exist* $g \in G$ *and* $\alpha \in \mathbb{R}$ *such that* $\succsim^*_{O,g,\alpha}$ *associated with* $g$ *and* $\alpha$ *is a subrelation of* $\succsim^*$.

Finally, replacing weak preference consistency with strong preference consistency in Theorems 5.4 and 5.5, we obtain the following axiomatizations of the critical-level utilitarian catching-up and the critical-level generalized utilitarian catching-up social welfare relations. The latter result was presented by Kamaga (2016). We omit their proofs because they are analogous to the proof of Theorem 5.4.

**Theorem 5.6** *A social welfare relation* $\succsim^*$ *on* $\Omega^{\mathbb{N}}$ *satisfies strong Pareto, finite anonymity, intratemporal incremental equity, weak existence of critical levels, existence independence, strong preference consistency, and indifference consistency if and only if there exists* $\alpha \in \mathbb{R}$ *such that* $\succsim^*_{C,\alpha}$ *associated with* $\alpha$ *is a subrelation of* $\succsim^*$.

**Theorem 5.7** (Kamaga 2016) *A finitely complete social welfare relation* $\succsim^*$ *on* $\Omega^{\mathbb{N}}$ *satisfies strong Pareto, finite anonymity, weak existence of critical levels, existence independence, restricted continuity, strong preference consistency, and indifference consistency if and only if there exist* $g \in G$ *and* $\alpha \in \mathbb{R}$ *such that* $\succsim^*_{C,g,\alpha}$ *associated with* $g$ *and* $\alpha$ *is a subrelation of* $\succsim^*$.

## 5.5 Population Ethics

In this section, we review the analysis of population ethics properties conducted in Kamaga (2016) for the critical-level generalized utilitarian overtaking and catching-up social welfare relations. In Kamaga (2016), Parfit's (1976, 1982, 1984) repugnant conclusion and Arrhenius's (2000, 2011) very sadistic conclusion—two of the major issues in population ethics—are reformulated in the infinite-horizon framework. The repugnant conclusion pointed out by Parfit (1976, 1982, 1984) is the ethically unacceptable conclusion that classical utilitarianism leads to when evaluating social states with finite and variable population sizes, namely, some social state in which each member of the population has a high level of utility is declared to be worse than some social state with a much larger population in which each member has a utility level corresponding to a life barely worth living, i.e., the utility level of positive but close to zero. Using the dominance in each generation's population size, Kamaga (2016) reformulated the repugnant conclusion in the infinite-horizon framework as follows. A social welfare relation $\succsim^*$ on $\Omega^{\mathbb{N}}$ implies the *repugnant conclusion* if and only if, for any stream of population sizes $(n_t)_{t\in\mathbb{N}} \in \mathbb{N}^{\mathbb{N}}$ and for any stream of positive utility levels of generations $(\xi_t)_{t\in\mathbb{N}}, (\epsilon_t)_{t\in\mathbb{N}} \in \mathbb{R}^{\mathbb{N}}_{++}$ satisfying $(\xi_t)_{t\in\mathbb{N}} \gg (\epsilon_t)_{t\in\mathbb{N}}$, there exists a stream of population sizes $(m_t)_{t\in\mathbb{N}} \in \mathbb{N}^{\mathbb{N}}$ with $(m_t)_{t\in\mathbb{N}} \gg (n_t)_{t\in\mathbb{N}}$ such that $(\epsilon_t \mathbf{1}_{m_t})_{t\in\mathbb{N}} \succ^* (\xi_t \mathbf{1}_{n_t})_{t\in\mathbb{N}}$.

The following axiom, presented by Kamaga (2016), requires that the evaluation avoid the repugnant conclusion. For the axiom requiring the avoidance of the repugnant conclusion in the finite-horizon framework, see Blackorby, Bossert and Donaldson (2005).

**Avoidance of the Repugnant Conclusion**: There exist $(n_t)_{t\in\mathbb{N}} \in \mathbb{N}^{\mathbb{N}}$ and $(\xi_t)_{t\in\mathbb{N}}$, $(\epsilon_t)_{t\in\mathbb{N}} \in \mathbb{R}^{\mathbb{N}}_{++}$ with $(\xi_t)_{t\in\mathbb{N}} \gg (\epsilon_t)_{t\in\mathbb{N}}$ such that for all $(m_t)_{t\in\mathbb{N}} \in \mathbb{N}^{\mathbb{N}}$ with $(m_t)_{t\in\mathbb{N}} \gg (n_t)_{t\in\mathbb{N}}$, $(\xi_t \mathbf{1}_{n_t})_{t\in\mathbb{N}} \succsim^* (\epsilon_t \mathbf{1}_{m_t})_{t\in\mathbb{N}}$.
Note that this axiom implies the negation of the repugnant conclusion.

Adding this axiom to the axioms of Theorems 5.5 and 5.7 implies the critical-level generalized utilitarian overtaking social welfare relation and the critical-level generalized utilitarian catching-up social welfare relation must be associated with a positive critical level. See Kamaga (2016) for a proof.

**Theorem 5.8** (Kamaga 2016)

*(i) A finitely complete social welfare relation $\succsim^*$ on $\Omega^{\mathbb{N}}$ satisfies avoidance of the repugnant conclusion in addition to the axioms in Theorem 5.5 if and only if there exist $g \in G$ and $\alpha \in \mathbb{R}_{++}$ such that $\succ^*_{O,g,\alpha}$ is a subrelation of $\succsim^*$.*

*(ii) A finitely complete social welfare relation $\succsim^*$ on $\Omega^{\mathbb{N}}$ satisfies avoidance of the repugnant conclusion in addition to the axioms in Theorem 5.7 if and only if there exist $g \in G$ and $\alpha \in \mathbb{R}_{++}$ such that $\succsim^*_{C,g,\alpha}$ is a subrelation of $\succsim^*$.*

In the context of evaluating finite-horizon utility distributions with variable population sizes, (Arrhenius 2000, 2011) pointed out a drawback of critical-level utilitarianism. Specifically, if a positive critical level is employed, critical-level utilitarianism leads to the very sadistic conclusion that, for any population with negative utility levels, there is a population with positive utility levels declared to be worse. Letting $\Omega_{++} = \cup_{n\in\mathbb{N}}\mathbb{R}^n_{++}$ and $\Omega_{--} = \cup_{n\in\mathbb{N}}\mathbb{R}^n_{--}$, the very sadistic conclusion can be reformulated in the infinite-horizon framework as follows. A social welfare relation $\succsim^*$ on $\Omega^{\mathbb{N}}$ implies the *very sadistic conclusion* if and only if, for any stream of negative utility vectors $\boldsymbol{u} \in \Omega^{\mathbb{N}}_{--}$, there exists a stream of positive utility vectors $\boldsymbol{v} \in \Omega^{\mathbb{N}}_{++}$ such that $\boldsymbol{u} \succ^* \boldsymbol{v}$.

The following axiom, presented by Kamaga (2016), implies the negation of the very sadistic conclusion.

**Avoidance of the Very Sadistic Conclusion**: There exists $\boldsymbol{u} \in \Omega^{\mathbb{N}}_{--}$ such that $\boldsymbol{v} R^* \boldsymbol{u}$ for all $\boldsymbol{v} \in \Omega^{\mathbb{N}}_{++}$.

As shown in the following theorem, the criticism that is raised against critical-level utilitarianism applies to the critical-level generalized overtaking and catching-up social welfare relations. See Kamaga (2016) for a proof.

**Theorem 5.9** (Kamaga 2016) *Let $\succsim^*$ be a social welfare relation on $\Omega^{\mathbb{N}}$ that includes $\succsim^*_{O,g,\alpha}$ associated with $g \in G$ and $\alpha \in \mathbb{R}$ as a subrelation. Then, $\succsim^*$ satisfies avoidance of the very sadistic conclusion if and only if $\alpha \leq 0$.*

Since the critical-level generalized overtaking social welfare relation associated with $g \in G$ and $\alpha \in \mathbb{R}$ is a subrelation of the critical-level generalized catching-up social welfare relation associated with $g$ and $\alpha$, the restriction of $\alpha$ in the theorem applies to the critical-level generalized catching-up social welfare relation. Consequently, when we use the critical-level generalized overtaking and catching-up social welfare relations, we face the trade-off between avoiding the repugnant conclusion and avoiding the very sadistic conclusion.

## 5.6 Concluding Remarks

We examined infinite-horizon extensions of critical-level (generalized) utilitarianism in the welfarist framework for intergenerational social evaluation with variable population size. The axiomatizations we presented for them show that intragenerational evaluation restricts permissible social evaluation between generations. Besides the infinite-horizon reformulation of the repugnant conclusion and the very sadistic conclusion, other population ethics properties could be reformulated in the infinite-horizon framework. In the finite-horizon variable-population framework, Asheim and Zuber (2014) recently proposed and axiomatized rank-discounted utilitarianism. Further, they showed that rank-discounted utilitarianism satisfies most of plausible population ethics axioms, including avoidance of the repugnant conclusion and the very sadistic conclusion. A future research to be addressed is to reformulate and axiomatically analyze rank-discounted utilitarianism in the infinite-horizon variable-population framework.

## References


Arrhenius, G. (2000). An impossibility theorem for welfarist axiologies. *Economics and Philosophy*, *16*, 247–266.

Arrhenius, G. (2011). *Population ethics: The challenge of the future generations*. Oxford: Oxford University Press. (forthcoming).

Asheim, G. B., & Zuber, S. (2014). Escaping the repugnant conclusion: Rank-discounted utilitarianism with variable population. *Theoretical Economics*, *9*, 629–650.

Atsumi, H. (1965). Neoclassical growth and the efficient program of capital accumulation. *Review of Economic Studies*, *32*, 127–136.

Blackorby, C., Bossert, W., & Donaldson, D. (1995). Intertemporal population ethics: Critical-level utilitarian principles. *Econometrica*, *63*, 5–10.

Blackorby, C., Bossert, W., & Donaldson, D. (1998). Uncertainty and critical-level population principles. *Journal of Population Economics*, *11*, 1–20.

Blackorby, C., Bossert, W., & Donaldson, D. (1999). Information invariance in variable population social-choice problems. *International Economic Review*, *40*, 403–422.

Blackorby, C., Bossert, W., & Donaldson, D. (2002). Utilitarianism and the theory of justice. In K. J. Arrow, A. K. Sen, & K. Suzumura (Eds.), *Handbook of social choice and welfare* (Vol. I). Amsterdam: North-Holland.

Blackorby, C., Bossert, W., & Donaldson, D. (2005). *Population issues in social choice theory, welfare economics, and ethics*. Cambridge: Cambridge University Press.

Blackorby, C., & Donaldson, D. (1984). Social criteria for evaluating population change. *Journal of Public Economics*, *25*, 13–33.

Broome, J. (1993). Goodness is reducible to betterness: The evil of death is the value of life. In P. Koslowski & Y. Shionoya (Eds.), *The good and the economical: Ethical choices in economics and management*. Berline: Springer.

d'Aspremont, C. (1985). Axioms for social welfare orderings. In L. Hurwicz, D. Schmeidler, & H. Sonnenschein (Eds.), *Social goals and social organizations: Essays in memory of Elisha Pazner*. Cambridge: Cambridge University Press.
d'Aspremont, C. (2007). Formal welfarism and intergenerational equity. In J. E. Roemer & K. Suzumura (Eds.), *Intergenerational equity and sustainability*. Palgrave-Macmillan: Basingstoke.
d'Aspremont, C., & Gevers, L. (1977). Equity and the informational basis of collective choice. *Review of Economic Studies, 44*, 199–209.
Hammond, P. J. (1979). Equity in two person situations: Some consequences. *Econometrica, 47*, 1127–1135.
Kamaga, K., & Kojima, T. (2010). On the leximin and utilitarian overtaking criteria with extended anonymity. *Social Choice and Welfare, 35*, 377–392.
Kamaga, K. (2016). Infinite-horizon social evaluation with variable population size. *Social Choice and Welfare, 47*, 207–232.
Parfit, D. (1976). On doing the best for our children. In M. Bayles (Ed.), *Ethics and population*. Cambridge: Shenkman.
Parfit, D. (1982). Future generations, future problems. *Philosophy & Public Affairs, 11*, 113–172.
Parfit, D. (1984). *Reasons and persons*. Oxford: Oxford University Press.
Sen, A. K. (1970). *Collective choice and social welfare*. Amsterdam: Holden-Day.
Suppes, P. (1966). Some formal models of grading principles. *Synthese, 6*, 284–306.
Svensson, L.-G. (1980). Equity among generations. *Econometrica, 48*, 1251–1256.
von Weizsäcker, C. C. (1965). Existence of optimal programs of accumulation for an infinite time horizon. *Review of Economic Studies, 32*, 85–104.

# Chapter 6
# Conclusion: Further Issues

**Abstract** This chapter discusses further issues regarding intergenerational social welfare evaluation that are not covered in the previous chapters. First, we review the analysis of representable social welfare orderings and the possibility of strongly anonymous social welfare orderings. Second, we will discusses a choice-theoretic approach to intergenerational resource allocation problems with variable population size.

**Keywords** Representability · Strong anonymity · Choice function · Economic environment

## 6.1 Representability and Strong Anonymity

In Chaps. 3 and 4, we considered social welfare quasi-orderings—reflexive and transitive but not necessarily complete binary relations for evaluating the relative goodness of infinite streams of utilities of generations. We produced general results showing how a social welfare evaluation applied to finite generations can be extended to an infinite-horizon social evaluation. Then, we obtained axiomatic characterizations of several kinds of specific social welfare quasi-orderings utilizing the axiomatizations of specific social welfare orderings and social welfare quasi-orderings we presented in Chap. 2. As we noted in Chap. 1, analyzing social welfare quasi-orderings is not the only possible approach to evaluating infinite utility streams. Besides the two other approaches mentioned above, another approach was proposed by Basu and Mitra (2003). It is closely related to the method that examines continuity properties that are compatible with a social welfare ordering satisfying the strong Pareto and finite anonymity. Specifically, Basu and Mitra (2003) examined a social welfare function

$$W : X \to \mathbb{R},$$

where $X$ is the set of possible utility streams $\boldsymbol{u} = (u_1, u_2, \ldots, u_i, \ldots)$ defined by $X = Y^{\mathbb{N}}$ and $Y \subseteq \mathbb{R}$ with $|Y| \geq 2$ and, for each $i \in \mathbb{N}$, $u_i$ is interpreted as the utility level of the $i$-th generation.

 
K. Kamaga, *Social Welfare Evaluation and Intergenerational Equity*,
Development Bank of Japan Research Series,
https://doi.org/10.1007/978-981-15-4254-1_6

If a social welfare function is assumed to be ordinal, the analysis of a social welfare function $W$ is related to that of a social welfare ordering $\succsim$ on $X$. Formally, a social welfare ordering $\succsim$ on $X$ is said to be *representable* by a social welfare function $W$ if, for all $\boldsymbol{u} = (u_1, u_2, \ldots, u_i, \ldots)$, $\boldsymbol{v} = (v_1, v_2, \ldots, v_i, \ldots) \in X$,

$$\boldsymbol{u} \succsim \boldsymbol{v} \Leftrightarrow W(\boldsymbol{u}) \geq W(\boldsymbol{v}).$$

Thus, $\succsim$ ranks infinite utility streams $\boldsymbol{u}$ and $\boldsymbol{v}$ according to the large-small relation of $W(\boldsymbol{u})$ and $W(\boldsymbol{v})$. The sup norm continuity of a social welfare ordering $\succsim$, which was employed in the impossibility result of Diamond (1965), is a sufficient condition for $\succsim$ to be represented by a social welfare function. Thus, the approach taken by Basu and Mitra (2003) is seen to weaken the continuity property employed by Diamond (1965), but it does not examine continuity properties that are compatible with a social welfare ordering satisfying the strong Pareto and finite anonymity, while the representability of a social welfare ordering is assumed to be given.

According to the definition of representability, Paretian axioms for a social welfare function are defined analogously to those defined for a social welfare quasi-ordering in Chaps. 3 and 4. The finite anonymity axiom for a social welfare function is defined in the same manner as that for a social welfare quasi-ordering. Basu and Mitra (2003) examined whether a social welfare function exists that satisfies a Paretian axiom and finite anonymity. They employed two Paretian axioms—a slightly strengthened variant of weak dominance and the weak Pareto principle; see Chap. 4 for the definitions of weak dominance and the weak Pareto principle. They obtained the following impossibility results: There is no social welfare function that satisfies the weak Pareto principle and finite anonymity; and, if $Y = [0, 1]$, there is no social welfare function that satisfies the variant of weak dominance and finite anonymity. (For these results, see Theorems 1 and 2 of Basu and Mitra (2003).) Clearly, these impossibility results are a generalization of Diamond's (1965) impossibility result since, first, the strong Pareto principle was employed by Diamond (1965), and, second, the representability of a social welfare ordering is logically weaker than the sup norm continuity.

Since the appearance of Basu and Mitra (2003), several authors have examined the possibility of a social welfare function (or a representable social welfare ordering) satisfying some plausible axioms. However, the results obtained so far are virtually all impossibility results. Banerjee and Mitra (2007) examined the nature of the domain of a social welfare function that satisfies the strong Pareto but violates finite anonymity (in the sense of impatience in Koopmans (1960)). Alcantud and Gracia-Sanz (2010) showed that, if $Y$ contains at least four distinct elements, there is no social welfare function that satisfies the strong Pareto principle and Hammond equity. (see Chap. 3 for the definition of an infinite-horizon reformulation of the equity axiom of Hammond (1976).) A related impossibility result was obtained by Dubey and Mitra (2012). Banerjee (2006) showed that there is no social welfare function that satisfies weak dominance and the weak equity axiom introduced by Asheim et al. (2007) under the name of "Hammond equity for the future." An exceptional social welfare function result is the possibility result of Basu and Mitra (2007b), who showed the existence of a social welfare function satisfying weak dominance and finite anonymity. However, their proof relies on the use of the Axiom of Choice, so that no explicit description is given of the social welfare function satisfying these axioms. (For a related possibility result using the weak Pareto principle and a certain form of restriction of $Y$, see Basu and Mitra (2007b) and Dubey and Mitra (2011).)

Zuber and Asheim (2012) provide an analysis closely related to the social welfare function approach. They impose the sup norm continuity on a social welfare ordering, so that it is representable by a social welfare function. They also insist on the strong anonymity axiom defined by the set of all possible permutations of generations. As we saw in Chap. 4, strong anonymity is incompatible with the strong Pareto principle. Insisting on strong anonymity, Zuber and Asheim (2012) consider the restricted version of the strong Pareto principle that requires the same property as the strong Pareto principle only for infinite utility streams that can be rearranged in a non-decreasing order. (See also Asheim and Zuber (2013) for a work employing strong anonymity.) Zuber and Asheim (2012) introduced a representable social welfare ordering called "extended rank-discounted utilitarianism"; then, using other axioms in addition to strong anonymity and the restricted version of the strong Pareto principle, they presented its axiomatization. Extended rank-discounted utilitarianism performs a comparison of the discount sums of utilities defined with respect to the utility ranks of generations. Consequently, extended rank-discounted utilitarianism can exhibit inequality aversion.

## 6.2 Choice Function Approach

Apart from the welfarist analysis of a social welfare ordering or quasi-ordering, the choice function approach to intergenerational resource allocations was proposed and analyzed by Asheim et al. (2010). They considered a simple dynamic economic environment consisting of a single resource and a stationary technology of production. The choice function approach to intergenerational resource allocations in this setting is to examine a social choice function that associates a single feasible consumption stream with a given initial amount of the resource. There are two major differences between the choice-theoretic analysis of intergenerational resource allocations and the welfarist analysis of a social welfare ordering and social welfare quasi-ordering. First, the choice-theoretic approach to intergenerational resource allocations entails the explicit consideration of feasible consumption streams according to the technology, while the welfarist analysis of a social welfare ordering or quasi-ordering is intended to rank all logically possible streams of utilities of generations, such as all possible streams $\boldsymbol{u}$ and $\boldsymbol{v}$ in $\mathbb{R}^{\mathbb{N}}$ as in Chaps. 3 and 4.[1] Second, the choice-theoretic approach to intergenerational resource allocations does not require that all feasible

[1]It should be noted that it is also possible to analyze social welfare orderings or quasi-orderings for feasible consumption streams of a dynamic economic model; see, for example, Asheim (1991), Asheim et al. (2001), Asheim et al. (2012), Basu and Mitra (2007a), and Zuber and Asheim (2012).

consumption streams be ranked coherently in the sense of transitivity, which may increase the possibility of resolving the conflicts between generations in a way that respects both the efficiency and impartiality considerations (even in their strongest form, such as strong anonymity).

Asheim et al. (2010) employ the Suppes–Sen axiom, which requires that a social choice function be consistent with maximality according to the grading principle, following Suppes (1966) and Sen (1970). An infinite-horizon extension of the Suppes–Sen grading principle corresponds to the conjunction of the strong Pareto principle and an anonymity axiom. Notably, the Suppes–Sen axiom employed in Asheim et al. (2010) is defined as the maximality of the Suppes–Sen grading principle in the sense of strong anonymity. In other words, it requires that a social choice function must be consistent with the maximality of the conjunction of the strong Pareto principle and strong anonymity. Using other axioms in addition to the Suppes–Sen axiom, Asheim et al. (2010) characterized a social choice function satisfying all the axioms.

In light of the possibility result of Asheim et al. (2010), the choice-theoretic approach to intergenerational resource allocation problems involving variable population size (as in Chap. 5) should be addressed. In the context of an intergenerational resource allocation problem with variable population size, a social choice function could be defined as a choice function that associates a pair of a feasible stream of consumption vectors and a feasible stream of population sizes of generations with a given initial amount of a resource, where the feasibility comes from a technology assumed in a dynamic economic environment with endogenous population growth. However, no attempt has been made to axiomatically analyze a social choice function in a dynamic economic model with endogenous population growth. On the other hand, Kamaga (2016) suggested that the choice-theoretic approach to intergenerational resource allocation problems with variable population size seems promising, particularly when focusing on several population ethics axioms. Among studies on finite-horizon variable population social choice, the choice-theoretic approach has been employed only by Blackorby et al. (2002). Further, their analytical framework is welfarist in the sense that a choice function selects a variable-dimensional utility vector from each set of feasible variable-dimensional utility vectors, and their primary purpose is to analyze a rationalizable choice function. Therefore, future studies should analyze the choice-theoretic approach to both intra- and intergenerational resource allocation problems with variable population size.

## References

Alcantud, J. C. R., & Garcia-Sanz, M. D. (2010). Evaluations of infinite utility streams: Pareto-efficient and egalitarian axiomatics. Munich Personal RePEc Archive, (MPRA Paper No. 20133).

Asheim, G. B. (1991). Unjust intergenerational allocations. *Journal of Economic Theory*, *54*, 350–371.

Asheim, G. B., Bossert, W., Sprumont, Y., & Suzumura, K. (2010). Infinite-horizon choice functions. *Economic Theory*, *43*, 1–21.

Asheim, G. B., Buchholz, W., & Tungodden, B. (2001). Justifying sustainability. *Journal of Environmental Economics and Management, 41*, 252–268.
Asheim, G. B., Mitra, T., & Tungodden, B. (2007). A new equity condition for infinite utility streams and the possibility of being Paretian. In J. E. Roemer & K. Suzumura (Eds.), *Intergenerational equity and sustainability*. Palgrave-Macmillan: Basingstoke.
Asheim, G. B., Mitra, T., & Tungodden, B. (2012). Sustainable recursive social welfare functions. *Economic Theory, 49*, 267–292.
Asheim, G. B., & Zuber, S. (2013). A complete and strongly anonymous leximin relation on infinite streams. *Social Choice and Welfare, 41*, 819–834.
Banerjee, K. (2006). On the equity-efficiency trade off in aggregating infinite utility streams. *Economics Letters, 93*, 63–67.
Banerjee, K., & Mitra, T. (2007). On the impatience implications of Paretian social welfare functions. *Journal of Mathematical Economics, 43*, 236–248.
Banerjee, K., & Mitra, T. (2008). On the continuity of ethical social welfare orders on infinite utility streams. *Social Choice and Welfare, 30*, 1–12.
Basu, K., & Mitra, T. (2003). Aggregating infinite utility streams with intergenerational equity: The impossibility of being Paretian. *Econometrica, 71*, 1557–1563.
Basu, K., & Mitra, T. (2007a). Utilitarianism for infinite utility streams: A new welfare criterion and its axiomatic characterization. *Journal of Economic Theory, 133*, 350–373.
Basu, K., & Mitra, T. (2007b). Possibility theorems for aggregating infinite utility streams equitably. In J. E. Roemer & K. Suzumura (Eds.), *Intergenerational equity and sustainability*. Palgrave-Macmillan: Basingstoke.
Blackorby, C., Bossert, W., & Donaldson, D. (2002). Rationalizable variable-population choice functions. *Economic Theory, 19*, 355–378.
Diamond, P. (1965). The evaluation of infinite utility streams. *Econometrica, 33*, 170–177.
Dubey, R. S., & Mitra, T. (2011). On equitable social welfare functions satisfying the weak Pareto axiom: A complete characterization. *International Journal of Economic Theory, 7*, 231–250.
Dubey, R. S., & Mitra, T. (2012). On monotone social welfare orders satisfying the strong equity axiom: Construction and representation. SSRN Discussion Paper. https://doi.org/10.2139/ssrn.2202389.
Hammond, P. J. (1976). Equity, Arrow's conditions, and Rawls' difference principle. *Econometrica, 44*, 793–804.
Kamaga, K. (2016). Infinite-horizon social evaluation with variable population size. *Social Choice and Welfare, 47*, 207–232.
Koopmans, T. C. (1960). Stationary ordinal utility and impatience. *Econometrica, 28*, 287–309.
Sen, A. K. (1970). *Collective choice and social welfare*. Amsterdam: Holden-Day.
Suppes, P. (1966). Some formal models of grading principles. *Synthese, 6*, 284–306.
Svensson, L.-G. (1980). Equity among generations. *Econometrica, 48*, 1251–1256.
Zuber, S., & Asheim, G. B. (2012). Justifying social discounting: The rank-discounted utilitarian approach. *Journal of Economic Theory, 147*, 1572–1601.

# Correction to: Social Welfare Evaluation and Intergenerational Equity

**Correction to:**
**K. Kamaga, *Social Welfare Evaluation and Intergenerational Equity*, Development Bank of Japan Research Series, https://doi.org/10.1007/978-981-15-4254-1**

The original version of the book was inadvertently published with error in copyright holder name as "© The Author(s), under exclusive license to Springer Nature Singapore Pte Ltd. 2020". This has been corrected to "© Development Bank of Japan" from "© The Author(s), under exclusive license to Springer Nature Singapore Pte Ltd. 2020" at book and chapters level.

---

The updated version of the book can be found at
https://doi.org/10.1007/978-981-15-4254-1



K. Kamaga, *Social Welfare Evaluation and Intergenerational Equity*,
Development Bank of Japan Research Series,
https://doi.org/10.1007/978-981-15-4254-1_7

# Index






K. Kamaga, *Social Welfare Evaluation and Intergenerational Equity*,
Development Bank of Japan Research Series,
https://doi.org/10.1007/978-981-15-4254-1

The manufacturer's authorised representative in the EU is Springer Nature Customer Service Centre GmbH, Europaplatz 3, 69115 Heidelberg, Germany. If you have any concerns regarding our products, please contact ProductSafety@springernature.com

Printed and bound by CPI Group (UK) Ltd, Croydon, CR0 4YY
30/09/2026
02225468-0017